DEDICATION

This book is dedicated with respect, gratitude
and affection to the staffs of the schools in which we worked

Whole School Curriculum Development in the Primary School

Jennifer Nias
Geoff Southworth
Penelope Campbell

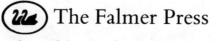 The Falmer Press

(A member of the Taylor & Francis Group)
London • Washington, D.C.

UK   The Falmer Press, 4 John St, London WC1N 2ET
USA   The Falmer Press, Taylor & Francis Inc., 1900 Frost Road, Suite 101, Bristol, PA 19007

© J. Nias, G. Southworth & P. Campbell 1992

First published 1992

A catalogue record for this book is available from the British Library

ISBN 0 75070 064 5 cased
ISBN 0 75070 065 3 paperback

Library of Congress Cataloging-in-Publication Data are available on request

Set in 11/13pt Bembo
by Graphicraft Typesetters Ltd., Hong Kong

Printed in Great Britain by Burgess Science Press, Basingstoke on paper which has a specified pH value on final paper manufacture of not less than 7.5 and is therefore 'acid free'.

Contents

Acknowledgments

We gratefully acknowledge the research grant from the Economic and Social Research Council (ref. no. R000231069) which enabled us to undertake the research upon which this book is based. We could not, however, have undertaken it or carried it through without the co-operation and forbearance of the school staffs whose practice we have reported. We are immensely grateful to the headteachers, teachers and ancillary staff in the schools where we worked.

We should also like to thank for their patience and help in transcribing, typing, editing and photocopying: Angie Ashton, Penny Collyer, Marguerite Farmer, Rita Harvey, Mavis Hulford, Gill Kimber, Jo Larkin, Mavis Robinson, Lesley Seaber and Barbara Shannon. We are deeply indebted to all of them for their painstaking work and their tolerance of our scribbled notes and amendments.

Introduction

'Whole school curriculum development' has recently gained currency and importance in educational debate. Yet despite its increasingly widespread use this term has no clear definition and there is no empirical evidence to suggest what it might mean in practice. In this book we seek to explore the meanings that might be attached to the phrase and to share the ways in which staff at five primary schools sought to engage in 'whole school curriculum development'. The descriptions of the teachers' practice which follow are not intended as a model of the ways in which such development ought necessarily to be carried out. Rather, they serve as examples of the activities of particular staff groups over the space of a single year as they sought to develop the curriculum of their schools. Each group experienced a unique set of circumstances, national and local, professional and personal. Though common themes emerge from comparing and contrasting the schools and the actions of those within them, we were, as observers, often most conscious of their differences. We are cautious, therefore, of suggesting that what was appropriate for any one group of people in a particular context at a particular time will be appropriate for all. Nevertheless we are confident that our analysis will provide others with opportunities for reflecting not only upon the experiences of the teachers described here, but also upon their own. We have certainly found this to be so ourselves.

Background to the Research

The book is based on the findings of a research project (The Whole School Curriculum Development and Staff Relationships in Primary Schools Project) funded by the Economic and Social Research Council

1

(ESRC ref. no. R000231069) from June 1988 to August 1990. The research was founded on and grew out of a previous research project (The Primary School Staff Relationships Project) which was funded by both the Economic and Social Research Council (ESRC ref. no. C09250003) and the Cambridge Institute of Education. The main concept to emerge from this earlier research was that of 'organizational culture' where culture was loosely defined as 'the way we do it here', that is, as a set of norms about ways of behaving, perceiving and understanding underpinned by jointly held beliefs and values. The research team (Jennifer Nias (Director), Geoff Southworth and Robin Yeomans) found that each of the five schools involved in the project had its own culture embodying strongly held beliefs about the social and moral purposes of education. These beliefs originated with the headteachers. In three of the schools the heads had worked for over ten years to develop and sustain an organizational culture which enabled the teaching and ancillary staff to work closely together. The project team described this as a 'culture of collaboration'. In the other two schools the heads were endeavouring to develop a similar culture but were impeded by conflicting values held by long established staff members. The culture of collaboration rested on four interacting beliefs: first, individuals should be valued; second, because individuals are inseparable from the group of which they are a part, groups too should be fostered and valued; third and fourth, the most effective way of promoting these values is by developing a sense of mutual security and openness.

Puzzlingly, in two of the schools identified as having a culture of collaboration, staff shared curricular goals and worked together to implement them, while in the third good working relationships existed amongst teachers with different educational aims. Furthermore, social cohesion appeared to lead in some schools, but not in others, to curricular development. Any connection, therefore, between positive staff relationships and curricular planning and development appeared ambiguous. These observations raised questions about which aspects of school organization and of adult relationships made it possible for productive working relationships to coexist with an explicit commitment to whole school curricular planning and development. It seemed especially pertinent to explore these questions further since the potentially widespread adoption of school development plans (ILEA, 1985; House of Commons Select Committee, 1986) and the imminence of a National Curriculum made it likely that there would be increasing pressure on teachers to collaborate and cooperate in the formulation and implementation of whole school curricular policies. Indeed, the 1988 Education Act made the questions we were seeking to address of national importance and particularly highlighted the need to explore the nature of 'whole schools' and the activities of teachers who together attempted to develop and implement agreed curricular policies.

Accordingly, the Whole School Curriculum Development Project (WSCD) was established, with four aims in mind. First, to enable us to identify and study the formal and informal ways in which curricular decisions affecting all the staff were made, and in which teaching and non-teaching staff sought to implement these. Second, to examine whether agreement to implement specific curricular policies had any effect upon pupils' learning experiences. Third, by studying closely the ways in which teachers worked together, to provide further analysis of the concept of collegiality and, fourth, to identify and study the location and nature of curricular and social leadership.

Immediately before the project began the 1988 Education Act was passed. This had wide-ranging effects on schools and those who worked in them. We did not set out deliberately to explore these effects. Nevertheless, as the proposals for the core subjects (mathematics, science and English) were published and discussed at a national level, and later placed on the statute books, we saw the teachers in most, though not all, of the project schools discuss them extensively. This provided us with increased opportunities to gain insights into the processes by which the teachers characteristically sought to develop the curriculum.

We need to make four further points. First, our account is primarily concerned with teachers. This is not to undervalue the work of many other adults who contributed to the smooth running of the schools as organizations and to their organizational cultures. However, it does emphasize the unique nature of the responsibility that the teachers held for the curriculum. Usually, therefore, when we use the term 'staff' we are referring to teachers. However, sometimes it will be clear from the context that we are also including non-teaching staff.

Second, our focus is on the work of the teachers in direct relation to the curriculum, whether this work was carried on within or outside the classrooms. This does not allow us to do full justice to the complexity of their working lives either in terms of the tasks they performed or the numbers of people (adults and children, members of, or visitors to, the school) with whom they regularly or intermittently interacted.

Third, where we have felt it to be appropriate we have distinguished between the perspectives of the heads and the teachers. Otherwise it may be assumed that what is written reflects professional views that seemed to be widely held in all the schools.

Fourth, we deliberately restricted our enquiries to schools with between five and twelve teaching staff (including the headteacher), a caretaker (or cleaner-in-charge), a secretary and at least one other ancillary. We were aware that size might affect the nature of whole school curricular decision-making and implementation. However, we made this decision with two facts in mind. First, about half of all children of primary school age in England and Wales attend schools with this number of teaching staff. Second, as participant observers we felt that it might be difficult to gain a sufficiently 'whole school' perspective, over a year, in larger schools.

Finding the Schools and Negotiating Entry

The schools were selected by non-random sampling. A long list of possible schools was compiled. It was based on the extensive knowledge of, and contact with, schools which we had gained through many years of INSET, on consultations with colleagues at the Cambridge Institute of Education and on informal discussions with LEA officers. We contacted the headteachers by telephone and described the nature and purposes of the research. Where headteachers expressed an interest in the project one of us visited their school, provided a fuller description of what was intended and discussed the likely implications for staff. Those heads who were still interested were asked to discuss with their staff the possibility of the school's involvement and, given no dissension, to organize a staff meeting at which one of the project team described the research and answered questions. During this meeting it was made clear that the research was to be conducted in accordance with an ethical code which gave each staff member the right to veto use of any interview material for which s/he was responsible and any observations of events in which s/he was involved, and the staff as a group to comment on the case studies to be written at the end of the year of data collection. The staff were then asked to take time to consider whether or not they were willing to open themselves to our scrutiny. As well as informing staff about the nature of the research these visits also allowed us to learn more of the schools.

In all but one case the heads contacted us within a short time to express a willingness on the part of all the staff to allow us to become temporary, part-time teachers and to observe them at work for a year. We then chose five schools which represented, as broad as possible a cross-section of characteristics which seemed, at a common sense level, to be important to the focus of our research. There were two infant schools, two primary schools and a junior school, drawn from two LEAs. One was a community school and one a Church of England Voluntary Controlled school. Two headteachers were men and three women, their experience of headship ranging from one-and-a-half to fifteen years. Two schools had a single sex staff group. Two schools had open-plan designs, one of these also having three mobile classrooms. Three schools had a cellular design. Two schools were in rural and three in urban locations. However, they all had similar catchments, incorporating substantial numbers of children from white, professional, middle class families. They are not therefore typical of, and our findings consequently may not be relevant to, the full range of primary schools. This bias was not of design. Simply, staff in schools serving diverse ethnic populations or impoverished urban communities responded to our initial enquiries that they were not 'whole schools' or that involvement might be 'too sensitive'. We formed a tentative and untested hypothesis that where the attention of staff is directed towards acute social or linguistic problems they are less likely to feel able to commit time and energy to out-of-classroom contact with one another and so to whole school curriculum development. This may be significant, since underlying the growing emphasis on whole school approaches to curriculum development is the assumption that this is equally easy to achieve in all schools.

Further details about the schools are given in table 1 and fuller descriptions follow.

Collecting, Analyzing and Checking the Evidence

For an academic year we acted as participant observers. We were willing to be deployed in ways that best suited the staff of each school. Between us we team taught, acted as supply teachers and ancillaries, attended a variety of meetings, participated in school camps and journeys, helped with plays, assemblies and displays, cleared cupboards, sorted resources and joined in extra-curricular activities. We worked a notional one day a week in each school, though occasionally we were in a particular school for a week or more at a time.

We used standard ethnographic methods for our research. We

Table 1:   School details

		Carey	Fenton	Ingham	Orchard	Upper Norton
1	Male head		1		1	
2	Female head	1		1		1
3	Head's time in school	12 yrs	13 yrs	6 yrs	10 yrs	1½ yrs
4	Head's experience	16 yrs	13 yrs	6 yrs	15 yrs	1½ yrs
5	School size group	4	4	5	4	3
6	Teaching staff group size (including head)	8	8.3	11	9	6.1
7	Gender	8f	6.3f 2m	11f	5f 4m	6.1f
8	Staff mostly 15+years experience	1		1		1
9	Staff mostly 15-years experience		1		1	
10	Open plan		1		1	
11	Cellular	1	1	1		1
12	Denominational					1
13	Suburban	1		1	1	
14	Rural		1			1
15	Infant school	1		1		
16	Junior school				1	
17	4–11 Primary		1			1
18	Special features			Assessment unit	Community school	

studied documents (governors' reports; school brochures; curriculum guidelines). We made briefly written notes of our observations during each visit and tape-recorded long, reflective fieldnotes based on these notes as soon as possible thereafter. These were later transcribed. Towards the end of the year (or earlier in cases where staff left the schools) we interviewed all but one member of staff. This one (at Ingham Infant School) preferred not to be interviewed though she allowed the researcher at that school access to her classroom throughout the year. All but one of the interviews were tape recorded with the participant's permission, and transcripts (or, in the one case, a summary) were returned to individuals who then had the opportunity to alter, add or delete material before we made use of what they had said. Almost all the interviews took place in school, some during school time and others after the school day had ended. They were loosely structured around key issues which appeared, from our observations, to be significant to our study. Interviewees were encouraged to talk freely and for as long as they wished.

We were aware, at an early stage in our selection procedure, that, notwithstanding their expressed willingness to be involved in the project, most teachers felt understandably apprehensive about being observed at work. It took some more time than others to overcome this apprehension and it is possible that there were a few who never did. If so, we are not aware of it. On the contrary we were often told that our presence was welcome and were made to feel that our help was appreciated. As much as it is possible to become members of staff whilst retaining an ability to observe, record and comment with detachment, we felt we did. We cannot claim that our presence in the schools did not affect what occurred. It seems likely that it did, if only in making the staff more self-aware and conscious of the processes in which they were engaged. However there were occasions on which staff expressed what appeared to be undissimulated surprise when reminded that we were taking notes. They seemed honestly to have forgotten our presence or our purpose.

At the end of the year's fieldwork we wrote individual case studies for each of the schools, using themes suggested by what we had seen and heard, progressively sorting and resorting the evidence, refining the categories that emerged, looking for contradictions and using these to help in the clarification. Each case study was written independently and reflects, as accurately as its author could ensure, the circumstances of that school. We took each draft case study back to the school, where we first asked individuals to clear the use of materials from interviews and comment on our interpretations and the meanings we had attributed to words, events and behaviours, and, second, asked the staff as a group to discuss and comment on what we had written. Very few changes, none of them substantial, were made during either of these stages.

During the final research stage the three of us compared and contrasted the validated case studies, looking for common themes and overarching concepts. It is from this analysis that the ideas in this book are derived. In drawing on the case studies for illustration we are aware of having used the same evidence in several different contexts. We did not attempt to eliminate what may appear to be repetition partly because we wanted to show that the evidence does indeed illustrate many different points simultaneously, and partly because we are conscious that each chapter of the book may be read separately.

Introducing the Five Schools

Carey Infant School

Carey Infant School is situated in an attractive market town, predominantly populated by professional, middle class families. It was opened

Table 2:   Carey Infant School

Number on roll (September 1988)	Group size	Number of teachers (excluding head)	Number of ancillaries	Head's tenure	Staff changes during year	Number of classes
173 (approx) growing to 215 (approx)	4	7(f)	2 ancillaries (f) 1 secretary (f) 3 welfare assistants (f)	12 years (f)	change of welfare assistant; additional welfare assistant appointed; caretaker appointed (m); deputy left replaced by temporary appointment	7

twenty-four years before the start of the research and was a single-storied, largely wooden structure with a flat roof built on two levels and set in pleasant grounds shared with the junior school of the same name. There were two mobile classrooms on the grass at the front of the school, one of which was used as a music room by the junior school. At the beginning of the school year the building was in a poor state of repair. The exterior was drab and uninviting. Inside, walls and roof were supported by exposed timbers — the evidence of previous repair work. The roof sometimes leaked, damaging equipment and children's work. Rebuilding was scheduled for the summer term. Nevertheless, the internal environment was light, spacious and colourful with displays of children's work. A small entrance with administrative rooms off to the side gave way to a large hall. Half a dozen steps ran its width at one end. At the other full length windows flooded the room with light. To one side was the kitchen and a classroom. From the top of the steps doors opened into four other classrooms through one of which a sixth classroom was reached. Each room was large and included a cloakroom, toilets, sink, cupboard, tiled and carpeted areas. Windows formed a major part of the external walls and a door led from each classroom into the playground. There were seven classes, the seventh being housed in a mobile classroom without water or toilets.

It was local authority policy that the school should be staffed in September on the projected numbers for the summer term, although children entered the school during the term in which they were 5 years old. Consequently the two parallel reception (YR)[1] classes began the school year with eight or nine pupils in each. They reached their full size in January, and a new reception class was formed in the summer term. In the days when the school consisted of six classes, each teacher had taken pupils from reception to top infants, moving classrooms each year. Growing numbers had complicated this organization and during this year a solution was found by splitting a middle infant (Y1) class between three other classes, one of which became a vertically grouped reception and middle infant class. Seven classes were then organized as follows: one reception class with summer born children (YR); one reception class with children who had entered school in September and January; one vertically grouped class with reception children from the January intake and middle infants (YR + Y1); two middle infant classes (Y1); and two top infant classes (Y2).

During the second half of the summer term rebuilding began, behind schedule. Two classes at a time moved out of the main building into mobile classrooms which had been temporarily added to the complex. A third class spent the final week of term in the hall.

The school had a stable staff, the average length of service being around eleven years. The most recent teaching appointment, an additional one, had been made three years previously. It was six years since any teacher had left the school. At the start of the year the school staff consisted of the head (Ella), deputy (Ivy), six full-time teachers (Kate, Christine, Thelma, Kay Harvey, Kay Hale, Naomi), two welfare assistants (Mrs. Evans and Mrs. Shane), two ancillary helpers (Carrie and Mrs. Vance) and a secretary (Nerys). For most of the year the school had no caretaker, though one was appointed towards the end of the summer term. All the staff were between 30 and 60 years of age.

Kay Hale had an 'A' allowance. All staff had a responsibility for an area of the curriculum. Ivy was the INSET Coordinator and was also responsible for curriculum development in maths. She was assisted in this latter role by Christine and Kate because maths was intended as a focus of development for the year. Naomi was responsible for science, Kay Hale for art and display, Kay Harvey for English and Thelma for music. In addition to these, Mary Carroll, who had been employed at Carey some years previously and had left to have a family, now regularly covered absences for ill health or in-service training. She took Kate's class for one day each week (when Kate was acting as a member of a LEA Working Party on Assessment) and frequently joined the class at other times on a voluntary basis.

Some changes took place during the year. Ivy Brandon left un-

Table 3:   Carey Infant School teaching staff

Name	Years taught	Responsibilities
Ella Rhys		Headteacher
Ivy Brandon	Top infants 6–7 years	Deputy Head Maths INSET Coordinator
Naomi Ingram	Top infants 6–7 years	Science
Kay Hale	Middle infants 5–6 years	'A' allowance Art and display
Kay Harvey	Middle infants 5–6 years (September to March) Reception infants 4–5 years (April to July)	Writing
Thelma Thomas	Middle infants 5–6 years	Music
Christine Gilroy	Reception infants 4–5 years	Maths
Kate Rowan	Reception infants 4–5 years (September to March)	Maths
Frances Osborn	Top infants 6–7 years (April to July)	Deputy Head (acting)

expectedly at the end of the spring term and was temporarily replaced by Frances who took over both her class and her role as Deputy Head. Frances was a Head of several years standing who had a peripatetic role within the LEA. Mrs. Evans left the school through ill health at Christmas and was replaced by Kathie Howell who was also a dinner lady. Ros Gryffydd was employed as a welfare assistant during the summer term.

Fenton County Primary School

Fenton County Primary School was situated on a new housing estate on the edge of a rural village. It opened in 1975. The building was of brick and had a flat roof. It was set in the centre of a rectangular plot of land. To one side was a swimming pool and a mobile classroom housing the local playgroup. There were two asphalt playgrounds. On the one where the infants played there were three mobile class-rooms and on the other a smaller mobile building used to store many of the resources held in common — art and craft materials, science equipment, fabrics, materials for craft, design and technology. At the rear of the school was an expanse of grass marked out with games pitches. Enclosed by wooden fencing was an environmental study

Table 4: Fenton County Primary School

Number on roll (September 1988)	Group size	Number of teachers (excluding head)	Number of ancillaries	Head's tenure	Staff changes during year	Number of classes
210 (approx) some part-time in Sept.	4	7.3 (6.3f) (1 m)	1 ancillary (f) 1 secretary (f) 3 welfare assistants (f) 1 caretaker (f)	13 years (m)	Head left; 1 teacher left; 2 teachers appointed on temporary contracts; welfare assistant replaced	7

area with a pond, meadow and woodland. In front of the school was another expanse of grass with ornamental trees.

The entrance to the school was small. To one side were the Head's and secretary's offices and to the other the staff room used by teaching and non-teaching staff, parent helpers and governors. Beyond the entrance was a large hall. Here, as throughout the school, children's work was prominently displayed on boards and tables and there were interesting things to look at — the twisted branches of trees, stuffed birds, lovely fabrics, weaving, reproductions of famous paintings, vases of dried flowers. Children's work and that of commercial artists jostled for attention. To one side of the hall were the kitchens. To the other the infant classrooms. These were open plan with three small class bays, an open area between them, a quiet room, two cloakrooms and toilets. The Headteacher had argued successfully in the past that one of the bays was not large enough for a class group and at the start of the year it was used, at different times, by teachers or parents working with small groups and by parents running a bookshop. The other two bays accommodated reception (YR) classes. Beyond the hall was a corridor leading to two junior classrooms. These were approached through a small library where there were shelves of books, some low tables and comfortable chairs. A tank full of fish was against one wall. Two small classrooms opened out of this area, each with a screen that could be drawn across, but which was, almost always, left open. Beyond these two classrooms opened another shared area used mainly for art and craft activities. A number of small animals — hamsters, guinea pigs — were located there.

The housing in Fenton was largely 'first time buyer'. A substantial number of families moved away from the village during the years of their children's primary schooling. Consequently the reception (YR) classes were usually larger than the top year classes (Y3–Y6), necessitating annual reorganization. At the time of the research there were four infant (YR–Y2) classes and three junior (Y3–Y6) classes. Two reception classes, each with a few middle infant (Y1) pupils in them, were sited in the open plan infant bays. Children who were rising 5 attended these classes, mornings only, from September. One middle infant (Y1) class was sited in a newly arrived mobile classroom with toilets attached. One top infant (Y2) class, with some middle infants in it, was sited on the other side of the playground. This mobile had no toilets, but did have a sink and running water. A mixed first and second year junior (Y3–Y4) class was based in a mobile classroom next to the top infant class. A mixed second and third year (Y4–Y5) class and a mixed third and fourth year (Y5–Y6) class were both based in the main building.

At the start of the academic year the Headteacher was Simon, who had opened the school thirteen years earlier. The rest of the staff were the Deputy (Rob), six full-time teachers (Kathryn, Susan, Dawn, Barbara, Verity and Rebecca), one part-time teacher (Tamsin), a secretary (Kirsty), a general assistant (Norah), three welfare assistants (Ros, Emma, Celia) and a caretaker (Patricia).

Rebecca had an 'A' allowance with responsibility for the lower school. Susan was given a temporary 'A' allowance in January to develop an agreed policy document on art and an agreed policy on handwriting. Dawn held a responsibility for music, Barbara for lower school science, Verity for parental involvement (a responsibility which reflected the importance attached by the teachers to the parents' role in the education of their children) and Tamsin for special needs. Most of the teaching staff were in their thirties or early forties. Some had recently returned to teaching after a break to have children. At the start of the academic year only Dawn (who had just completed her probationary year elsewhere) was completely new to the school, yet there was a sense of newness about the staff group as a whole. Simon Riley had been seconded to fulfil an advisory role within the county two years before. A number of staff changes had occurred immediately before, during and after this period, including the appointment of Rob as Deputy Head only a term before he took over as Acting Head. Barbara, though she had held temporary posts for a year, had been permanently appointed at the same time as Dawn. Kathryn had been appointed temporarily at the start of the previous summer term and her appointment became permanent the following January. Conse-

Table 5: *Fenton Primary School teaching staff*

Name	Years taught	Responsibilities
Simon Riley		Headteacher
Robin Mortimer	Top junior 9–11 years (September to March)	Deputy Head Acting Head (April to July)
Kathryn Edgar	Junior 8–10 years	Acting Deputy (April to July)
Susan Nicholas	Junior 7–9 years	'A' allowance Art and display Handwriting
Dawn Clark	Infant 5–7 years	Music
Barbara Kerr	Infant 5–6 years	Science
Verity Frederick	Infant 4–6 years	Parental involvement 'A' allowance — Lower School (April to July)
Rebecca Vincent	Infant 4–6 years	'A' allowance — Lower School
Tamsin Daley		P/t for children with special needs

quently the staff, as a group, had not been together for long, even though some of them had worked in the school for as long as four years. Simon continued to hold responsibilities attached to his advisory role after his return to the school and this meant that he was absent every Thursday when a supply teacher was used to release staff with curriculum or other responsibilities.

The feeling of instability arising from these changes and discontinuities provided a major challenge and Simon's main concern, at the start of the year, was to re-establish the educational beliefs on which the school had been founded. At the time he believed that the staff would be reasonably settled for the next two or three years. However, this was not to be and there was actually increased uncertainty, instability and insecurity. Firstly, Simon himself was appointed to a new headship elsewhere and left Fenton at the end of the spring term. The knowledge that he was to do so came as a shock to the majority of the staff. As one teacher said to another, 'I can't imagine Fenton without Simon', (Fieldnote, Fenton). The unexpectedness of his resignation together with the shortness of the spring term meant that staff had little time to adjust to his impending loss.

Secondly, Rebecca took maternity leave from the end of the

spring term. As the longest serving member of the staff she played a significant, though unobtrusive, role within the school.

Rob became Acting Head for the second time and Kathryn became Acting Deputy, having been a deputy elsewhere. Verity took over the responsibility for the lower school (YR–Y2). Celia and Brid, who was new to the school, were appointed on temporary contracts, Celia to take responsibility for Rebecca's reception class and Brid to share the responsibility for Rob's top junior (Y6) class. Laura was appointed to take Celia's place as welfare assistant. The general feeling of insecurity within the school as a consequence of these changes was further exacerbated by the resignations of Tamsin and Kathryn, which took effect from the end of the academic year. It is not surprising then that the staff's major preoccupation during the final part of the year was to hold things together until the new Head arrived the following September. They worked hard to do this.

Ingham County Infant School

Ingham County Infant School served a growing village community close to an old but growing city. It began life as a separate school in 1980 when the junior department of what had been a 5–11 primary school moved to new buildings and a new headteacher was appointed to the infant school. The two schools continued to share the same governing body.

The original building was Victorian but had been added to over the years. It was a long building, running parallel to the road, and was well maintained and pleasant to look at with white cladding, red brick

Table 6: Ingham County Infant School

Number on roll (September 1988)	Group size	Number of teachers (excluding head)	Number of ancillaries	Head's tenure	Staff changes during year	Number of classes
300 (approx) growing to 340 (approx)	5	10 (f)	2 ancillaries (f) 1 secretary (f) 4 welfare assistants (f) 1 caretaker (m)	6 years (f)	1 additional teacher (f) appointed for summer term; 3 teachers left; 3 arrived (2f, 1m)	10

and a red tiled roof. At the rear of the school was an asphalt play-ground and at the front, on the opposite side of the road, a large field where the children played when it was dry underfoot. Entering through the main door a visitor was first conscious of a long, narrow corridor, to the left of which were classrooms and to the right cupboards, toilets, offices and open areas used as cloakrooms or for art activities. At the end of this corridor, past three classrooms, was the hall, a large, rectangular room running the full width of the building. Beyond the hall the corridor continued past three further classrooms on the left, the middle one of which had been made into a library, and more cupboards and cloakrooms on the right. Internal, semi-circular windows opened from the classrooms into the corridors. The classrooms themselves were roughly square. Brown tiles covered half the walls from the floor up and made the rooms seem smaller than they actually were. Notwithstanding, the rooms appeared colourful and bright, partly because they were in excellent decorative order and partly because children's work was displayed in every available space. The typically high Victorian ceilings had been reduced in recent refurbishments. All the floors in this section of the building were wood block and beautifully cared for. At the end of the second corridor was a more recently built area commonly called the 'green carpet area'. This was used for classes of children to watch the television and by parents who, amongst other things, ran a 'Share-a-Game' project from there. There was a noticeboard for parents on one wall. A bay, partitioned from the main area by free standing cupboards, was used to store maths resources and contained a table and chairs where groups of children could work with an adult. Beyond the 'green carpet area', and at a slight angle to it, ran the main extension to the building. Its internal design was similar to that of the original building consisting of another long, narrow corridor with three more, slightly larger, classrooms on the left and a staffroom, toilets, cloakrooms and cupboards on the right. Against the walls of all three corridors were free standing cupboards and tables which, as well as providing much needed storage and working space, served to break up the length. Cupboard tops and corners were used to display a variety of objects (flowers, stuffed birds and animals, for example) as well as children's work. Display boards were fixed wherever there was wall space for them and these too were used to display children's work. Only one of the classrooms had a direct water supply. Eight classes were based in this building.

Separate from the main building was another brick building containing a further classroom with toilets and cloakroom, and alongside it, because of continued growth in numbers, a single mobile classroom on the edge of the playground. Also in the playground was another small building, called 'The Acorn', used as a base for parents running a Book Savings Club, by visiting speech therapists, physiotherapists and, at certain times, as a creche for the children of parents helping in the school. On the far side of the larger brick building was a small pond and wildlife area. At the opposite side of the playground, and separated from it by a wooden fence, was a slightly larger garden area with a sand pit and adventure playground used by the children, under supervision, during the summer months. Close to this area was a rabbit in a hutch. At the far end of the main building was a second large mobile which served as a canteen.

The immediate impression was of a well maintained, carefully considered, beautifully cared for environment. Though staff tended to be aware of the building's limitations in terms of space, storage and water supply and the difficulties it posed in terms of communication, it was clear that they were making imaginative use of its odd corners and that every effort was made to overcome disadvantages and to perceive potential.

There were ten classes in the school. One of these, based immediately opposite the headteacher's room and just inside the main entrance, was an assessment unit to which children with a variety of educational learning difficulties (related to developmental problems in physical, emotional, social and educational growth) were referred from a number of schools in the area. After spending sometime in this unit children were either reintegrated into mainstream education or moved on to a form of special education appropriate to their particular needs. Six of the other nine classes were vertically grouped. Five of these began the academic year with around twenty children aged between 5 and 6 years (YR–Y1) and grew to a size of around thirty-two during the summer term, children being admitted to the school at the start of the term during which they were 5 years old. The sixth class began the year with just fifteen children (YR) and was kept deliberately smaller than the others in order to accommodate a child with Down's syndrome, who joined the class on Monday and Wednesday afternoons. The three remaining classes contained just over thirty top year (Y2) infants.

The school's catchment area was predominantly professional middle class. A large number of parents were involved in every aspect of the school's life and parental expectations for their children were high.

The staffroom was a small, though pleasant, rectangular room to one side of the corridor in the extension to the main building. It was often crowded at breaktimes since not only staff but any visitors to the school, as well as the parent helpers, also congregated there. Not only were there not enough chairs to accommodate the numbers but space to stand was very limited. Consequently, staff sometimes chose to fetch a mug of coffee and return to their classrooms and, on certain days when they knew the pressure was likely to be greatest, chose not to go down to the staffroom at all. There was, then, no central place where all the staff commonly gathered other than for formal meetings.

The Headteacher (Evelyne) had been appointed four years previously. Other staff members at the start of the year were the Deputy (Lori), nine full-time teachers (Tina, Rosie, Kirsten, Theresa, Karen, Natalie York, Edith, Marilyn, Beth), a secretary (Elaine), two general assistants (Hazel and Tara) and four welfare assistants attached to the assessment unit (for most of the year, Alice, Kim, Nyree, Nadia).

Tina and Beth had 'B' allowances. Both fulfilled a management role. Beth was in charge of the assessment unit. Natalie York had a temporary 'A' allowance to develop the use of information technology throughout the school. Each member of staff held curriculum responsibilities, some of which were shared. Tina was responsible for maths and the 'Share-a-Book' project (a home/school reading programme), Rosie for topic, Kirsten for language and the 'Share-a-Book' project, Theresa for RE, Karen for the reading scheme and music, Natalie York for science and information technology, Edith for maths, Marilyn for multicultural education, special needs and topic, Beth for the environment, computers, display, health education and special needs. Some members of staff had administrative responsibilities in addition to their curriculum related ones. Most, because of particular curriculum interests and strengths, played a supporting role in the small working groups which sought to develop the curriculum.

The staff were between 30 and 55 years of age with the exception of Kirsten, who was in her early twenties and who had completed her probationary year at the school in July 1988. Several of the staff had been at the school for six or more years. There were relatively few staff changes during the year. Beth left at Christmas to take up a deputy headship. She was replaced temporarily by Fran and later Eliot, who was permanently appointed to the post. Kirsten left and was replaced temporarily by Natalie Yarborough. Evelyne was on a long course and was absent one day a week for much of the year. Lori took on her responsibilities at these times and her class was then

Table 7: *Ingham Infant School teaching staff*

Name	Years taught	Responsibilities
Evelyne Upton		Headteacher
Lorraine Nicholls	4–6 years	Deputy Head INSET
Tina Eves	4–6 years	'B' allowance Maths 'Share-a-book'
Rosemary Clift	4–6 years	Topic
Kirsten Yeardley	4–6 years	Language 'Share-a-book'
Theresa Inglis	4–6 years	RE
Karen Dalgety	4–6 years	Reading scheme Music
Natalie York	Top infants 6–7 years	'A' allowance Information Technology Science
Edith Challis	Top infants 6–7 years	Maths 'A' allowance from January 1989 for introduction of 'Kidscape'
Marilyn Kaczmarek	Top infants 6–7 years	Multi-culture Special needs Topic
Elisabeth Kempe	Assessment unit	'B' allowance Environment Computer Display Health Education Special needs
Francesca Devonport	Assessment unit (January – March)	Special needs
Eliot Chapman	Assessment unit (from April 1989)	'B' allowance Special needs
Natalie Yarborough	4–6 years (April to July 1989)	
Rhiannon Evans	0.6 support for the six vertically grouped lower infant classes	Music

taught by Marion, a supply teacher regularly used by the school. Other adults regularly associated with the school were Irene, a main grade teacher employed at a nearby special school. She was attached to Stewart, who spent the afternoons in Tina's class, and Betty, who spent the mornings in the Assessment Unit. Both children suffered from Down's Syndrome. Gayle, an advisory teacher, spent some time during the summer term working with groups of children in a number of classrooms in the school. During the second half of the autumn term, Malcolm, a teacher from the junior school, joined the staff for half a day a week, an exchange organized between himself and Edith. Isla was a speech therapist who regularly worked in the school, mostly with children from the Assessment Unit.

Orchard Community Junior School

Orchard Community Junior School originally served a village community. However, the village had, over recent years, become a dormitory suburb of an expanding city. During the year of the research once open vistas around two sides of the school field were closed in with new housing developments. This growth did not significantly affect the size of the school since a new school had recently been built in the locality. The children at Orchard came from mainly owner-occupied homes. The children were fashionably dressed, few of them were on free school meals and they were extrovert and friendly.

The school was two form entry, of open-plan design. It was built in three distinct parts. The main entrance led to a central administrative area with a foyer serving both the school and the community centre, offices, a staffroom, a quiet room and a large hall. It was not unusual to see children in this area, but it nevertheless tended to be quiet since the rest of the school was separated from it by a pair of red glazed doors leading off to the right. Beyond these were four 'units', each the base for two classes. Three were in a straight line, but the first year unit was 'round a corner' and staff working in it sometimes felt isolated. All doors had large glass portholes, screens were of clear glass and two units did not have doors. This meant that it was easy for anyone passing through to see and gain access to what was happening. The school was carpeted throughout. Each unit had a

Table 8: Orchard Community Junior School

Number on roll (September 1988)	Group size	Number of teachers (excluding head)	Number of ancillaries	Head's tenure	Staff changes during year	Number of classes
198	4	8 (5f) (3m)	1 ancillary (f) 1 secretary (f) 1 welfare assistant (f) 1 caretaker (m)	10 years (m)	1 teacher left; 1 arrived	8

central art and craft/wet area, sinks and store cupboards. The staff used the term 'unit' to apply not only to these architecturally discrete areas of the school but also to the two classes which worked within them. At the rear of the school there was a swimming pool and a mobile classroom which was used for music. To the left of the administrative area was the community part of the building. Here there were a coffee bar, a small hall, the Community Development Officer's office and a community meeting room. During the school day it was not unusual to meet OAPs (some of whom dined with the children each Monday) or very young children (members of a play-group meeting in the small hall each morning) as well as other users of the community buildings.

The Headteacher (Ron) had opened the school in 1979. The headship of Orchard was his third. At the start of this academic year he had been a headteacher for fifteen years. He held an overall respon-sibility for the work of the community centre as well as for that of the school. He was in his mid-40s and was the oldest member of staff. In September there were eight full-time members of the teaching staff ranging in age from early twenties to early forties. Each had a class responsibility. Marion and Helen taught in the first year (Y3) unit, Dave (the Deputy) and Jean in the second year (Y4) unit, Sarah and Michael in the third year (Y5) unit and Marie and Ken in the fourth year (Y6) unit. There was an explicit expectation that the teachers in each unit would work together. Thus, whilst the teachers were indi-vidually responsible for their own classes, they also shared a respon-sibility for planning and teaching the curriculum within their units. When difficulties arose, as they occasionally did, the Head sometimes exerted pressure to ensure that the working partnership did not break down. An ancillary worked in each unit during the week, often employed on art and craft activities. Parents also helped in the units. In addition, Lesley, a special needs teacher, was attached to the school, though also working in neighbouring schools. Lesley sometimes attended staff meetings and was often involved in discussions about the curriculum.

Marion, Dave, Sarah and Marie were 'unit leaders' and as such were expected to take a lead in planning the unit's work. They played an important part in helping their less experienced partners adjust to the school's approaches and policies. Marie held a scale 'A' incentive allowance as the INSET co-ordinator. Sarah was responsible for music, Ken for teaching guitar, Michael for drama and Ron and Michael for inter-school football. In addition, any member of staff who had a particular curriculum interest took an informal leadership

Table 9: *Orchard Community Junior School teaching staff*

Name	Years taught	Responsibilities
Ron		Headteacher
Dave	8–9 years	Deputy Head Unit leader
Jean	8–9 years	
Marion	7–8 years	Unit leader
Helen	7–8 years	
Sarah	9–10 years	Unit leader Music
Michael	9–10 years (until December 1988)	Drama
Graham	9–10 years (from January 1989)	
Marie	10–11 years	Unit leader 'A' allowance INSET Coordinator
Ken	10–11 years	Guitar

role in providing advice and support for colleagues. There had been a regular turnover of staff through the years and none, apart from Ron, had been at the school above five years. At the start of the academic year Helen and Jean were both newly appointed although Jean had done some supply teaching in the school. Ken had been in the school for one term. Michael was in his second year of teaching. He left the staff at Christmas and was replaced by Graham, a probationary teacher. During the school year the deputy head applied for a number of headship posts, was interviewed for three of them, but was unsuccessful. Marie was also interviewed for a post in another school.

Upper Norton Church of England Voluntary Controlled Primary School

Upper Norton Church of England (Controlled) Primary School closely resembled many other village schools founded, as it was, around 1870. Adjoining the village street and next to the church, it presented a characteristic picture when approached for the first time. Part of the building was Victorian red brick, with high windows and narrow doors. Added on, at right angles to this rectangular structure, was a low, flat-roofed hall well lit by high windows and flanked by the school kitchens. In, and stretching a little beyond the angle formed by

Table 10:   Upper Norton Church of England Voluntary Controlled Primary School

Number on roll (September 1988)	Group size	Number of teachers (excluding head)	Number of ancillaries	Head's tenure	Staff changes during year	Number of classes
143 Some part-time in September	3	5.1f	1 secretary (f) 3 welfare assistants (f) 1 caretaker (m)	18 months (f)	—	5

these two buildings, was an asphalt playground surrounded by a brick wall. It was used by the infant children. A narrow path led from it, round the kitchens, to a second asphalt playground used by the older children and, beyond that, to a large, level playing field, dotted with a few trees and marked at the boundary by shrubs and hedgerows. On the side of the playing field nearest the school was a mobile classroom, in a poor state of physical repair. During the summer term repairs were put in hand and Class 3, whose base it was, moved temporarily into the art room in the main building. In addition a major repair and redecoration programme, affecting the rest of the school, was carried out in the summer term. Immediately beyond the mobile was a small conservation area, used for environmental studies. Between the mobile and the main school was a small swimming pool, administered after school by the PTA but used in school time by every class.

Once inside the main entrance, which was in the angle of the two constructions, the old building stretched to the left, where the Head's and secretary's rooms and Class 1 (YR–Y1) were situated, and to the right, where Class 2 (Y1–Y2) and Class 4 (Y4–5) had been added some years before. Beyond these were two new classrooms — Class 5 (Y5–6) and one used as an art room — an enclosed, carpeted audio-visual/music room and a second set of toilets. The art room was separated from the hall and kitchens by a walk-through library/resource area. The hall, which also served for physical education and school dinners, was big enough to seat the whole school and, when a larger space was needed for any reason, the doors separating it from the library/resource area could be folded back. Class 4 (Y2–3) was based in the mobile classroom at the rear of the school building.

The walls of the narrow corridor which ran through the school from one entrance to the other were decorated with pictures and children's work. In the foyer, facing the main entrance, low storage cupboards formed a flat surface on which changing art work was displayed. The main central areas in the school also served as cloak-rooms for the children and were commonly dotted with coats, boots, kit bags and satchels. The general impression was homely, workman-like and cheerful.

The school served three villages, each of which fell within what might be described as the rural commuter belt. Children attended the school from a variety of homes, some having parents who were born and brought up in the area and still worked on the land, whilst others had moved from other parts of the country in connection with their white-collar employment. Children were admitted to the school at the beginning of the year in which they were 5.

The headteacher was Dorothy who had been appointed to the post eighteen months before our research began. She was a mature entrant to the profession and had worked in two schools (in the second as deputy) for ten years before coming to Upper Norton. She attempted to maintain a regular teaching commitment, taking groups from all classes, except the reception class (YR–Y1), for language and art and craft. Other full-time members of the teaching staff at the start of the year were Helen, Wendy, Katherine (the Deputy) and Nancy. Robert King had been unexpectedly seconded during the summer holidays leaving Class 3 (Y2–3) without a permanent teacher for the first three weeks of the school year. Noreen was then appointed, on a temporary contract, to take his place. This appoint-ment was made permanent towards the end of the summer term. Kirsty was an experienced music teacher who worked part-time at several schools in the area, of which Upper Norton was one. Other adults working at the school (excluding kitchen, cleaning and dinner-time staff) were Nina (part-time nursery nurse, part-time care assis-tant), Tessa (secretary), Hope (welfare assistant), Gina (care assistant), who came into school one day a week to work with a child with special educational needs and Harry (caretaker). The staff were aged between mid-thirties and early fifties, except for Harry who retired at the end of the summer term.

At the beginning of the year Katherine was responsible for special needs, but there were no other official curricular responsibilities. Dur-ing the year, however, an 'A' incentive allowance was divided equally between Wendy for the development of information technology with-in the school, Helen for the early years and reading, and Nancy for environmental studies. During the spring term the school received regular visits from advisory teachers in information technology and art.

Table 11: *Upper Norton Primary School teaching staff*

Name	Years taught	Responsibilities
Dorothy Simon		Headteacher
Katherine Ivey	8–10 years	Deputy/Special Needs
Helen Davies	4–6 years	Early years and Reading*
Wendy Grant	5–7 years	IT*
Noreen Newland	6–9 years	
Nancy Richards	9–11 years	Library/Resources* Environmental Studies*
Kirsty Thompson	.1	Music

* During the year an 'A' allowance was divided equally between these three teachers for the named responsibilities.

Main Themes

There are three recurring and closely associated themes in this book which relate to an understanding of whole school curriculum development: first, the beliefs held by the teachers in the five project schools about the purposes of education and how these might best be achieved; second, the variety of ways in which the teachers worked together, and by so doing developed, established and sustained shared beliefs about their purposes and practice; third, the ways in which the teachers learned from and with one another and so developed the curriculum in accordance with these developing or established beliefs. These themes deserve some introduction here, particularly in relation to the concepts of a 'whole school' and 'whole school curriculum development'. They are not easily disentangled and, to some extent therefore, must be considered simultaneously.

During initial contacts with schools we used the phrase 'whole school' in explaining our research purposes to staff. For example, in a booklet describing the project to prospective participants we stated:

We have contacted schools which we believe to have whole school approaches to curriculum development.

We neither offered nor sought any definition of the term, since we hoped to discover in the process of the fieldwork what it might mean to those for whom it had currency. Nevertheless we recognized that many teachers and heads attached some importance to the idea of 'wholeness' or 'likemindedness' within a school. Nias (1989a), in a longitudinal study of primary teachers, had already argued that most teachers want to work in an adult environment in which they receive help, sympathy, guidance and friendship at an individual level and where they share with their colleagues common beliefs about education, working with them towards common ends and extending their professional thinking and practice through their formal and informal contacts, their agreements and disagreements.

We were also aware that, at an official level, a succession of policy statements, surveys, inspection reports and enquiries from central government, HM Inspectors of Schools and other committees (for example, DES, 1978, 1980, 1982, 1984a, 1984b and 1987; Welsh Office, 1985, ILEA, 1985, House of Commons, 1986, Schools Council, 1981 and 1983) had, over a period of years, emphasized a model of school management in which all professional staff participate actively in negotiating an agreed curriculum and contribute jointly to planning, implementing and evaluating it. References to unity of purpose, to the value of a collegial approach to management and of collaborative planning and shared decision-making, and to the need for the curriculum to be planned as a coherent whole are common in these documents. The emphasis on these ideas has continued to the present and is more and more frequently summarized in the phrase 'whole school'. There should be, says the National Curriculum Council, 'a step by step approach to curriculum planning from a whole school perspective' (NCC, 1989). Again, 'The planning approaches to the curriculum should...ensure a whole-school approach to implementing the National Curriculum' (*ibid*) and, 'The successful management of the whole curriculum depends upon a corporate plan for the whole school, embracing all the aspects of the whole curriculum' (NCC, 1990). But however frequently and in whatever context the phrase 'whole school' is used, its definition remains imprecise. Consequently its repeated use raises a number of questions. What is a 'whole school'? Why is it perceived as desirable that a school should be 'whole'? By what means does a school become 'whole'? What are the implications of being a 'whole school' for curriculum development? What does it mean to have a 'whole-school approach' to the curriculum? How is a 'whole-school' approach to the curriculum achieved and sustained? What benefits accrue from having a 'whole-school' approach?

Despite the uncertainties surrounding these questions, our evidence suggests that the teachers in the project schools, like those cited earlier (Nias, 1989a), wanted to work in institutions which they thought of as being 'whole schools' and to which they attributed certain characteristics (see chapter 1). The headteachers, likewise, had

a vision of their schools as 'whole' and, attributing particular meanings to that phrase, they worked towards its development in ways that
we explore in greater depth in chapter 3. The emphasis placed on
'whole school' by the DES, HM Inspectorate and others, sharpened
by recent political events and given a new thrust by the National
Curriculum Council, thus complements and reflects the desire of
teachers to be members of 'whole schools' and of headteachers to
create 'whole schools'.

In chapter 1 we explore the understandings teachers in our study
had of the term 'whole school'. Briefly, they regarded 'whole schools'
as communities within which people share the same beliefs about the
purposes of education, agree on ways in which those purposes might
be fulfilled and in accordance with the resulting policies behave in
similar ways in their classrooms. The notion of beliefs is central to
an understanding of the concept of 'whole school' because 'whole
schools' are perceived as ones where beliefs are shared, articulated and
enacted by all staff. Likewise, it is central to the notion of 'whole
school curriculum development' because this, as we argue in chapter
4, is the means by which shared beliefs are progressively translated
into practice and are deepened and extended in the process.

The ways in which teachers individually behave in their professional roles, within or outside their classrooms, is governed by their
beliefs. Beliefs determine the values that teachers hold and, consequently, the aims and purposes of their teaching. They are of two
kinds. They concern, firstly, the purposes of education, the intentions
and aims of educational provision, and, secondly, the means by which
those aims might best be achieved. For example, two teachers may
share a belief that one purpose of education is to teach children to
spell. They may, however, differ in their beliefs about how best to do
so and consequently their practice differs also. One may believe that
learning to spell is a visual skill. S/he may teach spelling by encouraging children to look closely at a word, cover it, write it and then
check it. S/he may also teach children to identify letter families and
common letter strings by their appearance. The teaching of spelling is
divorced from the teaching of phonics in which the visual and the
auditory are linked and which may be perceived as more appropriate
to the teaching of reading. Another teacher, however, may believe
that the teaching of spelling and the teaching of reading are closely
allied, in which case s/he may encourage children to think about the
sounds of words and use the letters and letter blends that commonly
represent those sounds in order to spell. Exceptions to common rules
may be taught separately. In both cases the teachers' practice is deter-

mined by their beliefs. Because of this close association between beliefs and behaviour we have often described teachers' professional practice as 'beliefs in action'. This notion is similar to that described by Elliott (1976) as teachers' 'practical theories'.

It is important to realize that beliefs are often implicit in teachers' behaviour and not easily recognized, expressed or challenged either by themselves or others. However, if 'whole schools' are perceived as being places where beliefs and purposes are shared then, of necessity, they must also be places where beliefs are openly recognized and agreed upon. We would not claim, since none of the teachers in them so claimed, that any of the schools in our study were 'whole' in the sense that all staff fully shared the same beliefs and purposes. However, each school did have explicitly expressed beliefs. The school brochure for Upper Norton, for example, opened with two statements of belief:

> We believe that all children are individuals, each with talents and interests which need to be nurtured.

> We believe that our school provides a secure and happy environment which enables children to fulfil their potential and achieve high standards in personal and social development as well as academic achievement.
>
> (Upper Norton School Brochure)

And the Head at Upper Norton believed that children learned through talking. In her daily interactions with staff and pupils the value she placed on oracy exemplified this belief. At Fenton five beliefs were readily recognizable, expressed both in the school brochure and repeatedly by the Headteacher in both formal and informal discussions with staff and visitors to the school. These were: a belief in the value of the individual; a belief in the value of first-hand experience to the learning process; a belief that parents had a vital role to play in the work of the school; a belief that high expectations should be held of children; a belief in the importance of promoting progression and continuity through the provision of a balanced curriculum. At Orchard, clearly stated aims sprang from broadly similar beliefs and at Carey and Ingham too, both in formal documents and daily practice, like beliefs were apparent.

There was evidence that such beliefs originated with the headteachers, since they were either expressed in documents for which the Headteacher had been wholly or partly responsible or were openly talked of by the heads. Additionally, at all five schools the heads actively sought to promote these explicitly stated beliefs in the work of their colleagues (see particularly chapters 3 and 4). The fact that they did so suggests that they also believed strongly in the value of having a staff group whose members shared a common set of beliefs about what was said and done within the school. This was the corner stone upon which their vision of a 'whole school' was founded.

Desirable as it might appear that teachers, working as colleagues within the same school, should share the same beliefs about educational purposes and practice, it cannot be assumed that they do so nor that they are easily brought to do so. Hence the importance of the second theme we identified — the ways in which teachers worked together, and by so doing developed, established and sustained shared beliefs about their purposes and practice. The variety of ways in which teachers worked together are explored in greater detail in chapter 3. Here we need only say that our evidence suggests that shared beliefs developed over time, were established only gradually in the thinking and practice of individuals and were sustained at a cost in time and effort to those who subscribed to them. Indeed, attaining shared beliefs could sometimes be a painful process, since tensions existed between the desire to work in concert with one's colleagues and the desire to retain an autonomy over classroom practice which was consistent with the responsibility that teachers felt at an individual level for their pupils and the curriculum (see chapter 1). As teachers worked increasingly closely together, differences in thinking as well as similarities were exposed and this could be disturbing. For example, at Ingham, where the staff worked together to produce an agreed curriculum policy on English, just such differences in the approach to the teaching of spelling as have been described above were highlighted by the Headteacher during the course of a curriculum discussion. Several of the teachers became confused and unhappy. The process of resolving the differences in belief between them was neither quick nor easy, indeed it was not achieved during the period of the research. However, the staff were sustained in the attempt by a more fundamental belief to which they had all come to suscribe, namely that they should, in the interests of their pupils, agree a common approach. Their commitment to working together reflected this belief and was so well established that it could not be reneged upon despite the tensions that had been exposed. Though the differences between the teachers with regard to spelling were unresolved during the period of the fieldwork, the need to resolve them and the determination to do so were often expressed.

Whilst this example shows how a commitment to working together helped shared beliefs and shared approaches to teaching and learning to develop amongst staff, it also suggests that beliefs themselves vary in importance to those who hold them. The centrality of any particular belief to an individual's educational philosophy will determine the degree of their willingness to compromise in their own practice for the sake of reaching agreement with their colleagues, to tolerate differences in practice between themselves and their colleagues or to tolerate delay in reaching agreement. The greater the agreement between them on what they regard as their core beliefs the greater the likelihood that they will be able to resolve or tolerate minor differences. The more central their belief in the importance of having shared beliefs, that is, of being a 'whole school', the more likely they are to address the differences between them and seek to resolve them.

Working together also served another, and equally important, purpose which is central to the third theme that we identified. Collaboration provided teachers with opportunities to learn. Learning was the means of both individual and 'whole school' curriculum development, as we demonstrate in chapters 2 and 4. There were, of course, many ways apart from working together in which individual teachers learned, but in a 'whole school' teachers' learning had added significance. As they worked with and so learned from one another, they developed the curriculum in staffrooms and classrooms in accordance with the beliefs they already shared or were coming to share with their colleagues. Whole school curriculum development occurred when beliefs were interpreted in classroom practice in similar ways by those who shared them. The processes by which such development took place are described in chapter 4.

The majority, if not all, of the teachers in the project schools valued the opportunities to work together and to learn from and with one another because they wanted, as we have already seen, to work in schools which they thought of as being 'whole'. They were willing therefore to seek to establish such schools and progressively to develop the curriculum within them. The headteachers recognized the importance of teachers both working and learning together and consistently encouraged them to do both (see chapter 3). By so doing they were, in fact, involving staff in the process of developing 'whole schools', places where beliefs about educational purposes and the means by which they might best be achieved were shared by their members and interpreted in broadly similar ways by them.

Notwithstanding this shared commitment, the evidence in chapter 5 suggests that whole school curriculum development does not occur all the time in any school. At Upper Norton in the summer term, for example, much happened that contributed towards the development of elements of a 'whole school' but very little occurred that might be termed 'whole school curriculum development'. At Orchard there was much evidence of a history of 'whole school curriculum development' but during the year of our research there was apparently none. What seems certain is that, whatever the circumstances of a school, the process of becoming 'whole' and of developing a 'whole school curriculum' is generally slow and halting, is sometimes subject to decay, yet may occasionally move forward at a surprisingly rapid pace.

In this book we first explore, in chapter 1, what the teachers in the project schools understood by the terms 'curriculum', 'curriculum development' and 'whole school'. In chapter 2 we argue that the curriculum was developed in the classrooms only as teachers themselves learned. We offer explanations as to why teachers wanted to learn, describe the opportunities which existed for them to learn, analyze the means by which they learned and examine how their learning was encouraged and facilitated within the schools. In chapter 3 we describe the actions of the headteachers as they sought to encourage the development of 'whole schools' and the ways in which teachers, as they worked together, came to share beliefs about their professional purposes and practice and so to behave in similar ways within classrooms. Chapter 4 demonstrates how closely allied were teachers' learning and the development of shared beliefs in the processes of bringing about whole school curriculum development, and provides examples of those processes. Chapter 5 outlines the conditions that appeared on the one hand to facilitate development and on the other to impede it. Finally, in chapter 6, we summarize the main findings of the project, consider some conclusions we feel may be drawn from them and discuss the implications these have for those who work in primary schools and are concerned with their development.

We hope that you will enjoy reading this book as much as we enjoyed working in the schools about which it is written, and that at the end of it, you will share our respect for the teachers who engaged in the complex and difficult task of whole school curriculum development.

Note

1 We have used the terms common within each school to describe the year groups. The National Curriculum usage follows in brackets.

Chapter One

Understanding Whole School Curriculum Development

This book, and the research project from which it stems, is based upon a study of five schools in each of which the staff were consciously trying to develop policies which would affect the practice of them all — that is, in whole school curriculum development. Their efforts to think about what and how they taught as if it were the professional concern of them all and not simply, as is still the case in many schools, of individual class teachers predates our research. In this respect, these schools were in the van of a trend which has been quickened and made obligatory by the introduction of the National Curriculum. In Orchard, Fenton and Carey, in each of which the heads had been in post for at least ten years, the staff had been steadily reviewing the curriculum for almost as long as the heads had been in post. At Ingham and Upper Norton, relatively new heads had initiated, soon after their arrival, school-based and staff-led curriculum development. In all these schools the National Curriculum therefore, to some extent, cut across existing practice.

Sometimes, it complicated the staffs' purposes and increased the pressure upon them, by distracting their attention from plans which they had already made and taking them in directions which did not always fit comfortably with existing long-term aspirations and strategies. At Upper Norton, for example, the scrutiny of the school's mathematics, which had begun the previous year and was planned to continue into the next one, was informally suspended, to await publication of the National Curriculum Council's final report. The effect upon many teachers at Orchard of the flood of NCC and DES documents and related local authority training was to slow down existing school-based initiatives and to induce a sense of frustration. Staff at Ingham were also conscious that their attention was being fragmented and distracted from some of their on-going plans.

However, the schools also turned the impending introduction of the National Curriculum and the nature of the NCC's recommendations, as these appeared during the year, to some positive effect. In particular these proposals gave heads and interested teachers a reason to direct the staffs' attention to aspects of curriculum or pedagogy which they felt could be used to serve their schools' long-term educational purposes. In this respect, the National Curriculum gave an impetus to school review and to the growth of structures and strategies appropriate for development. The positive use to which the staff of these schools turned national legislation, with which they were not necessarily in sympathy, recurs as a constant theme in successive chapters.

Indeed, the teachers worked together in ways which may offer a way forward to other primary staffs who are struggling in response to the National Curriculum to find ways of developing and implementing through-school policies. For over a decade, HMI and the Department of Education and Science (for example, DES, 1978, 1980, 1982, 1985a, 1985b and 1987) have repeatedly argued that the curriculum in primary schools, both in individual subject areas and as a whole, had insufficient coherence, breadth and balance and that not enough attention was paid to continuity and progression. They have in consequence urged teachers to work together and to develop 'collegiality' (though the precise meaning of this phrase has never been made clear, Campbell and Southworth, 1990). There have been other initiatives, notably GRIDS (McMahon *et al.*, 1984) whose purpose was to stimulate the collective involvement of teachers in school-based review and development. During the 1980s many local authorities developed their own ways of persuading teachers both to undertake systematic reviews of their practice and to work collaboratively towards greater curriculum coherence and continuity. Individual headteachers too have worked towards these goals.

However, these have often been influences upon primary schools, rather than requirements. The obligation now placed on teachers to think about what and how children learn from the ages of 5 to 16 is a new one. So too is the inference that individuals will have no option but to alter their practice in the light of these deliberations. The introduction of the National Curriculum, the requirement that schools produce development plans, and the related pressure on heads and teachers to move towards the production of whole-school policies call for a fundamental change in the attitudes of many primary teachers.

This change is the more radical because involvement in the formation and implementation of whole-school policies is not simply new, but also alien to many primary teachers. Campbell and South-worth (1990) showed that the teachers in the project schools were not particularly conscious of the 'whole school' in which they worked. This is not surprising; the traditions of individualism, self-reliance and curricular autonomy are deeply engrained in English primary schools (Nias, 1989a). Over the years, some schools have been at pains to develop an institutional culture built upon particular beliefs about teaching, learning and the nature of knowledge (see, for example, Holmes, 1952; Jackson, 1968; Clegg, 1980), but by long-established custom, primary teachers have been expected to reflect upon and assume responsibility for the learning of only those children whom they teach.

This tradition has been fostered by the nature of teachers' profes-sional development. Alexander (1988) suggested that teachers on ad-vanced in-service courses are more aware than their less experienced colleagues of multiple perspectives on classroom phenomena. Nias (1989a) argued that as teachers mature their concerns shift from class-room survival to a consciousness of their impact on children and other adults. Both accounts stress a shift from preoccupation with self to awareness of others. Young or inexperienced teachers, or those who, for whatever reason, are temporarily finding classroom work a strug-gle, may be disinclined, even unable, to see beyond the boundaries of their own practice. A willingness to engage wholeheartedly in the formation of whole-school policies and, more particularly, to be con-cerned about their implementation may be a hallmark of profes-sional maturity. Therefore, not all staff may be capable of it at all times. Indeed, we found that though almost all the teachers in the project schools valued learning, only a minority were actively con-cerned to foster the learning of their colleagues or to effect changes in other people's practice.

So, the National Curriculum requires that primary teachers radi-cally alter the ways in which they conceptualize and carry out their responsibilities. They are not, however, unused to change, since schools are in any case dynamic rather than static institutions, as Nias *et al.* (1989a) makes clear:

Primary schools are constantly changing, in unpredictable ways. Teachers' classroom lives were changing, almost by the minute, numbers of adults (teaching, ancillary and support, visiting, part-time volunteer, full-time) daily came and went from the head's office, the staffroom and the school, their mood and their numbers affected by predictable events (such as in-service courses) and unpredictable ones (such as illness or vandalism), the tempo, rhythm and content of school life altered with the seasons and in response to specific events (such as medical inspections and fire drills). The feelings and the energy levels of headteachers and staff rose and fell, following the dictates of their personal lives as well as of events in school. More dramatically, staff left, requiring the attention of those who remained to be focused upon replacing them, upon the subsequent socialization of newcomers and upon their own accommodation to new colleagues and fresh ideas. These constant modifications to the personnel, tasks, climate and feelings of the staff created an endemic potential for disequilibrium within each school. (p. 124)

These schools were no different. During the year, they faced constant interruptions which had little to do with the National Curriculum and were independent of their own ongoing curriculum reviews. Individuals dealt with personal upheavals such as severe illness, bereavement, marital breakdown and family disruption. They were absent from school for reasons such as jury service, illness, hospital appointments, courses, interviews for other jobs, school journeys. Sometimes they were replaced by supply teachers, at others their absence disrupted the work of the head or of other teachers. Students, visitors, tradespeople, governors, parents, and related professionals such as social workers and school doctors came and went. So too did children, either absent, sick, or, with increasing frequency, on out-of-season holidays. Some pupils left, others joined. One school celebrated a tenth anniversary, the others altered their timetables and internal arrangements for musical or dramatic productions, to fundraise, to involve parents in school activities or to show them their children's work. Four of the schools lost staff. In one the Deputy left and was replaced by a temporary appointment, in another the Headteacher left to be succeeded for a term by the Deputy as Acting Head. Often these changes had an effect on organization, such as the composition of teams or the frequency of meetings. Teachers' roles and responsibilities also altered in response to them. Two schools ended the summer term facing unexpected cuts in staffing because of falling rolls, with the attendant need for organizational modifications. All of them began to anticipate budget cuts and the likely effects of LMS. All had new governing bodies, either at the start of the year or at its end (Upper Norton was a controlled school). Two lived with major building programmes.

Our study then, took place in schools whose staff were already finding their own ways towards a more holistic view of the school curriculum than is customary in many schools and who, simultaneously, faced during the year a considerable number of changes which owed little or nothing either to internal review and development or to the National Curriculum. Our focus was the ways in which these staffs were working together to develop and implement whole school policies. National innovations and unpredicted events cut across these efforts and had an impact upon them. But neither was the initial cause of school-based developments nor was either responsible for the continuing pursuit of quality in children's education which inspired the schools' continuing search for improvement. It was the heads and teachers in these schools who undertook and carried out, in the absence of any established blueprints or models, their own reflective attempts at 'whole school curriculum development'.

In this chapter we analyze and interpret teachers' and head-teachers' understandings of the words which made up this phrase. We did not directly ask them what they understood by 'curriculum' or 'curriculum development'. During many years of teaching on in-service courses, we had learnt that when primary teachers think or talk of the curriculum they use the term in very broad, ill-defined ways. Moreover, our fieldwork coincided with the impending introduction of the National Curriculum and with active preparation for it, especially in Key Stage 1, so it seemed likely that formal questions about the meaning of 'curriculum' would elicit responses reflecting what was known about the National Curriculum, rather than about individuals' own classrooms or schools. Similarly, we did not directly probe teachers' or headteachers' understanding of 'curriculum development', relying instead on observations of what they did and said. In respect of these terms, we have therefore relied on inference. By contrast, we did feel it appropriate towards the end of the year, after we had made our own observations, to ask the staff in each school what they understood by 'whole school', because we had selected these schools on the grounds that they were seeking to formulate and implement specific policies throughout the 'whole school'.

One further point needs to be made. It was often difficult to determine whether or not a particular development was curricular (for example, at Upper Norton, the review of the school's discipline policy). Accordingly we felt it would be misleading to dismiss any change as too trivial or localized to merit attention. Consequently, evidence, both for this book, and for the case studies from which is drawn, has been sifted from a mass of detailed observation. We have chosen to present the main themes which emerged but at the cost of laying to one side many smaller changes or innovations which might in time prove to be of even greater significance than those upon which we have focussed.

Understanding 'Curriculum'

Children's Learning

In every school, the curriculum was conceived in terms of children's learning. All the staff appeared to assume, and sometimes openly said, that the first and main purpose of schools is to educate children. The referent for curriculum was unambiguously the learning of individual pupils.

This showed itself in a number of ways. No school tried to build its curriculum on children's own interests, though the Head of Fenton said that this had been one of his original aims. However, in all of them we found evidence that teachers allowed their classes' enthusiasms to shape the course of topic work, that individual children were given the opportunity to pursue in detail particular aspects of a common theme and to develop specific talents, that teachers' expectations of achievement altered in response to their perceptions of children's social, emotional and physical states, that, when levels of adult help allowed, they gave additional assistance to individuals with particular difficulties, that they constantly talked about, and made informal assessments of, individuals' abilities and levels of attainment and tried to tailor to them the nature and pace of the tasks they set. It is impossible to generalize in a way that does justice to the subtle nuances of teacher behaviour or to shifts in individual attitudes and practice in five schools over a year, but, that said, the teachers evidently wanted their pupils to make progress and to enjoy learning, were responsive to what they felt were individual and collective talents, interests and needs and selected much of the content of the curriculum, especially in topic work, by reference to their classes' likely or actual involvement in it. Heads, too, frequently referred to the learning or progress of individuals and classes, supported teachers in their efforts to be responsive and flexible (for example, by working with individual children, by the provision of specialized resources, by giving advice on classroom organization or the management of resources) and encouraged choices of curriculum content and pedagogy which were likely to motivate and stimulate as many children as possible. As the Curriculum Policy Statement at Fenton stated,

> Our aims are to ensure that the needs of each individual are catered for to the best of our abilities.

The Head said,

> At the centre of it all is still the individual child and wanting to do the best for the individual child... As a staff I don't think I could find a group of people who are more concerned with each individual in their classes. They do know them pretty well and...if you listen to their conversations...it's very much about the individual child and the individual child's problems and how do you deal with them.

Teachers' Right to Choose

Though the central purpose of each school was, then, to ensure the maximum possible learning of all its pupils, teachers directly or indirectly determined much of the content of the curriculum and almost all the ways in which it was transmitted. That they assumed this as a right emerges very clearly from their planning of topic work. They frequently chose themes which stimulated them personally. Typically:

> I think a lot of it boils down to inclination and interest from your own point of view. If you aren't interested in a topic it's really a bit of a non-starter, because you are the one who has got to spark the enthusiasm. It's also partly based on expertise, in that different teachers have different inclinations and different expertises. (Teacher, Orchard)

Often, however, these topics were then negotiated with the children:

> I find if I've chosen something I'm really interested in, the children get much more out of it than something I'm not too keen on... I had chosen Space for this (term), but since our outing was fairly late in the term I decided we must have a little mini-topic. We had a few subjects and then out of those we voted. (Teacher, Carey)

Choice was also determined by the teacher's previous experience:

> I think the main thing is that you bring certain things with you... When I plan my work, I plan it now (that I'm teaching full-time) the way I've planned it ever since I've left college. (Teacher, Upper Norton)

or, by reference to other activities in the school:

> This half term we've done the life, times and work of Charles Dickens. The reason for it is partly due to the fact that we did *A Victorian Christmas* as a production and then Mrs. Clark started working with the choir on *Oliver*. We've been to see a production, so I thought that it would be rather nice to continue with that. (Teacher, Fenton)

Even on the occasions when staff were working within the framework of a topic agreed at school (in Ingham, Fenton and Upper Norton) or unit (Orchard) level, they felt free to exploit individual expertise or to pursue particular interests:

> Often what's happened is that, well with Graham for example, last term he wanted to do something on the local area and the Fens and I think he was very enthusiastic about doing that. I was doubtful whether I would be able to string it out for fourteen weeks and also whether it would have been valid to do that. So what we came up with in the end was a topic on water...and we've now included a big chunk on the Fens specifically. That can carry on for as long as we want it to and as long as it's useful. But I think it's important not to feel completely tied down. People do have different enthusiasms. If one is dead keen on something and the other can't think of anything about it that they would like to do, or can't see a way into it, then if you've got a specific topic it can be really restricting. (Teacher, Orchard)

Teachers also assumed that they had freedom of choice in most areas of their teaching behaviour and classroom management. Within a single school we noted considerable differences in organization and teaching style. The temporary teacher at Ingham who worked in six classes said, 'It's been very interesting seeing how different people work and the different approaches and the different responses from the children'. Though it was mandatory at particular schools to teach within certain structures (for example, mixed age classes at Upper Norton; unit pairs at Orchard; and at Fenton teachers were expected to strike a balance between individual, group and class teaching), individuals otherwise took for granted their right to decide how they would run their own classrooms and select their teaching methods.

> If somebody came in and said to me to do something different to what I was doing I wouldn't like it at all. I'd listen but...obviously, if you're quite an experienced teacher you know which way you can give yourself best. It might not be the best for somebody else, but...if the children are learning and getting a good education, then I think you can't change very basic things like that... Everybody works in different ways. (Teacher, Upper Norton)

Moreover, they seldom made any distinction between 'curriculum' and classroom practice. As the Fenton School Brochure, in its description of the curriculum put it:

> The actual teaching will vary according to the type of activity or the aims of the particular session. Children will be taught as classes, in small groups and as individuals. Sometimes it is more efficient to talk to the whole class but at other times, because of ability differences or the needs of the children, it is more productive to teach in other ways.

A teacher said:

> I start off with a flow diagram and at the start of that flow diagram there will be headings, maths, science, English, art. Music is sometimes written down, sometimes not. Then under those headings are listed the amount of work that I want to get through, the amount of basic work that I see in each and then, of course, after that, topic books are ordered from the library. The whole thing will be elaborated using those books. Poetry and the art work will then be elaborated again from using those books and the materials that we have in school. (Teacher, Carey)

We noted:

> (In assembly) Noreen's class showed their work on wheels... Noreen talked about the kinds of wheels people have brought into the classroom, the different things that they've done with them in technological terms (for example, making a wheel that fulfilled the conditions of standing upright and rolling down a line) and were going on to (now they've got to make a wheel that will follow a curved line). They'd all had to make these; they started from a 60 cm diameter piece of cardboard and then could use anything else that they could find around the classroom. The children told us what they'd used. We also looked at some art that one group had done. (Fieldnote, Upper Norton)

'Curriculum' then, was a comprehensive term, covering all the aspects of classroom activity for which teachers felt responsible and in respect of which they therefore expected to make choices. It included teaching methods, because through them children learnt skills (such as how to solve practical problems, how to work productively together) and attitudes (such as perseverance, curiosity, a willingness to listen to others). It also encompassed classroom organization, because this underpinned and facilitated pedagogy. Also included in 'curriculum' were the provision, organization and display of material designed to stimulate interest or teach concepts and the display of children's work, since the latter emphasized for adults and children alike acceptable standards (for example, of neatness, originality) and approved ways of working. Resources too, such as books, technology apparatus, physical education equipment, art materials, were viewed as an important part of the curriculum, since they constrained, shaped and facilitated the choice of both content and teaching methods. In some instances the organization of resources, in particular whether they were controlled by adults or freely accessible to pupils, was explicitly perceived as part of a teacher's pedagogy.

Constraints: 'Breadth', 'Balance' and Avoiding Repetition

To stress that individual teachers expected to be able to make most of the decisions which directly affected their classes' learning is not, however, to claim that they operated without any constraints. The availability of resources limited or encouraged certain types of work and ways of working, but teachers had only a limited control over the purchase, organization and use of those which were not in their rooms. In all the schools heads had expectations, in some schools more openly stated than in others, about the ways in which, for example, work was displayed, discipline was exercised, groups were used. These constraints are more fully explored in chapter 3, because they played an important part in developing among staff a sense of being a 'whole school'. Here, we simply draw attention to them.

Similarly, although teachers expected to exercise a good deal of control over curriculum content they did not look for complete autonomy. They showed a respect for many of the considerations which official publications (for example, DES, 1978, 1985a, 1985b and 1985c; ILEA, 1985; NCC, 1989 and 1990) have described as 'breadth', 'balance' and 'continuity'. First, they expressed, tacitly or openly, a belief that the curriculum should provide a rich and varied diet of learning experiences and should cater for the different physical, intellectual, emotional and cultural needs and abilities of individual children. Hence content was selected so as to cover a number of frequently mentioned areas (English, mathematics, science, the visual arts, music, technology drama and/or dance or movement, history, and less commonly geography, religious education, games and physical education). Indeed, teachers felt lacking if they could not teach such a broad curriculum and actively sought the knowledge or re-training of which they felt in need.

> First, I read about it. I get the topic books from the library about two weeks before... (Teacher, Carey)

> I haven't learnt enough technology. I have said openly within the staff that I do not feel qualified to teach technology and science... Frankly I don't know enough... I need retraining for science teaching. (Teacher, Upper Norton)

Four other aspects of children's learning were seen to be important. One were so-called extra-curricular activities (for example, clubs, sports, musical and dramatic activities) which went on outside school time in most of the schools and in which many teachers were involved. The others were moral, social and health education. All the teachers appeared to view aspects of their schools' 'hidden curriculum' (for example, its multicultural policy, its reward and punishment systems, the conduct and subject matter of assemblies, behaviour on school journeys) as serious and worthwhile topics in their own right.

At Ingham, the staff worked together for several weeks, using Kids-cape, to increase their understanding of, and sensitivity to, issues of child abuse. At Upper Norton, in-service time was devoted in and out of school to considering problems of racism and sexism in the curriculum and in teaching. In all the schools teachers attached considerable importance to good manners, respect for other's convenience and property, tolerance for differences in custom, belief and attainment. Moral and social teaching were often direct and, because they frequently arose from incidents within the school, sometimes occurred within, and took precedence over, the formal curriculum.

> Marion asked the children 'What hasn't the Tin Man said so far?' 'Please' said all the children. 'That's right. And that reminds me', said Marion, 'the other day, when you were going into the dining hall one of the dinner ladies held the door open for you and not one of you remembered to say "thank you".' She then recommenced reading the story. (Fieldnote, Orchard)

> Dorothy came in to talk briefly to Nancy, who gathered the class together from the art room and corridor. She asked them to sit down, made them shut the door and then talked about the nuts that had gone missing from the display in the art room. She said very directly, 'There's been some stealing'. She explained what had happened, making it quite clear in uncompromising ways that she felt it was dishonest. (Fieldnote, Upper Norton)

At other times (for example, for sex education; certain aspects of religious education), these curriculum areas were taught separately, as all areas were at some time, in all the schools.

Assemblies and school 'events' (such as *Starship Silver Grey* at Ingham or *Oliver* at Fenton) were also seen as part of this broad curriculum. Both types of activities frequently recur in later chapters, but a typical brief fieldnote reads:

> At the end of the fourth year's showing assembly Ron said, 'We've seen some lovely work, science work, structured work, maps, photographs, a lot of maths work, poetry, factual writing, art work'. He listed all areas of the curriculum that had been covered in this work and said whilst looking at

the children, 'All that work is of a high standard'. (Fieldnote, Orchard)

Another constraint of which teachers were aware was the need to strike a balance in the amount of time allocated to different curricular experiences, though English featured in some form in most activities and mathematics, taught as a separate subject, took up a good deal of time for most children. Few people seemed to feel that such a balance needed to be achieved over short periods, such as a day or a week. More often they thought in terms of half-terms, terms or even a year. Typically:

> The only maths work that I'm going to get in this topic is money...because there isn't really any maths in it, so I will, perhaps, make sure there is a bit more maths in the next topic. I do tend to look at it like that, perhaps not enough science in this one and not enough maths. There's more art and writing in here, so the next project I decide on will be something to do with science or something like that — that's how I try to work it out. (Teacher, Carey)

Often, too, 'balance' was analyzed retrospectively (as when the Head of Upper Norton listed to a parent the curriculum areas which had been included in *The Firebird*) or was sought through intensive bursts of focussed activity (for example, day trips to a castle, windmills, farms; residential journeys to Holland, Derbyshire and the Isle of Wight; sports days, musical productions). A teacher said of the *Summer Garland* at Ingham,

> It was really a kick back from having to do all the nitty-gritty National Curriculum work. I thought 'Wouldn't it be nice to do something really aesthetic through the summer term'?

Some teachers were also constrained by a sense, itself, so they claimed, the product of experience, that the learning of skills (and more rarely of concepts, especially in mathematics) was hierarchical and sequential. They therefore had what a teacher at Upper Norton described as 'ladders in my head', or as someone else less vividly put it:

> A prerequisite of planning is to go through the children's folders so you can see exactly what they have done in learning

terms and where gaps might be, or where something has been begun and could be developed. (Teacher, Orchard)

Fenton, and to a lesser extent Carey, were unusual, a fact to which we return in chapter 4, in that the teachers there showed an awareness of progression in the curriculum and planned their work with this in mind:

> It's got to be down to what we've agreed as a staff, what we're going to follow as progressions. That's one of the first things I've got to look at — where they've come from in each of the main areas and where they are going to... It'll either be a class-based topic where I decide the content knowing the skills levels I want them to achieve or it might be a school-based topic where again, the content has been agreed, perhaps with one or two people at the junior level. Then I decide on the particular levels of skills that the children have got to achieve...the sort of levels that we've as a school identified for third and fourth year children (Y5 and Y6) (Teacher, Fenton)

At Carey, classes were reorganized and merged in the summer term:

> Kay Hale (said) that her class had done a lot of work on 'Time', but Kay Harvey's class had not. She has to be aware that these pupils need to cover 'Time'. (Fieldnote, Carey)

In the remaining schools teachers were more conscious of their responsibility to build on what children already knew and could do than to prepare them for what was to follow. Most teachers were however at pains to avoid repeating work which they knew, often from the records sent to them by other teachers, had already been tackled.

'Ownership': Control and Internalization

In everything that we have so far said we have emphasized the fact that teachers expected to be able to exercise choice, within limits, in relation to every aspect of the widely-conceived curriculum which they felt responsible for transmitting to children. Indeed, in many respects they behaved as if they 'owned' the curriculum. By this term we wish to convey two notions. One is control:

> The teachers felt they needed a flexible structure that would
> give them control over the teaching of reading... Verity was
> particularly adamant about the need for the teachers to take
> control. (Fieldnote, Fenton)

So great was teachers' desire to control the curriculum to which 'their'
children were exposed that it affected the way in which they worked
with other teaching and non-teaching staff, a point to which we return
in chapter 3. Only in a very few instances (for example, Kate and
Mary, who shared a class at Carey; Jean and David, a unit pair at
Orchard) did teachers feel that they shared their responsibility for a
class or a teaching situation with others and so were able to share
control of it as well. In every other case, no matter how many adults
were involved, one of them assumed overall responsibility, and hence
control, while the others acted as 'helpers' or took on delegated
responsibilities for particular parts of the task. Individual teachers'
reluctance to surrender control of the curriculum for which they felt
responsible was evident in the overwhelming majority of cases, no
matter who the adults were (for example, support teachers; class
teachers, part-time specialists), what the context (for example,
teachers sharing a working space or a class; school journeys; preparing
for a school production) or who they were working with (for example, welfare and care assistants; other teachers; the headteacher).

The other major component of curricular 'ownership' is internalization. Teachers in the project schools often behaved in relation to
the curriculum, as if it came from within them or was part of them. It
was 'their' curriculum in the sense that it resided inside them and did
not have a separate and possibly alien identity. In the same way, they
did not perceive constraints upon their autonomy as limitations, because these too had been internalized and had become part of their
thinking:

> I think probably topic work has a genuine hold on us now...
> We've actually internalized the topic approach since I've been
> here. It's not something you do on an odd afternoon. It
> permeates everything you teach. (Teacher, Carey)

This notion of 'ownership' as both control and internalization is
important because it highlights the contrasting fact that in each school
there were parts of the curriculum which seemed to be external to the
teachers and which they therefore perceived as burdens, obstacles or,
even sometimes, as fetters.

The dual nature of curriculum ownership is clearly shown in the attitudes of heads and teachers to 'schemes' such as Peak Mathematics, Oxford English, SRA, Ginn 360, or graded worksheets. All of the schools used such schemes, particularly in mathematics and English. None of the heads liked the limitations implicit in the idea of a curriculum confined within books, its philosophy and scope decided by people outside both the school and the individual teacher's classroom. They all, however, sanctioned the use of schemes as a means of providing continuity, progression and individual progress in children's learning, to add to the teachers' repertoire of pedagogical skills and to provide teachers, supply teachers and, sometimes, parents, with a sense of security. However, they encouraged their staff to use them so that they fitted in with rather than dominated their classes' learning programme and to go beyond them when they saw fit. As the Head of Upper Norton said,

> It's teachers who teach reading, not schemes...Ginn 360 is a fairly average reading scheme if it's used by the teacher and if the teacher doesn't follow it slavishly.

At Ingham, a recently appointed teacher reported:

> I was told, 'We use the Maths scheme, but you can veer from it. You need to supplement it. You need to put something more into it.'

For their part, teachers varied in their liking for schemes and the use they made of them. They also showed different levels of understanding of the curriculum rationale underlying the particular 'scheme' that they were using.

Teachers advanced two sets of reasons for liking or using schemes or worksheets. One was organizational. Commercial materials frequently involved minimal preparation, marking was usually straightforward, children using them could often get on with relatively little teacher intervention (or with the help of a parent or volunteer) and, provided the task matched the child's capabilities, some pupils enjoyed using them.

> I still teach phonics... They must know the letter sounds... And part of the reason for doing it this term is in fact that I've got thirty-three children in the class and you can give them worksheets. You've got to survive. (Teacher, Ingham)

I've got the Oxford Junior English which is more or less a sleeper activity so that a group...know what is expected of them and they know where to do it and how...then I can have a couple of groups for an oral activity. (Teacher, Fenton)

The teachers involved have got their children into a real routine of using these books. The children evidently love them — they're thin, there's just sufficient work that it's not going to take them too long to get through it, it gives them a sense of achievement to say, 'I've finished this one, I'm going on to this one and then I can do that book.' They can see their way ahead, they can see where their path lies. (Teacher, Upper Norton)

The second set of reasons was epistemological. For some teachers structured curriculum materials provided 'bread and butter' (Teacher, Ingham), that is, practice in routine but necessary skills such as handwriting, comprehension or mathematical tables. Others found that schemes provided guidance in subject areas in which they felt insecure (for example, 'Until recently I kept entirely to the Maths scheme', Teacher, Upper Norton). Different from either of these reasons was the suggestion, more rarely made, that schemes were written by experts who knew the curricular area well and could structure it so as to allow for the introduction of progressively more complex and difficult concepts and skills.

A reference to Oxford English raised the question of its value... In spite of some reservations they concluded that it has some worth in providing the opportunity for regular and systematic developmental work in language. (Fieldnote, Fenton)

In all these cases, teachers voluntarily used schemes because they facilitated classroom organization or because they appeared to offer a simpler or better way of helping children to learn than the unaided teacher could devise. However, teachers themselves controlled the use they made of them, incorporating them into their individual pedagogies and epistemologies. Schemes in this sense became part of the 'beliefs in action' (see Introduction) of individual teachers. As the case of SPMG worksheets at Upper Norton suggests, under these circumstances they would go to considerable lengths to protect them.

Teachers' reactions to schemes which they did not understand or like also stresses their felt need to 'own' them. Sometimes they subverted them, by using them for ends other than those intended by the authors.

> In the afternoon I worked with a Ginn 360 group. I got in a fearful muddle with these, as they were on three separate levels and some of the worksheets didn't seem to go with the books. The children were quite happy when doing the worksheets, but the three working together wanted only to gallop through the text and weren't interested in discussion. I apologized to the teacher at break for having to interrupt her a couple of times; I realized afterwards it was my fault for not having realized that she was using Ginn 360 as individual readers, with accompanying worksheets for comprehension. She explained: 'Helen and I decided to start them off on Ginn at this stage so that it could be properly used as a group reader later on'. (Fieldnote, Upper Norton)

On other occasions they ignored or abandoned them, or paid them token attention:

> I've taught first year for about twelve years, on and off...what I've taught in the first year has been based on my own experience and my own standards, particularly where maths is concerned, rather than what is laid down by the school, although I've covered what's on the maths curriculum sheets. (Fieldnote, Orchard)

They also sought to replace them with more congenial materials, as happened individually over Sound•Sense at Upper Norton or collectively with SRA at Carey and the introduction of Breakthrough at Fenton. Whatever the strategy adopted, teachers who objected to the use of a particular set of curriculum materials indicated by their words or their actions their desire to control the curriculum and to feel that it was a natural part of 'this vision in my head that I want to carry through' (Teacher, Upper Norton).

'Owning' the National Curriculum

This powerfully expressed desire to 'own' the curriculum influenced teacher's reactions to the impending introduction of the National

Curriculum. In general, the nature of their anticipation of it
a great deal upon whether or not they felt that they coul
control it and make it part of their own thinking and practi
the schools, some teachers initially saw it as an overwhelming constraint upon their own practice.

> I was very wary when the National Curriculum was coming
> — if that meant I was going to have to change the way I was
> teaching, I couldn't have done it. I would have to have left,
> because there's no way I feel I could do the job I was doing,
> to the best of my ability, in a different way. You feel you
> couldn't work in any other way. (Teacher, Upper Norton)

Yet collectively the staff at Ingham, Upper Norton and, in some
curriculum areas, Fenton turned the situation round during the year,
demonstrating how they could use the National Curriculum to develop or extend the realization in action of their school's educational
purposes. In each case, the Head (in Fenton, it was the Deputy who,
in the summer term, became the Acting Head) forestalled a feeling
of collective impotence by taking the initiative. The Head at Carey
summed up the way she and her colleagues behaved:

> We've got this idea that we want to be one stage ahead of the
> game, so that when somebody does put pressure on, we can
> say, 'Oh, but that's not the way we do it here!' We wanted to
> find our own way through... I actually wanted us to be one
> step ahead of the game in a way that I saw was useful to
> education in the school.

Typically, the staff, led by their heads, fastened upon one or more
features of the National Curriculum Council's publications, or upon a
related local authority initiative (for example, on assessment). This
then became the basis for a programme of learning and dissemination
activities in which all the teachers, and often the non-teaching staff,
participated. In chapters 2, 3 and 4 we examine some of these activities
in detail. The point we wish to stress here is that aspects of the
National Curriculum were actively used in all these schools to foster
policies and practices which already existed or with which the Head
and key staff members were already in sympathy. As this happened
teachers and headteachers began to absorb the National Curriculum
into their thinking and to serve their own purposes through it. In the
process they collectively reasserted their own sense of control over

and personal identification with the school curriculum for which they felt responsible. In addition, individuals used the opportunities offered by the coming of the National Curriculum to increase their own learning and, through the acquisition of new knowledge and skills, to expand their own classroom potential. So, the National Curriculum was made, often simultaneously, to serve three related ends: the development of a sense of belonging to an educational community with shared purposes, individual learning, collective learning in the interests of the 'whole school' (see chapter 4).

In the summarized example which follows we show how the Head of one school used an in-service day based upon the requirements of the National Curriculum to help her staff extend their sense of 'ownership'.

With the agreement of the staff, Evelyne, the Head at Ingham, led an in-service day, based upon the proposals for English in the National Curriculum. It took place on one Saturday in the summer term; the choice of day had been a collective one. The teachers worked initially in the same groups as they had in the previous term when drawing up policy documents for the implementation of the English National Curriculum. They were asked to itemize what resources they thought there should be in the classrooms in order to fulfil the needs of English in the school and then to report back to the whole group. There was a fairly lively discussion about resourcing, storage, play, display and possible approaches to the teaching of the reading, writing, speaking and listening. Then:

> At about 10.50am Evelyne introduced the second task of the morning. She asked the teachers to pair up, or perhaps be in threes, and look at each other's classrooms as 'critical friends'. She said, 'Choose somebody to work with that you trust and think about possible ways of reorganizing the classrooms'. She went off to photocopy the sheets with the lists of resources on and the rest of the staff sat around for a bit just chatting generally before eventually dispersing around the school. There were some questions about which classrooms they would be in next year. Some clearly felt that when thinking about reorganizing classrooms, their main intention would be to begin September with a new organization... There was a lot of laughter both now and throughout the morning... I found Eliot and Karen together in Karen's room talking about a reading area, a place for carpet play, a place to put the maths equipment and an area for working at maths. They were

discussing the possibility of getting rid of some tables to create more space. How many children would she need to have seated at any one time, David asked her. 'Well, perhaps three out of five groups', she replied. Evelyne, she said, had told her that getting rid of tables would be Fearghus's (the caretaker's) problem and not something that she should worry about. Karen had drawn a plan of her room and marked on it the various suggestions she and Eliot had made... I went into Lori's rooms to find Edith, Lori and Rhian just finishing their discussion on Lori's room. Lori too had a plan. She had particularly asked Edith to join her because she admired Edith's own classroom organization. Clearly Edith, and probably Rhian too, had made lots of suggestions and Lori was quite excited about what she was going to do, even saying that she would like to do it straight away. We all went over to Edith's classroom. Rhian said, 'Oh, you've changed this round even since last week'. During these discussions, all the teachers occasionally shared their own teaching practices through comments like 'I do a lot of teaching from here' or 'I move around and hear reading in different places'. (Fieldnote, Ingham)

Several of the teachers found this to be a useful exercise and some wished it could have been extended, though not all of them found it easy. Nor did the process of thinking stop with the immediate changes. Teachers became more aware of the use of space in the classrooms, made alterations in their own rooms, and continued to mull over the advantages and disadvantages of particular types of arrangement. Individuals also fed their growing awareness of alternative forms of organization into changes they were coincidentally making in their teaching of other areas of the curriculum. Using the National Curriculum, they moved over the term closer towards the 'shared way of working that we're edging towards' (Head, Ingham).

To sum up: In this section we have made four claims about these teachers' perceptions of the curriculum. First, its scope, suitability and relevance were judged by reference to children's learning. Second, teachers expected considerable freedom to decide upon curriculum content and upon the many aspects of their practice which they saw as inseparable from it, particularly pedagogy, classroom organization and management, display, resources. Third, this freedom was exercised within constraints, especially those imposed by a respect for 'breadth', 'balance' and a desire to avoid repetition. These restrictions were freely espoused and were not therefore seen as irksome. Fourth, they wanted to 'own' the curriculum, including the National Curriculum, that is both to control it and to feel that it was part of their own thinking rather than external to them and, at times, imposed upon them.

If these teachers are typical, practitioners see 'curriculum' as a complex, many-faceted, interrelated notion which is the servant of, and the vehicle for, their intention to educate individual children. The key to understanding this comprehensive view of an ill-defined term lies in their sense of accountability to, and for, their pupils. Teachers feel deeply responsible for the children whom parents and others have placed in their charge. Elliott *et al.* (1981) found that secondary teachers had a dual sense of accountability. They felt formally accountable to those (for example, headteachers, governors) to whom they had legal or bureaucratic obligations, but whom they often perceived as being distant or remote from their practice. They also, and much more powerfully, felt morally accountable for their pupils and through them to the latter's parents. This sense of moral accountability arose through, and was inseparable from, interpersonal contact and knowledge. The better they knew their pupils, the more likely they were to feel morally committed to their progress and in many cases to their overall well-being. Nias (1989a), in a study of primary teaching as work, made a similar claim. She argued, in the words of the teachers themselves, that to 'feel like a teacher' is to experience concern, responsibility and a desire to control. These feelings were inter-linked. Concern arose from personal knowledge of individuals and from the sense of 'belonging' and 'wholeness' which came from working as a classteacher. Responsibility was fuelled by concern, and so by interpersonal knowledge, but also resulted from the sense of isolation and self-reliance which primary teaching traditionally imposes on its practitioners. The felt-need to control was inseparable from responsibility, particularly in the tense, crowded, swiftly-changing conditions of primary classrooms where children's safety, happiness and above all learning depended upon the teacher's capacity to maintain a finely-poised balance amidst all the conflicts, dilemmas and tensions which were inherent in the job.

Now, teachers are heirs to many curricular traditions (see Alexander, 1984). One of these is 'Romanticism' or 'progressivism', a set of ideas with a history of at least two centuries which stresses the importance of educating the 'whole child' and therefore of having an undivided curriculum. Many primary practitioners are socialized into this tradition and therefore feel responsible for children's development and learning across a vast and interrelated curricular field. In turn, this sense of responsibility leads them to feel that that they must exercise control over all aspects of the curriculum in order to meet their perceived obligation to educate the 'whole child'.

Furthermore, the isolated and individualistic conditions under which in the past much primary teaching has taken place has encouraged practitioners to invest a great deal of their sense of personal identity in the job (Nias, 1989a). There is a widespread assumption that much of what individuals say and do should, indeed must, come from within themselves. Concern, responsibility and the urge to control are compounded by a felt-need for self-reliance and self-expression. Small wonder, then, that teachers make as much of the curriculum as they can, including the National Curriculum, part of their own thinking; internalization and control go hand in hand.

Understanding Curriculum Development

Given the vast and comprehensive nature of 'curriculum' and its implicit roots in the individual teacher's sense of personal identity and self-investment in work, it follows that 'curriculum development' too will be a broad concept and a complex, personal process.

Most obviously, it was perceived in the project schools as inseparable from the development of the individual teacher. This often meant providing opportunities for, or motivation towards, the acquisition and practice of fresh knowledge, skills, attitudes. On occasions it meant helping a newly-appointed teacher to fit into a school. Similarly 'curriculum development' could involve persuading one or more teachers to internalize a new set of beliefs about knowledge, learning, teaching, the nature of children and the purposes of schooling. It could also include the extension of existing knowledge and skills or of specific interests. Sometimes too it meant responding to the individual's need for personal recognition, refreshment or growth. Teacher development is so central to our understanding of curriculum development and to that of others (notably Stenhouse, 1975) that we have devoted the next chapter to it.

Headteachers and teachers showed through their actions and, less frequently their words, their awareness that the curriculum could be 'developed' in different ways. Sometimes, some or all of the staff focussed upon a particular curriculum area, changing, modifying or extending their practice, either on a small scale or throughout the school. Such development could happen almost spontaneously (for example, at Orchard, where the arrival of fresh resources stimulated the third year team to undertake some new work in technology). At others it arose from the initiative of the head, a curriculum coordinator or an interested staff member and involved some, but not all, of the teachers (for example, music at Fenton). More formal reviews of particular policies also took place, often, though not invariably, stimulated by the headteacher, but requiring the participation and attention of all the staff (for example, special needs at Upper Norton where the coordinator's attendance on a course required her to produce specific information from every class). There were occasions too when someone, or a group, sought to broaden the curriculum which was being presented to particular children. At Ingham, for example, two teachers became extremely interested in the concept of creativity and of how the local environment could be used to help children become more creative, while one unit pair at Orchard consciously introduced open-ended enquiry work into their teaching of science.

Headteachers had a particular view of curriculum development because they had a formal and a felt responsibility not just for all of the curriculum but also for the learning of every child. In addition they all had educational beliefs around which they wished the practice of the school to be built. So they wanted their staff to accept these as their own, or at the least to show adherence to them. 'Development' in this sense meant developing a 'whole school' curriculum, that is, doing what they could to ensure that all the staff behaved in accordance with these basic tenets and that their understanding of them was deepened and enriched. This was an aspect of the heads' work which required them to educate their colleagues, to monitor their work and to be constantly aware of staff selection and of the processes of induction into and socialization by the staff group (see chapter 3). At the same time heads tempered their search for a 'common approach' (Head, Upper Norton) by respect for the individuality of staff members. Seeking to establish shared beliefs about the ways in which children learned, about the value of individual pupils and the breadth and standard of the learning of which they were capable was an educative activity and not an exercise in cloning. It was also an important aspect of developing a sense among all participants that their school was 'whole'. These are ideas that we explore further in the next section and in chapter 3.

In all the schools, the heads also sought to foster a climate in which every aspect of the school, except its fundamental beliefs, was perceived as open to question and as capable of improvement. Consequently, each school engaged in continual, though often informal, processes of review, development and change which encompassed both the apparently insignificant (for example, altering the start of the infant day at Fenton) and the fundamental (for example, at Carey giving systematic thought to the place of science in the curriculum, in the light of proposals for the National Curriculum). Although we saw little evidence of formal evaluation, all the heads encouraged their teachers to treat their choice of curriculum content and their pedagogy as open to question. In this sense curriculum development was a form of critical enquiry into current practice and future goals. Initiating and fostering this state of mind was, like ensuring a 'common approach', an educative aspect of the head's job (see chapter 2).

The meaning of 'curriculum development' varied then with its context. In addition, it was possible for development in all the senses that we have identified to take place simultaneously or in any combination for varying lengths of time. All in all, it was not a tidy, neatly defined or predictable phenomenon.

It is slightly easier to make generalizations about the processes through which it took place. We examine these in detail in chapters 2, 3 and 4. Here we suggest their defining characteristics and the reasons for these. The processes of curriculum development were gradual and did not proceed at a uniform pace, because teachers needed to reassure themselves that change was likely to benefit their pupils, would not interfere with their freedom to select and teach the curriculum in ways which they felt were appropriate, did not impose unacceptable constraints upon them and could be made part of their own thinking. They were piecemeal, for the same reasons and because development often started with an individual concern or enthusiasm. Similarly, they were opportunistic, in the sense that any event, activity or stimulus could be used to make learning broader, deeper, more purposeful or more in keeping with the school's fundamental beliefs. They were complex and interdependent because the curriculum was seen as all-embracing and interlocking. Paradoxically, however, the processes by which the curriculum was developed were also fragile, because teachers had relatively little time and attention to spare from the consuming task of helping children of all abilities, talents and interests to learn in many ways, across a vast and indivisible spectrum of attitudes, knowledge and skills. They were both formal and informal, because neither type of activity was by itself sufficiently flexible or rigorous to encompass the curricular preferences and differences of every individual staff member. Finally, they offered participants opportunities for stimulation, enjoyment, laughter and companionship. In consequence, the development of the curriculum, though slow, halting, fragmentary and often apparently cumbersome, did not appear an unnatural or frustrating activity to most of those who participated in it.

To introduce the idea of 'whole school' into understandings of curriculum and curriculum development is to offer a further complication. This is particularly the case because teachers attached specific meanings to this term, some of which do not at first glance seem to have much to do with curriculum. However, it is our contention that 'whole school curriculum development' can be understood only in the context of these meanings. It is to those that we now turn.

Teachers' Understanding of 'Whole School'

The project schools were selected because their staffs agreed that they were trying to develop a 'whole school curriculum'. Not surprisingly, therefore, the teachers said they wanted to be members of 'whole schools' and felt that the development of a 'whole school' was something they should work towards. During interviews with them we asked them what, in their view, characterized a 'whole school' and whether or not the school they were presently working in could be called 'whole' according to the definition they gave us. Their responses revealed that teachers in all five schools shared similar beliefs about the nature of a 'whole school'. These were: First, each member of the staff group aspired to belong to a community. Second, they shared the same educational beliefs and aims and interpreted these in similar ways in their actions. Third, they worked together as a team to develop and implement policy, share decision-making and cope with crises. Fourth, they each exercised autonomy within their own classrooms, felt able to play an individual role within the school and readily called on one another's expertise. Fifth, the members of the group related well to one another. Sixth, their knowledge of the school was not limited to matters of immediate concern to themselves and their own classes but encompassed the concerns, practice and classes of their colleagues. And, finally, they valued the leadership of their headteacher.

These characteristics suggest an ideal which the teachers associated with improved and improving educational practice. Yet it was always beyond, though it grew out of, this personal experience. They often identified the match, or the mismatch, between the ideal and their present experience in comments like these:

> I think, to a large extent, we do that. I think some things we don't do, but obviously no place is perfect. (Teacher, Fenton)

It's probably as near as you get. (Teacher, Carey)

It's getting there! (Headteacher, Ingham)

The first characteristic of an idealized 'whole school' was, then, its wholeness. Many of the teachers had a sense of the school as a community which created the context within which individuals carried out their professional tasks. The membership of the community included non-teaching staff, most commonly parents as well and sometimes governors and children.

> It's all children, all staff and all the parents and governors, and when I say all the staff I mean the caretaker, the cleaners, the kitchen staff, everybody. (Teacher, Ingham)

It was regarded as important that there should be a sense of unity among the members of the community and that no-one should feel excluded from it.

> There's such an atmosphere with us all, whether I'm a teacher or whether I'm a caretaker or whether it's a cook in the kitchen, we're all one. That's how this school seems to be. (Caretaker, Upper Norton)

It was equally important that members of the community should be closely involved with one another's activities. This applied most particularly to the teachers and the children.

> I think 'whole school' is involving all the children with one another...children with children whatever age, doing whatever, and helping each other and sharing in what each other is doing, and I think, to a large extent we do that... Staff being prepared to be involved with other children, not necessarily your own class. (Teacher, Fenton)

Whilst such involvement took place within the smaller community of the school there was a sense in which the members of the wider community of which the school was a part were also involved. They had both a right and perhaps an obligation to contribute to and take part in the activities of the school.

> I believe the school is part of its community, so I do feel that all those people have an input and have a right to have an input. (Teacher, Fenton)

The benefits of this involvement flowed both towards and from the schools themselves.

> We've had people come in and contribute. We go out and give things to them. (Teacher, Fenton)

The most obvious way in which children and staff benefited from this wide interpretation of community was the contribution towards their activities that parents made.

> Parents are very involved and I suppose now I take it for granted. As an outsider you notice it, but once you've been here for a while you just accept that parents get very involved and come to help and wander in and out. (Teacher, Fenton)

Activities in which several or all shared helped to engender a sense of community and promoted feelings of belonging and ownership. Individuals identified with the school and felt pride in it.

> It should be our school no matter who is talking about it. (Teacher, Fenton)

> Everyone who's involved with the school feeling that it's their school...that they can identify with the school. (Teacher, Upper Norton)

> I hope...that everybody feels proud of the school. (Teacher, Ingham)

In all the activities in which the members of the community shared, there was a sense in which everyone was working for the good of the entire community and of the individuals within it.

> Everybody's trying to work together. Parents work with teachers for the benefit of the child. Everybody's trying to pull together. I think that's the thing that's one of the main features of the school. (Teacher, Fenton)

Although the primary focus of this corporate effort was the children, the good of the other members of the community was also considered.

> The fact that everybody works for the common good, that's the thing that makes the school tick over. The fact that everybody is prepared to work with everybody else, to put themselves out for each other and has a caring attitude to the adult members of the school as well as the children. (Teacher, Upper Norton)

This community, this coming together of children and staff, parents and governors, was important because it helped everyone to fulfil the main purpose for which the school existed. This was loosely expressed above as being for 'the benefit of the child'.

As they worked for 'the benefit of the child', teachers attached an overwhelming importance to the second characteristic of a 'whole school': they shared the same purposes with their colleagues, and not only some but all of them.

> If you are aiming for a 'whole school'...then everybody has got to agree about aims and purposes. (Teacher, Orchard)

When teachers felt that such agreement existed, they associated it with a sense of movement or direction.

> To me a 'whole school' is one when every single person shares compatible ideals and moves towards them. (Headteacher, Carey)

> We are subtly going in the same direction. (Teacher, Ingham)

In many of their remarks there was a direct link between belief and action. As one said:

> We believe in what we are doing overall. (Teacher, Ingham)

In other words, the notion of 'purposes' encompassed the beliefs, intentions and actions of all the teachers within a school. It was often impossible to separate references to each of these from one another. Ideally, to believe, to intend and to act were one and the same. By implication, if there was a break between belief and intention or intention and action, or if one or more persons did not believe, intend and act in similar ways to their colleagues, a 'whole school' did not exist. Indeed, none of the teachers claimed that the schools in which they worked were 'whole' in this sense, though several felt that they were moving in that direction.

Like the idea of community, that of shared purposes grew out of teachers' concern for children. There seemed to be general agreement amongst them all that children should be cared for and that what went on within the school should be considered with their interests and needs in mind.

> I think the 'whole school' here is the fact that we care, everybody here cares for the children...and that's what draws us together. (Teacher, Ingham)

> I think you can stretch it back to a point (where) everybody is looking at things with the best interests of the children in mind. Therefore I think at one level we're all in total agreement about something. We're all in agreement that the children are important and that it is important that the children actually get something from school, that they're happy in school. (Teacher, Ingham)

When everybody within the school accepted these two underlying principles, it became not only desirable but also feasible that teachers should reach agreement, at the level of beliefs, intentions and actions, about three things. These were: the ways in which they behaved towards children and their expectations of children's social behaviour; their policies in relation to the curriculum; and their approaches to the teaching of the curriculum. However, they realized that it was possible, though not necessarily desirable, for them to accept the social and moral imperative to care for children, without sharing the same educational aims, and to have both of these in common without acting similarly in the teaching and learning situation. As one said:

> We should have a consistent handling of the children whatever our philosophy is. (Teacher, Fenton)

In general though, the teachers interpreted 'caring for the children' in educational as well as in social and moral terms. Sharing the same purposes was not restricted in meaning to the social and moral beliefs, intentions and actions of teachers and others, but included their beliefs, intentions and actions in relation to educational aims, objectives and policies and to teaching behaviour. So, ideally, common policies were statements of intention which reflected all the shared beliefs of those who formulated them and were reflected in the practice of those who implemented them.

> I suppose everybody is thinking basically the same, so that there is a 'whole school' approach to things like general aims, a 'whole school' approach to parents, a 'whole school' approach to...multicultural issues...behaviour...special needs, those sorts of things that run throughout the curriculum. (Teacher, Ingham)

It was when policies both reflected agreed beliefs and were reflected in practice that teachers fully shared a sense of purpose and of moving together towards recognized and agreed ends. They were aware of contributing to continuity in curriculum provision, of the part they played in an educational process which extended beyond their classrooms, and they made decisions about their own practice in the light of agreed policy.

> I think we do try and have policies that go all the way through. I have said that some of the policies are old but they are ongoing in the practice and 'whole school' means that. Trying to know where you are going and what ends you are achieving and going for it. (Teacher, Fenton)

There was one exception to this general understanding. Apart from one brief reference to everybody caring for the children the teachers at Upper Norton made no mention of anything that pointed to the importance of shared purposes as a characteristic of a 'whole school'. The contrast with the other four schools is marked. In this school there appeared to be longstanding, but unacknowledged, differences between the staff regarding teaching and learning strategies and approaches to discipline. However, they did agree on their moral obligation to care for the children. Our hypothesis is that during the year the new headteacher (eighteen months in post) attempted to build on that common agreement and to begin to address the question of what, in the light of that imperative, she and her colleagues should be providing for the children educationally. As the staff started to address these educational issues, they began to move towards articulating and sharing a common purpose.

Since such importance was placed on believing, intending and acting in similar ways it is not surprising that teachers also emphasized working together as a team as a third characteristic of a 'whole school'. They commonly used phrases like 'working together', 'working as a team', 'working with others', 'pulling together' to describe what many felt to be a major feature of a 'whole school'. However, they did not necessarily attribute the same meanings to these phrases. 'Working together' could mean as little, in practice, as shared coping in a crisis, a practical response which was made regardless or in spite of interpersonal tension or professional difference. One teacher said:

> I know there is friction with the staff, but if there is a time when we all have to pull together, we do. (Teacher, Orchard)

By contrast, it could also mean shared responsibility for, and commitment to, the entire school.

> It's the goal of everybody giving as much, and everybody as much in charge, as everybody else. (Headteacher, Carey)

More commonly though to work together, to be a team, meant to be involved in decision-making, to participate in the formulation and implementation of policy and to be willing to place the common good before personal interests.

> Everybody...is contributing to decisions, to practice, to policy... Everybody concerned with the school, with the children, owns the practice because they have contributed, and are continuing to contribute, to it in terms of decision-making and in terms of managing, in terms of operating... It's a very high level of participation. (Teacher, Orchard)

> It's working together as a team, being able to share ideas in order to help each other, which will give a school its strength because you can't develop anything in isolation. (Teacher, Fenton)

> Everybody works for the common good. That's the thing that makes the school tick over. Everybody is prepared to work

with everybody else, to put themselves out for each other. (Teacher, Upper Norton)

Working together then was the means by which the staff of a 'whole school' agreed and achieved their aims. It was an inevitable corollary of sharing the same purposes.

Nevertheless, although it was important to the teachers that they should share the same purposes at the level of beliefs, intentions and actions, and that they should work together to achieve their aims, they also believed that individuality should be acknowledged and valued. This fourth characteristic of 'whole school' took three main forms. First, teachers accepted how unlikely it was that everyone on the staff of a school would agree about everything all the time. Differences would therefore inevitably occur. However, these should be valued and respected.

> Anyone can express opinions. People listen to and respect each other's views and thoughts. The staff are always willing to share ideas and take them on board, so I think there is a very good team spirit. (Teacher, Fenton)

Indeed, as we describe in chapter 5, a willingness to be open about differences might increase a staff's capacity to collaborate in pursuit of shared aims.

> The collaboration. I think people talk much more than they used to and express opinions and perhaps the feeling that everybody's opinion is worth it, even if it's not the same as anyone else's. I think that has developed through the years since I've been here. I certainly feel I can say things, even if it's completely different from everybody else. (Teacher, Ingham)

A second way in which teachers showed that they valued individuality was by acknowledging that individuals fulfilled unique roles within the school, as a result of their particular interests or expertise (see Nias, 1989a).

> Whole school? It's a collection of individuals using their skills, expertise and enthusiasms in whatever way they can to benefit the community. (Teacher, Orchard)

> Everyone who's involved with the school feeling that they
> have a part to play, no matter how big, no matter how small,
> no matter in what sort of capacity. (Teacher, Upper Norton)

And thirdly, teachers believed that as individuals they should exercise
some autonomy in relation to their own practice.

> Ingham is a 'whole school' near enough as it can be, allowing
> people still to maintain their individuality, able to operate how
> they want to operate in their own classrooms. (Teacher,
> Ingham)

> We are all very individualistic people and I think that most
> teachers are, and that we do each have a slightly different way
> of approaching the teaching of our children. (Teacher, Carey)

Although in general when teachers spoke about their 'individuality' or
'freedom', they meant the right to make all practical decisions about
what was done within the classroom, there were some who gave these
words a slightly different emphasis. For them it included the right to
try out new ideas and then talk them over with colleagues. As one
said:

> We all feel free to try things and genuinely ask for an opinion.
> (Teacher, Carey)

Such teachers felt that they exercised their autonomy in the context of
the group. They considered that what they did as individuals in the
classroom was of concern to their colleagues and contributed to the
thinking of them all.

Overall, then, individuals were highly valued within a 'whole
school'. The teachers believed that they should have opportunities to
voice their opinions, participate in decision-making processes, make
their own contribution to the work of the school by fulfilling unique
roles, develop their own expertise, exercise a degree of autonomy
over their own classroom practice and have their own professional
development needs met. As one said:

> I think a 'whole school' is everybody being able to have their
> say and perhaps their opinion being counted, not decisions just
> made over their heads...and everybody having different roles
> to play so that everyone can develop their own expertise

> perhaps... And it is being a community, that too, that you pull together if one teacher's not having a very good time, being able to help out. That sort of stuff...being able to operate how they want to operate in their own classrooms. (Teacher, Ingham)

The fifth characteristic of a 'whole school' was that relationships were marked by mutual caring and respect.

> I think that's it, the caring attitude, to say, 'This school cares, not only about the children but about the staff as well'. (Teacher, Upper Norton)

> There is certainly respect here among the staff and the ancillaries and everybody else, which often you don't get, and that makes a difference. The children respond to that I think. (Teacher, Ingham)

Teachers felt that, ideally, such caring and respect would extend to all the members of the community of the school. However they regarded their own relationships with one another as fundamental in helping to establish accepted patterns of behaviour within the school. These relationships had both a personal and professional dimension.

> It's how we react with one another... It's...relationships, personal as well as professional. (Teacher, Carey)

> As long as you are all working together and can get on together, strengths and interests and enthusiasms all rub off on each other. (Teacher, Fenton)

For these teachers 'getting on together' was not simply a means of providing pleasant social relationships and so making it more comfortable for them to work within the same establishment. Rather easy relationships between all members of the school community, but in particular the teaching staff, were important because these were directly related to the success of their work.

> I think that the ethos of the school is that we all work together as a team. We all like one another very much. (Teacher, Carey)

> The schools function best where the relationships are good —
> that really is the crux of it. (Teacher, Fenton)

Sixth, teachers felt that part of being a 'whole school' was having a knowledge of the school that transcended the individual's own class-room boundaries and encompassed the practice of colleagues. This knowledge was an important component of 'working together'.

> Everybody knows what everybody else is doing to a certain
> limit. (Teacher, Fenton)

For all the staff in the school to know what others were doing, two things were required of the teachers as individuals — a willingness to learn what was happening elsewhere in the school and a willingness to be open about their own practice.

> You have to look beyond your own boundaries. (Teacher,
> Carey)

> It's being open about things. (Teacher, Carey)

With openness came a readiness to share ideas, offer suggestions and make contributions to the work of their colleagues.

> Sitting in the staffroom people talk about what they're going to
> do and people come up with suggestions. (Teacher, Fenton)

When all the teachers knew about current practice in their school, about what had gone before and what came after, they were more able to support one another in their work. Shared knowledge could also contribute to continuity in the curriculum.

> The most sensible thing, . . . would be that everyone was aware
> of what the curriculum stood for and that there was some specific
> way of following it through, so that everybody knew what
> everybody else was doing. That is what is actually happening
> now. (Teacher, Ingham)

In other words, having a knowledge of the school which encompassed the practice of their colleagues enabled teachers, they believed, to work together both simultaneously and successively in pursuit of their shared educational purposes.

Lastly, teachers believed that a 'whole school' had an effective leader whom they identified as the headteacher. Such a person was one to whom they could talk and with whom they could discuss, who did not dictate, but made allowances for individual differences, who was affectively a part of the staff group and whose philosophy was both clear and shared by colleagues.

> Have a good leader that you can talk to and discuss things with. (Teacher, Carey)

> The majority of the staff are quite happy together. I think Ron's included in that. (Teacher, Orchard)

> We should have a consistent handling of the children whatever our philosophy is. I knew very clearly what Simon's philosophy was in handling the children and I liked his philosophy. (Teacher, Fenton)

Teachers acknowledged that there are different kinds of leader. Whatever the leader was like, however, in a 'whole school' s/he exercised that leadership as a member of a team.

> The whole school is so dependent on...the members of staff working in a cohesive team with good leadership... You do need good leadership. I think I have to say that, but I think that there's leadership and leadership and everyone is different in their approach. So long as the team work together and they have the best interests of the children and they're not vying for their individual glory, which doesn't seem to be the case here, then that to me is the whole school approach. (Teacher, Fenton)

What emerges from this analysis of teachers' descriptions of a 'whole school' is that it is a community of people, primarily teachers and children, but also other interested parties, who share the same beliefs, and behave in similar ways in accordance with them. Within this community teachers in particular, sometimes supported by non-teaching staff, parents and governors, work together to establish, sustain and develop their shared beliefs and to interpret them in practice. Individual members of the community are valued both for their own sakes and for their contribution to the shared task of interpreting beliefs in action. Two things are essential if teachers are to come to share the same beliefs and to interpret these in similar ways in their practice. They must have opportunities to find out what their colleagues believe and do, how they think about and carry out their professional tasks in both curricular and pedagogical terms, and they must get on sufficiently well with one another that they can cooperate on and support one another in their common work. Communities which are 'whole schools' in this sense have leaders who play a major part in establishing and sustaining the beliefs that underpin the educational activities of the members of the community and who act to further the interests of both the community and the individuals who are part of it. They articulate clearly the philosophy on which the community is built and act consistently with its beliefs. They foster the realization of these beliefs in action amongst the other members of the community and acknowledge the worth of individual contributions to the work of that community. The teachers in the project schools identified these leaders with the headteachers, who, in a 'whole school' should also act as a member of the staff team.

None of this means, however, that the members of the community have to do exactly the same in their classrooms. Rather they share a way of thinking which they can interpret in their practice in their own ways. A regular supply teacher at Carey, when expressing her understanding of a 'whole school', said of her colleagues:

> They are obviously all following the same ideas and trying to give the children similar experiences in different classes, but... I am sure, each teacher approaches this experience in a different way, and the way they fit in will be according to their topic and their particular personality and method. (Supply teacher, Carey)

It is this kind of likemindedness — made up of broad general understandings held in common, agreement on aims and an overall similarity of approach, rather than of the shared use of resources and exactly duplicated methods — which appears to be most important to teachers in their understandings of 'whole school'. As one said, when matching present experience with the ideal:

> I don't think we're quite right, but I wouldn't like to upset what is good. It's probably as near as you get. I think there's a level of understanding here that might not exist in a lot of schools where they print the same way and use the same maths scheme. In some ways we're absolutely hopeless, useless, but

we do have a sort of empathy with each other. I think we do teach in a similar overall way. We've got the same aims and we try our hardest to get those aims. (Teachers, Carey)

Running like a thread through all that these teachers said about a 'whole school' were frequent references to feelings. Being a member of a 'whole school' apparently had to do not only with working together, but also with feeling together. This affective component was one which they valued but it was, for these particular primary school teachers, incidental to, and derived from, their shared task. Their sense of mutual enjoyment and satisfaction sprang from the fact that they shared the same social and moral beliefs about the ways in which people should behave towards one another and held common educational beliefs about goals, in particular those relating to the curriculum and to pedagogy. One teacher said:

Whole school is, in a way, I think, working happily together at doing the best for the children, meeting their needs and doing the best for each other, enjoying it really. I think we do that. (Teacher, Fenton)

Conclusion

Teachers' understandings of curriculum, curriculum development and 'whole school' suggest that two kinds of curriculum development take place within schools in which teachers simultaneously believe in the value of individual learning and of wholeness. One takes the form of the improvement of individual practice in the classroom. The other shows itself as a gradual move towards the ideal in which a community of people share both a common educational philosophy and the responsibility for implementing that philosophy in practice. In pursuing both of these goals the teachers in the project schools made productive use of parts of the National Curriculum.

Most, probably all, of these teachers desired to improve their own practice, though some were more actively involved in exploring the opportunities to learn than others. Curriculum development in this sense was a well established and accepted characteristic of the professional lives of the teachers in these schools.

The heads in all the schools at all times and some teachers in all the schools for some of the time also desired to move towards the ideal of the 'whole school'. To this end a minority of the staff were actively concerned to foster the learning of their colleagues and to influence other people's practice. However, it was particularly difficult for the teachers consciously to work towards the development of shared beliefs and similar ways of working, however desirable these ends seemed to them. There were two reasons for this. One was that the activities of the classroom were inevitably the main focus of their attention from day to day; it was harder for them than for the headteachers to have a school-wide view. The second was the traditional isolation of primary school teachers and their sense of individual responsibility for the curriculum in their classrooms and the children in their care. Most primary teachers are unused to sharing this responsibility, to working together or to opening up their practice to others and may not welcome the changes which would result from moving in these directions. For both these reasons, headteachers are likely to be the main architects in their institutions of a shared sense of 'whole school'.

In the following chapters we explore first (chapter 2) how the heads and teachers in the five schools sought to develop the curriculum through improvement in individual classroom practice and second (chapter 3) how they tried to develop their schools as communities with shared beliefs and similar ways of working. Although for convenience we consider these two forms of curriculum development separately we are aware that, because a 'whole school' represents beliefs in action, the development of practice cannot be separated from beliefs. Any attempt to develop a 'whole school' has, by definition, to involve the development of practice within the context of shared goals. Though individual practice may be improved by, for example, course attendance or experience without the development of a sense of 'whole school' it will be encouraged and facilitated within a whole school context. Chapter 4 therefore explores the ways in which these two kinds of curriculum development interact in a way that justifies the use of the term 'whole school curriculum development'.

Chapter Two

Teachers' Learning

In the previous chapter we argued that for the teachers in the project schools curriculum development could not be seen as separate from the learning of the individual teacher. Teachers felt individually responsible for the learning and well-being of the children whom they taught and so for the curriculum that they offered. They therefore believed they needed to 'own' the curriculum, that is simultaneously to control and to internalize it. They also assumed the right to make choices about curriculum content and all other associated aspects of their practice, subject to certain constraints, such as the need to provide for breadth and balance, and to a lesser extent, for continuity and progression. Finally their deep sense of personal responsibility for the education of 'their' children and their belief that it was they who were in charge of it led them to seek ways of improving their own practice. Sometimes this was a matter of acquiring fresh knowledge (for example, in science or technology). At others it was a question of improving specific pedagogical skills (for example, story telling; asking open-ended questions; setting appropriate tasks for children with special learning needs) or mastering new approaches to the teaching of subjects such as reading or spelling. Teachers' practice also sometimes changed in more fundamental ways. On occasions they were faced with the need to reassess their beliefs about the nature and purposes of education, to accept challenges to the values which shaped their perspectives and practice or to consider how far they wished to fall in line with the views and standards of their heads or colleagues.

The headteachers in the project schools also felt responsible for the children in their charge and so for the curriculum. They all had strongly held beliefs about the social, moral and educational purposes of schooling and consequently about the nature of the curriculum and of practice within their schools. Furthermore their appointment as headteachers had confirmed them in their beliefs. Consequently they sought to ensure that the staff in their schools shared their beliefs and values and acted in accordance with them. So they too were concerned that teachers should learn, in two respects. They wanted to ensure that all the staff in their schools understood and accepted the fundamental principles which determined the curricular and pedagogical policies that they espoused. They also sought to increase the teachers' capacity to realize these principles in their practice. So, they did all they could to encourage their staff to learn in both these respects. They also demonstrated their personal commitment to learning by actively pursuing their own education, by talking to the staff about what they were learning and by showing their willingness to learn from others. At the same time their example carried two other messages for their schools: that the professional development of individuals could benefit everyone and that staff members could contribute to and assist one another's learning.

In other words, both teachers and heads saw professional learning as the key to the development of the curriculum and as the main way to improve the quality of children's education. Although they responded during the year to internal and external pressures for change, the main impetus for their learning came from the shared belief that existed in all the schools that practice could always be improved and hence that professional development was a never-ending process, a way of life. This generalized commitment to learning meant that all members of staff could initiate development in any curriculum area whether or not they were formally responsible for it. For example, Wendy was the coordinator for information technology at Upper Norton but Marilyn at Ingham had no such responsibility for multicultural education. Similarly anyone, out of shared interest or concern or with some encouragement from the headteacher, could support an initiative, as did a small group of interested colleagues who joined Marilyn to develop the multicultural policy at Ingham, or could even take on responsibility for it, as Barbara did with technology at Fenton. Involvement might also arise from a sense of responsibility for one's own classes' learning, as when Helen, at Upper Norton, persisted in learning about computers in spite of her own feelings of inadequacy. As individuals initiated or supported such developments they increased their own personal knowledge and practical skill, their understanding of the issues involved, and their appreciation of how others might benefit.

In all this the headteachers played a vital role, sometimes initiating developments themselves, but more often encouraging interests among their staff, supporting them by responding positively to their concerns, providing advice and appreciating their work and commitment. There was historical evidence to suggest that learning had not always been as highly valued by the staff of the five schools as it now was and that the attitudes and behaviour of the heads had significantly contributed towards its growing importance as a key factor in the schools' development.

It is the desire of heads and teachers to improve children's educational experiences by increasing their 'ownership' of the curriculum and their commitment to professional learning as the key to development that explains why we devote this chapter to teacher learning. Four things helped to increase the capacity of the teachers in the project schools to engage in effective professional learning. First, they were motivated to learn. Second, opportunities existed for them to learn both within and outside the schools. Third, appropriate means of learning were used and, fourth, learning often took place under favourable conditions. We examine each of these factors in turn.

Motivation to Learn

As we watched the teachers at work we became increasingly aware that they were characterized, both as individuals and as groups, by an eagerness to learn and a commitment to learning. There were several reasons for this. One was their own sense of personal responsibility for the curriculum. Another was the school context itself. It was clear that teachers joining any of the five schools expected, and were expected by their colleagues, to learn and to fit in with the accepted norms of the school. There were also external pressures for change which, at the time of our fieldwork, arose particularly from the *Education Act 1988*. Finally, learning was sometimes intrinsically satisfying. Each of these factors made teachers aware of their need to learn and the desirability of learning.

Teachers who wanted to improve their practice were characterized by four attitudes: they accepted that it was possible to improve, were ready to be self critical, and to recognize better practice than their own within the school or elsewhere, and they were willing to learn what had to be learned in order to be able to do what needed or had to be done. A detailed example will serve to illustrate these four points.

It was common for teachers starting at Fenton to be overawed by the standard of the artwork achieved by the pupils. Their first reaction was to be impressed:

> There was a very high emphasis on art and display which I was extremely impressed with. (Student, Fenton)

They also had doubts about whether the standards of work on display were really achievable by young children. These reservations were however quickly dispelled by the evidence in the school with the result that they changed their view of what it was possible for children to do.

> I remember visiting this school before I came to teach here and thinking, 'They can't possibly have done this artwork, fourth year juniors (Y6)!' But they do and that changed my thinking. (Teacher, Fenton)

Like Schiller, who said, 'We never dreamt that they could do anything like this' (Griffin–Beale, 1979, p. 96), these teachers were overwhelmed by the realization that children were able to achieve standards of which they had never before thought them capable. This new awareness of children's potential was followed by a sense of personal inadequacy. It was common for staff, recalling their early days in the school, to say things like:

> At the time I thought, 'I'll never get them to do that'. (Teacher, Fenton)

This sense of inadequacy was accompanied by feelings of discomfort. These were not alleviated by knowing one was 'good at art', for the issue was not whether teachers could draw and paint themselves but whether they could teach children to draw or paint.

> When I first came here it took me about half a term to really feel a part of the school. The standards and the expectations were phenomenal and I didn't see how I could meet them and get the children to meet them. Everybody seemed to really know that they were doing, particularly with art. I've got some sort of art training myself. I've done 'A' level art and I spent a year at art college, when I did a foundation course, so I don't know really why I panicked so much. (Teacher, Fenton)

Faced with the evidence of both the children's potential (to draw and paint) and the teachers' potential (to teach children to draw and paint) new staff had only two alternatives — to ignore what was happening in the school or to take steps to learn how to teach art. Given that some of the criteria for selecting staff were that they should be 'ready to learn' (Fieldnote), 'prepared to think' and 'concerned to improve' (Head, Fenton) they were unlikely to take the first alternative. Had they chosen to do so they would probably have lived uncomfortably with that choice. Indeed, there was evidence that in the past teachers unwilling to make a commitment to learn had not stayed long in the school. In taking the second alternative teachers were supported by the knowledge that their colleagues had taken the same path before them. Each of them looked primarily towards Simon, the Head-teacher, to teach them what they needed to know, not least because the high standards they admired and to which they aspired originated with him and he was perceived as possessing expert knowledge.

> I couldn't really see why Simon thought that young children could achieve such a high standard. I used to think, 'Well, why are they doing that? Infants can't do that sort of thing'. In the end Simon took me under his wing and used to come in and say, 'Well, what do you want me to do?' 'Painting please!' 'Right.' So he used to get the paints out and really show me how to do it and what he was after. (Teacher, Fenton)

Through a continuous process of watching, listening and experimentation, teachers learned not only from Simon but from the children, their colleagues and their own experience. As they did so their knowledge and skills increased and became deeply rooted in their classroom practice, as much of our evidence over the year shows. The following is a typical example:

> In one corner of the area, on the tiled floor, were four easels with pieces of grey sugar paper already set up on them. Underneath were a palette, a brush, water and powder paints. The children mixed their colours themselves and were encouraged to match tone and shade. Today they were going to paint pictures of themselves. Some children had quite determined ideas of their own about what they were going to do... It was interesting to see how the children differ in terms of skill, yet they are all already familiar with mixing paints and the procedures for clearing away. They have been in school about three weeks. (Fieldnote, Fenton)

'Learning' in this context meant that teachers increased their own knowledge and skills and improved their classroom practice. In addition they deepened their understanding of the school-wide curricular framework within which their teaching took place. They became conscious of their part in the continuous learning experience which all the staff were trying to create for the children.

> From being in reception as a supply teacher and watching them at work and then, say, being in the fourth year juniors (Y6) and seeing the end product, it was all there. It was obvious why we started it and went through the whole school, and I had never seen that in a school before. (Teacher, Fenton)

The case of art at Fenton is particularly vivid because the consciousness of what was possible came from within the school and its effects could be traced in the experience and practice of all the staff members. However Fenton was not unique. The staff in all the schools generally accepted that it was desirable, even necessary to be constantly seeking to improve. They recognized good practice in the work of their colleagues and others and this enabled them to appraise their own work. These twin forces (being aware of possibilities and ready to engage in self-appraisal) provided teachers with a powerful motivation to learn what they needed to know, in order to achieve what they were now aware could be achieved in the classroom. Seeing colleagues learning was an added encouragement, because individuals realized that they were not alone in their need to learn. Learning was regarded as a means of increasing one's ability, not as a sign of inadequacy. In addition, the case of art at Fenton illustrates the fact that when individuals recognized a school-wide framework for the curriculum into which their learning fitted, it increased their desire to learn. Similarly, they were particularly ready to adopt ideas and acquire skills which they could use in their classrooms, because they recognized these as part of a pedagogical approach which was characteristic of practice throughout the school.

The desire to improve practice also led to a constant quest for 'good ideas', that is ideas that were relevant to classroom practice. Sometimes these were absorbed into a teacher's general repertoire, but at others they required a fairly radical shift in pedagogy. An example of the first occurred when Natalie, temporarily appointed at Ingham, showed some of her colleagues how to make frogs with zigzag legs. These, adapted in a variety of ways, were soon evident in a number of displays throughout the school. Ideas like these tended to be either stored for future use (for example, Noreen at Upper Norton wrote them down for future reference) or used immediately and unquestioningly. An example of the second is the way in which Karen at Ingham gradually absorbed into her own practice the idea of using books other than those within the reading scheme to teach reading. It seems likely that she was influenced over several months by Kirsten who used only 'real' books. Karen and Kirsten were regarded by colleagues as being at opposite ends of the continuum that described the practice of teaching reading within the school. Kirsten's main concern was that Karen should understand what she (Kirsten) was doing. She described what she felt to be a significant event in enabling Karen to reach such an understanding:

> I remember Karen coming into my classroom one day... The door was open and she walked through and I was sitting in the book corner with a child actually reading with them you see, and she stood at the door and said, 'I understand what you say now about reading with your children, Kirsten. It's lovely,' and went off again. I think in that two seconds that she saw me sitting there, she learnt far more about what I was doing. (Teacher, Ingham)

Kirsten was unaware that any changes had taken place in Karen's practice as a result of such incidents and of their intermittent dialogue about reading. Karen however was conscious that she had modified her own practice. She attributed this to two possible causes — Kirsten's influence and her own willingness to learn:

> I have become, in the last year to eighteen months, much more flexible in the way I teach reading. It's been quite interesting. I still use the scheme for the very early stages because I think it provides a very sound, good structure for the little ones coming in...and somewhere, perhaps when they have been in just under a term, depending on the child, they will try some of the supplementaries that they can cope with and the enjoyment that they feel in really reading books is lovely. So I am much more flexible now than I have been in the past. Whether that was the result of Kirsten Yeardley I am not sure or whether it was just that I am always open to new ideas. (Teacher, Ingham)

Karen's gradual, experimental accommodation of 'real' books into the way she taught reading represented not merely the adoption of a 'good idea', something she could add to her personal resources, but a change of philosophy and approach. Marilyn who had made a similar shift away from total reliance on reading schemes spoke to the researcher of the way in which she tested the reliability of the approach against her experience:

> She kept a close eye on the children and brought them back to dip into the reading scheme again, to reassure her that they were making the kind of progress she felt they ought. (Field-note, Ingham)

The touchstone for both these teachers as they assessed the value of the changes in their pedagogy was the effect these might have on children's learning. Both were willing to question existing practice — their own and other people's — if they felt that children might benefit. In other words they were open to curriculum change because it was part of their individual search for professional improvement.

Teachers' willingness to learn was also affected by the feelings which accompanied the experience of learning. Some teachers found an inherent satisfaction in learning, an excitement which became a motivating factor in itself. This was particularly the case when they were aware of belonging to a community of learners. Their satisfaction came partly from their belief that their pupils benefited when they learnt, partly from the acquisition of new knowledge and skills.

> We were just saying yesterday, each person has different strengths and it's in combining those strengths that the children get the best out of all of us... Here everyone wants to learn from everyone else and that is what is so lovely. It's just so good. (Teacher, Fenton)

However, learning was not enjoyable and exciting all the time. For some teachers it was at times a necessity, for many it was often tiring, on occasions it was uncomfortable. Coming to terms with the standards expected at Orchard, for example, was not always easy, as Dave, the Deputy recalled:

> I came thinking I'd established good practice and found to my horror, shock and dismay that the practice wasn't good or not good enough. It was good enough in very narrow areas but

there were whole areas of the curriculum that were just not good enough, I had to embark on retraining myself which is quite difficult when you are Deputy Head.

Yet what Dave learned for himself became a means of support for others. The discomfort he experienced enabled him to work sensitively with new colleagues such as Ken whom he perceived as experiencing similar difficulties. Of Ken he said:

> When he first came there was a need to get his practice to an acceptable level. I mean, his idea of project work when he first came to the school was that you found a book about it and copied it out... And to his credit, he's actually, in the eighteen months he's been here, developed as a teacher, phenomenally. (Deputy, Orchard)

And of Dave, the Head, Ron, said:

> He's worked very hard on Ken, for example. (Fieldnote, Orchard)

Opportunities to Learn

Motivation was not by itself enough to ensure that individuals improved their practice. They also needed opportunities to acquire appropriate knowledge and skills. A wide variety of such opportunities existed in the project schools. They were of five different types.

Teachers as Learners

Firstly, there were occasions when teachers consciously took on the role of learners. Some writers suggest that the role of learner is central to that of teacher (for example, Schaefer, 1967; Schön, 1987). Our observations support that hypothesis, yet the teachers themselves did not identify learning as an essential characteristic of their work and they did not consider their workplace a centre of learning for themselves. Yet they attended in-service training courses with the intention of learning because they were conscious of their own weaknesses and inadequacies and believed their own practice could be improved. In this sense there were occasions when they were aware of being learners. Sometimes they sought out such opportunities for themselves. At others the attention of individuals was drawn to a course by their headteacher who wanted to foster their professional development, to meet their expressed needs or interests or to deepen their understanding of the educational principles which made the school 'whole' (see chapter 1) or to introduce new ideas to the school. These reasons could not easily be separated. For example, Ella, at Carey, recommended Kate for membership of the LEA Working Party on Assessment. She believed Kate would benefit personally from this opportunity for professional development and also that the school as a whole would profit from the expertise she acquired. Similarly Evelyne, in her early days of headship at Ingham attended, together with other members of staff, a course on reading which led to the introduction of a home-school reading programme. This started a slow revolution in the thinking and practice of several teachers with respect to their teaching of reading. On another occasion, she responded to Marilyn's concern about a racist incident in her classroom by drawing her attention to a relevant course and supporting her during her consequent work with colleagues, as they developed a multicultural policy for the school. The work Marilyn did with her class on Divali and the school's celebration of the Chinese New Year indicated the pervasiveness of the school-wide multicultural approach that resulted from this initiative.

In other words, individual interests and concerns, supported, and sometimes prompted by the headteachers' desire to develop 'whole schools' led teachers to adopt the role of learners and to go on courses. What they learned sometimes had an effect on their own practice and sometimes too on the work of their colleagues. Though teachers generally regarded courses as opportunities for individual growth, their heads saw them as a means of development not only for individuals but for the school as a whole.

In-service courses were not the only occasions on which teachers consciously saw themselves as learners. The five statutory professional development days provided other opportunities to learn. These days were akin to in-service courses in terms of focus, structure and activity, but distinct in that they involved all the teaching staff, and sometimes the ancillary staff, of a school in learning together. Sometimes such occasions were shared with nearby schools with whom there was a formal or informal link. Thus the staff at Carey joined with the staff of the junior school for half a day's in-service training on assessment. This was led by Kate, as a consequence of her membership of the LEA Working Party, supported by the Deputy Heads of both schools. The staff at Fenton joined a number of staff groups from a cluster of schools (to which they did not themselves belong) for a day on craft, design and technology led by a college lecturer. The staff at Ingham joined other staff groups for a talk on topic work by a headteacher from another LEA. The staff at Orchard attended various workshops on a day organized by the in-service coordinators of the schools forming the cluster of which they were members. The staff at Upper Norton similarly spent some of their in-service time with other staff groups in their cluster. As well as giving teachers the chance to learn from outside expertise such occasions also provided them with opportunities for professional dialogue within and between school staffs.

Teachers also frequently took advantage of planned opportunities to learn specific skills and concepts from colleagues and others with particular curriculum expertise. Sometimes, such expertise already existed within the school. For example, staff at Fenton learned about art from Simon, those at Ingham about computers from Natalie, those at Upper Norton about music from Kirsty. On other occasions advisory teachers worked within the schools. These teachers were usually invited by headteachers because they, some or all of their staff recognized a need to learn about a particular curriculum area and realized that the relevant expertise was lacking within the school. Occasionally, advisory teachers were attached to the school over a particular period of time because it happened to be that school's 'turn' to have access to their knowledge and skills. For example, Upper Norton had the chance to use Georgia on several days to assist in the development of information technology in the school. She used the computer and 'turtle' with groups of children in Wendy's, Noreen's and Nancy's classrooms, conducted in-service sessions with the whole staff group and worked with pairs of teachers, introducing them to programmes about which they wanted to know more. Her role was mainly responsive. She allowed the teacher's expressed needs to determine the provision she made. Similarly Gayle, leader of a team of advisory teachers concerned with the creative arts, taught art and pottery to groups of children in classes at Ingham. Fieldnotes describing the staff meeting during which she introduced herself and her work to the staff record:

> It was clear that she had a flexible approach and was willing to do whatever the school wanted her to. (Fieldnote, Ingham)

Observations in the classrooms showed that teachers, on the whole, organized their classes so that they freed themselves to observe Gayle at work. They also took note of Gayle's suggestion that before her next visit they should use her ideas with the other children in the class. In this way she encouraged the teachers to make what they were learning part of their own practice. However, whether individuals learnt from advisory teachers or not was also a question of motivation. We recorded some instances of teachers using their advisory colleagues as 'helpers' and as a result benefiting little from their presence.

When one or more teachers deliberately set out to learn from another, their learning often spread beyond those immediately involved. For example, Gayle's work at Ingham became the object of informal conversation amongst several staff and in the process Natalie Yarborough learnt from them. In the following extract Tina and Natalie York had observed Gayle at work and had learned directly from her. Natalie Yarborough had not.

> On the table was a basket with two plants in it with a lot of colourful flowers. Tina jokingly said to me, 'Let's all sit down and do a still life, shall we?' This led on to a discussion about Gayle's visit on Thursday. People talked about the fact that she had mixed the paint with a fungicideless polycell. Tina and Natalie York described the way in which she had got the children to use palette knives to paint with. Natalie Yarborough said she thought the idea of mixing paints to the correct shades to begin with was a good idea. She had tried to get her children to mix paints for themselves last week. She made a gesture of despair! It was she that asked Tina and Natalie York the most questions. (Fieldnote, Ingham)

Induction and Socialization

A second opportunity for teachers to learn occurred when they were inducted into a school's norms. We found examples of this procedure at Fenton and Orchard, but not at any of the other schools. This may be because both schools had long-established norms relating to curriculum and pedagogy to which all those teaching there were expected to conform. Yet both schools had experienced regular changes in staff membership. At Fenton none of the staff apart from Simon, the

Headteacher, had worked at the school for more than four years and for one of those Simon himself had been absent. At Orchard more than forty teachers had been appointed during the ten years since the school had opened. By contrast at Carey where strong school norms also affected the staff's thinking and behaviour, no teachers had left the school for six years and so induction was unnecessary; while at Ingham and Upper Norton teachers acted in accordance with a variety of educational beliefs and there was no clearly accepted approach into which newcomers needed to be inducted.

At Fenton and Orchard new staff took time to assimilate the school norms into their own practice, as the heads of both schools recognized. One of them said:

> New people come in and you spend a year, two years, getting them round to a way of working, and it probably takes three or four before they are properly confident in that. (Headteacher, Fenton)

Accordingly, each school had evolved ways in which new teachers were made aware of the expectations which others held of them. One was the work on display. One headteacher said of a new member of staff:

> She came into a classroom that was well set up and there was some good work displayed, visually very good. The writing and so on that was available to look at was good quality, so immediately there's that which says, 'This is what we are about. This is the sort of quality we're aiming for'. (Headteacher, Fenton)

Another was assembly. In the following example Simon not only acted as a model but also made his expectations of the teachers clear:

> As soon as they were seated one of the youngest children began crying loudly. Simon said, 'Whatever's the matter, Anna?' She replied, 'I want my mummy.' He said, 'Well, you'll have to put up with me', and waded in amongst the children to lift her up and cuddle her. Then he said generally, 'Who wants her?' She said she wanted her teacher and Simon passed her across to her teacher on whose knee she sat for the rest of assembly. (Fieldnote, Fenton)

Ron, the headteacher of Orchard, too made his expectations of staff clear by questioning children closely during 'showing' assemblies, about how they had done their work.

> Throughout... Ron would ask questions of the children, 'What was the propeller made of? How old is a penny farthing bike? When were they last used? Why were these bikes called penny farthings?...' He would ask questions about how the children did things. This was evident when examples of needlework were held up. 'Ah', he said, 'you did initial drawings of them and what types of stitching did you use?...' He enquired as to how the work had been organized, but he also took care to be positive... He never let the questions sound too inquisitive. (Fieldnote, Orchard)

Commenting on this one member of staff said: 'I think it's Ron's way of finding out exactly how much those children know', and another said, 'He's testing the staff... Yes, he asks very searching questions sometimes.'

Teachers also learned through 'apprenticeship'. This took more than one form. At Orchard it was to be found in the pairs who shared open-plan units. In these units teachers new to the school worked with longer serving colleagues who were called 'unit leaders'. The Head, describing how pairings had been decided for the current year, explained:

> The balance of experience was important, I think that was something that I and everybody else would think desirable. Helen and Ken being the most recent arrivals on the staff would have felt vulnerable if they'd been in a unit together... The unit leader...will know how the system in the school works, how the culture of the school works and know the rules of the game. You can impart those sometimes formally and sometimes informally to newly arrived colleagues. (Headteacher, Orchard)

A different and very effective form of apprenticeship existed at Fenton. Barbara and Celia both knew the school as parents. They were each employed first as supply teachers, then as special needs ancillary helpers. They had temporary teaching contracts before being given permanent ones. During their long association with the school, they had the opportunity to see all their colleagues at work in the classroom and to become familiar with the teaching and learning approaches common within the school. One of these approaches involved group work with which neither of these teachers had been familiar before. Yet as soon as each was given responsibility for a class she immediately used groups as a means of organizing children's learning opportunities. They were confident to do this because they were familiar with the practice of their colleagues. They knew that group work was one aspect of classroom organization and practice which was expected of them as teachers within the school and they were confident that it worked as a means of facilitating children's learning. They had learned from watching and working alongside others, from taking colleagues as models, with the result that as classteachers themselves they were able to put into effect without hesitation or uncertainty what was to them an innovative form of classroom organization. Although not all teachers had the same opportunities for 'apprenticeship', Simon, the Head, regarded it as a valuable way of ensuring that potential staff members could learn his preferred pedagogy. The following interview extract illustrates the powerful nature of this type of learning.

Interviewer: Would you say you all had similar approaches?

Teacher: Yes, following the same group arrangements and things like that . . . I think we all follow more or less the same daily routines. The children know the routine for group work and settle down well to it.

Interviewer: Do you think you've come with those kinds of approaches quite separately, or have you learned them from being here at the school?

Teacher: I would say I had learned a lot from being at the school, seeing group work and whatever. I have worked a lot in different classrooms. . . I came as a mum originally and I was a special needs assistant so I was in various classrooms and saw how all the group systems worked together and saw the theme throughout the school, because I didn't actually work like that before. I was more, half the class would do that and half the class would do that, but now I've got lots of little groups doing all sorts of things.

Interviewer: How did you make that adjustment?

Teacher: I think just by seeing how well it did work and

what output the children were giving back. I always used to think that if they were working in small groups, they would just be chatting about what they did last night, but they actually don't. Just being an outside observer looking in on the situation you could see that they were actually talking about what they were supposed to be doing.

Interviewer: So when you started officially as the teacher of the class you put that approach into effect straight away?

Teacher: Straight away.

Interviewer: With confidence?

Teacher: Yes, I would say with a lot of confidence, because I had seen how to arrange it and how to work it and seen what to do with one group when you're busy with two other groups...so I went in for it straight away.

Working Together

Thirdly, opportunities to learn existed whenever teachers worked together, which they did in all the schools in a variety of ways. Sometimes they worked together within a variety of teaching and learning situations. Examples were:

— a teacher with particular responsibility for special needs teaching within a colleague's classroom (for example, Tamsin at Fenton);

— a teacher with a support role teaching within a colleague's classroom (for example, Rhian at Ingham);

— teachers teaching together in open-plan areas (for example, in the units at Orchard or the reception area at Fenton);

— teachers sharing the responsibility for one class (for example, Kate and Mary at Carey);

— teachers working together on school journeys (for example, Nancy and Katherine from Upper Norton during a week on the Isle of Wight);

— teachers teaching together on an occasional basis related to specific initiatives associated with curriculum development (for example, all the teachers involved in paired teaching in the course of developing the maths, and later the science, curriculum at Carey);

— teachers teaching together on an occasional basis because they shared an interest or expertise (for example, Natalie and Beth at Ingham planning with the children where to plant trees; Marilyn and Evelyne preparing a dance with a group of children for the Summer Garland, a celebration of Summer at Ingham);

— putting on a performance (for example, the *Firebird* at Upper Norton, *Oliver* at Fenton, *Starship Silver Grey* at Ingham);

— celebrations (for example, the tenth birthday celebrations at Orchard).

At other times teachers worked together away from children. Examples included:

— sharing knowledge about children (as the Orchard teachers did regularly at the start of their staff meetings and other staffs did in breaks and informal gatherings);

— choosing topics together (for example, *On the Move* at Upper Norton);

— planning topics together (for example, *Clothes* at Fenton);

— evaluating classroom activities (for example, as the Carey staff did after teaching science activities together in the course of developing the science curriculum);

— sorting resources (for example, when the Ingham staff sorted the maths equipment and those at Upper Norton turned out a cupboard);

— holding open evenings for parents (for example, as when staff at Carey set up problem solving activities for parents);

— planning and holding workshops for parents (for example, when staff at Fenton sought to give parents guidance about what help they might give in the teaching of reading in the classrooms);

— involvement in school wide initiatives peripheral to the classroom (for example, the *Share-a-Book* and *Share-a-Game* initiatives at Ingham to encourage parents to get involved in reading and maths activities with their children at home);

— participating in the formulation and implementation of policy through agreeing an approach and/or writing a curriculum document (for example, agreeing a policy on handwriting at Upper Norton);

— sharing in decision making (for example, about how an extra 0.6 teaching time should be used during the summer term at Ingham).

In all these situations the possibility existed that teachers might learn from one another, particularly because, as they worked together, they became increasingly familiar with the ways in which each planned, taught and thought about the curriculum.

Increasing familiarity with other people's thinking and practice encouraged teachers to take on responsibility for aspects of one another's work. Sometimes they assisted and facilitated colleagues' work in relation to the curriculum. For example, one teacher said:

> I find if I go anywhere or do anything and I know that any-body else is doing something on birds or pollution I will pick things up like that, therefore I'm working for the whole school... You've got an extra pair of eyes to watch out for information or any other resource that you can handle.
> (Teacher, Fenton)

At others they sought to share their own newly-acquired knowledge, skills and understanding. So, for example, teachers disseminated, both formally and informally, what they had learned from attendance at courses, as when Edith at Ingham left her work from an art course on the table in the staffroom with a note inviting colleagues to look at it, or Rosie and Theresa, also at Ingham, set up a lunchtime meeting to share excitedly what they had learned from a course on the creative use of the environment. Occasionally too staff shared a learning opportunity with their colleagues during a piece of curriculum development which involved them all. (for example, the staff at Carey visited other schools in pairs to observe the ways in which children were involved in problem-solving activities and then reported to the rest of their colleagues what they had learned).

The experience of working together also enabled and encouraged teachers to challenge one another's thinking and practice. At Orchard, for example, pairs of teachers taught in close proximity in open-plan units. They planned their work together on a day-to-day, a weekly and a half-termly or termly basis. One teacher, either through interest, experience or enthusiasm, usually took the lead. This arrangement provided opportunities for teachers to support and challenge one another, as Graham describes:

Sarah played the major role, I think. We talked about what work we'd do, but she was the one who actually delivered the input to the children and I went along with it, because I'd had no experience of anything like this. Then gradually I was able to put in my own inputs. It's very much a joint thing, that we get together and decide what we'd like to do and whether that would be suitable for the children. To begin with I came up with lots of ideas and Sarah shot a lot of them down which at the time I didn't particularly like, but I can see that she was right. What I wanted to do was probably far too ambitious. (Teacher, Orchard)

Seeing and Hearing

Fourthly, other learning opportunities arose when teachers had incidental chances to see or hear about, and reflect upon, colleagues' practice. Though unplanned, these encounters enabled individuals to gain a knowledge of the school that transcended their own classrooms and encompassed the practice of colleagues. Sometimes such occasions arose naturally from the activities that teachers undertook together. In some schools (for example, part of Fenton; Orchard) open-plan architecture facilitated teachers' awareness of what and how their partners were teaching, whether or not they were deliberately working together. In addition teachers learned about what was happening elsewhere in the school through 'showing' or 'sharing' assemblies (ie. when children and/or their teachers shared current work with the rest of the school). Professional development days too could provide incidental opportunities for teachers to share aspects of their practice with one another. For example, at Ingham the teachers spent an INSET day sorting maths resources and as they did this they informally exchanged ideas about how these might be used in the classroom. This kind of professional conversation had not previously characterized their interactions as a group. A similar type of sharing occurred later in the year when Evelyne, the Headteacher, encouraged them to visit one another's classrooms in pairs during another in-service day, to discuss ways in which classrooms might be organized and resourced in order to implement the English National Curriculum. During these visits teachers talked about their own practice, exchanging professional insights and understandings. Once again they found it valuable to do so. One said:

> I think we should have had two or three days doing that. I think that would have been more adequate, not just looking at people's resources, but the whole question of personal development, well, the school's development. People had to express themselves in letting people into their classrooms and seeing other people's classrooms. (Teacher, Ingham)

Such incidental opportunities for mutual learning enabled teachers to share ideas, to offer suggestions and to make contributions to the work of their colleagues, while simultaneously picking up ideas that were useful to their own classroom practice.

> I do feel that I tend to know what is going on in the whole school. I do know, and I hope in some way I contribute to things that are going on in other units, even if it's only just with natural discussion with the children. (Teacher, Orchard)

Further, knowledge of what was happening elsewhere in the school enabled teachers to support and build on one another's work, and, by raising awareness of what had gone before and what came after, increased the likelihood of continuity in the curriculum.

> You can see what they're doing in reception, where it gets to as well, and I think that is vital... It's actually got some purpose. It's not done in isolation and you can see it following right the way through. (Teacher, Fenton)

Some teachers encouraged others to know what they were doing by opening up their classrooms, perhaps because it made them feel as though their work was acknowledged and approved by their colleagues and was part of a shared endeavour. At Upper Norton, for example, Noreen, the new, temporary staff member taught in the mobile classroom situated at the rear of the school. There were many occasions when she did not know about organizational arrangements that had been made. She was rarely visited in her classroom by other colleagues though Dorothy, the Headteacher, visited most days and, towards the end of the year, so did Wendy. Noreen sometimes wandered through the classrooms in the main school on her way to and from the staffroom and this enabled her to have some idea of what other teachers were doing, but they knew little of what was happening in her classroom. During the summer term Noreen and her class moved into the art room in the main building, while builders worked on the mobile classroom. She said afterwards:

I actually quite liked being over there. At one stage — I think we might have been there a week before I felt happy enough to do it — I folded back the doors onto the library area and had the classroom as open as I could to the library area. And that was rather nice. It was just the feeling that my classroom was open to anyone who walked past, who could look in, anyone could wander in if they wanted to. I think the fact that my doors were open was me saying, 'Here we are, here's my classroom. Come on in'. And people did wander in and out. I liked that. (Teacher, Upper Norton)

Taking Responsibility

Finally, opportunities to learn arose when individuals undertook some new responsibility within the school and so had to increase their own knowledge and understanding in ways that they otherwise might not have done. For example, Naomi at Carey was asked by Ella, the Headteacher, to take on the responsibility of Science Coordinator because she was the one member of staff with a scientific qualification. The learning that resulted for her and for others and the means by which this happened are described in further detail in chapter 4. Other examples are Nancy who undertook an informal responsibility for science at Upper Norton and in the process increased her own scientific knowledge and skills, and Beth in relation to health education at Ingham.

To summarize, teachers in the project schools had five different types of opportunity for professional learning, all of them actively promoted by their heads. These were: when they were consciously in the role of learners (for example, on in-service courses); while they were being inducted into school norms; when they worked closely with colleagues both within and outside the classroom; as they became more aware of and therefore more able to reflect upon colleagues' practice (for example, through assemblies, display, professional development days); when they fulfilled a responsibility held within the school. However, the mere existence of any of these activities did not ensure that learning would take place. The willingness of teachers to learn was the key which turned any activity into a learning opportunity. This willingness could not be assumed. For this reason if teachers did not perceive and take advantage of these opportunities, they sometimes came under pressure to do so. At Orchard, for example, teachers were aware that their work was monitored and evaluated, particularly by Ron, the Head, but also by the Deputy Head and the unit leaders. Southworth (1989) in the case study on Orchard, wrote:

> It has already been noted that unit leaders helped newcomers settle in, were a first point of reference for less experienced colleagues and modelled collaboration and cooperation. They also took an active lead in curriculum planning in the unit. When a colleague failed to pick up the approved way of doing things, ignored or was unaware of school policy, the unit leader felt free to intervene. If that did not resolve the issue matters were discussed with Ron.

Similarly at Fenton, gentle but deliberate pressure was put on Dawn to learn what was expected of her. This account records a discussion between Simon, the Head, Rob, the Deputy, and Rebecca who held a responsibility for the lower school.

> They agreed that Rebecca should talk to Dawn. Simon suggested that she should talk about systems for organizing reading in the classroom. He said that Dawn had had a term to settle in now and it was time to pick her up. Last term he was preparing to talk to her about certain issues but the fact that she had been ill, and that she wasn't really well even now, had prevented him from doing so. He said that his policy with her at the moment was to boost her on the writing and creativity that was going on in the classroom, which was very good. Simon said he had talked to her about the difficulties of having children queuing to see her. They reminded themselves that she was just out of her probationary year, a year that had been spent in an unsupportive environment in another school. They agreed that Rebecca's next release day should be spent largely with Dawn. Simon suggested that Rebecca emphasize her role as supporting Dawn...saying that Rebecca should let Dawn bring up her own problems for discussion. (Fieldnote, Fenton)

Means of Learning

Teachers, like other adult learners, found some means of learning more congenial and more effective than others. The success of the opportunities to learn, provided, promoted and used by headteachers and others depended in part on how they were carried out. We found that teachers appeared to make particularly productive use of four types of activity: talk, observation, practice and reflection. These means were valued by some or all of the staff, and particularly by the headteachers, who, as a result, worked to foster them.

Talk

Talk was an important means of communication about all aspects of school life, including the curriculum. At Carey it was explicitly recognized as a key means of spreading ideas amongst the group. An extract from the case study of Carey reads:

> Staff meeting discussions about the maths curriculum continued over several months. Fieldnotes confirm that every member of staff regularly took part and that ideas were derived from their own practice, from courses, from literature. Discussions took place in the belief that they were vital to the process of development. Ivy is recorded in field notes as saying to Ella, 'It's like you're always saying, it's the talking that's important...it can be a learning process with everybody chipping in ideas.' (Campbell, 1989b)

Talk was also given a high priority in informal situations. For example, at Carey lunchtimes and breaktimes the staff, with only rare exceptions, gathered in the staffroom. In any single day most spent between an hour and an hour-and-a-half in conversations which were a mixture of the personal and professional. Fieldnotes record the importance that the Headteacher attached to this informal chat.

> At the end of lunchtime when the staff were drifting away, Ella turned to me and said, 'It's surprising what a lot of discussion about school takes place at these times.' I knew what she meant. Even in the short time I've been at the school there have been several occasions when, in an informal and

casual way, conversations have been influencing quite important decisions about the curriculum and organization of the school. (Fieldnote, Carey)

One teacher summarized the value of the continuing interplay between formal and informal discussion in enabling teachers to learn from one another and so in bringing about curriculum development:

I think what happens is that everybody talks and you gradually integrate these things into your teaching. Occasionally you might say, 'That's a good idea. I'll do that', but also the good thing about having a formal meeting every Monday, is that you might go over the same ground, you might talk about different things, but things get mulled over and gradually ideas get taken on board...they become part of you... It's not only the Monday lunchtime discussions...you've seen for yourself that little ideas get thrown about, all sorts of times. (Teacher, Carey)

That the value of talk in spreading ideas was recognized in the other schools too is evident from the many occasions, formal and informal, on which it occurred and the importance that teachers attached to such occasions. For example:

We talk together quite a lot as a staff about what we are doing. I go away and take things on then. (Teacher, Fenton)

The importance of the (in-service training) day was that people came back discussing things. (Teacher, Ingham)

The best thing about the cluster INSET day was bouncing ideas off each other which I found very interesting. (Teacher, Upper Norton)

Talk was not only a means of sharing learning. It was also a way of providing mutual support and challenge. Both were valued, as this teacher makes clear:

It was really quite hilarious listening to Lori and her stories...and that was really good. Beth would say, well, she didn't like something. She thought something else was much better, and Lori would say, 'But you can't do this'... It was good because you listened to people's reasonings. (Teacher, Ingham)

Sometimes, however, challenging questions were regarded as less threatening if they came not from a colleague, from whom one might reasonably expect support, but from some third party, such as an INSET lecturer or an advisory teacher.

Having somebody there just to ask questions triggers off the thinking. In a way a third person can do it in an unthreatening way. (Head, Upper Norton)

Observation

Observing others at work was another popular and frequent means of learning. There were several teachers who, because of their status or role, believed they should provide an example for their colleagues. Heads were an obvious example of this and this aspect of their role is considered in greater detail in chapter 3. As teachers watched their heads, they learnt not only about classroom practice but also about leadership. For example, the staff at Fenton found it useful to observe Simon as, in his words, he 'delivered the goods with groups of children'. However they also recognized that they were learning other things from watching him at work. One described his role as 'subtle' rather than 'obvious', 'guiding' rather than 'authoritarian', 'leading' rather than 'confrontational'. Yet he informed the staff group of his own 'particular views' and motivated them 'to fall into the way he wants them to work'.

This teacher's ability to analyze Simon's leadership role argues a close attention given to all his actions. Teachers were evidently adept at learning from the subtle as well as the obvious messages contained within the actions of others.

Ivy, the Deputy at Carey, saw assemblies as a powerful opportunity for teachers to observe one another's work. She used them to share her practice with her colleagues and thus to fulfil some of the responsibilities of her role. She said:

The class assembly, I thought, was a really good way of sharing what one class had done and maybe give another teacher some ideas and, leaving apart what it was doing to children, it...could be used as a vehicle for getting across certain ideas and ways of working to other members of staff... It's a fine line between trying to do a wonderful assembly which everyone else thinks, 'Oh dear, I've got to follow that', or, 'She's showing off'... That's very difficult, but I felt being the deputy head removed the threat of competition. I could be seen doing that, because I was the Deputy and so no one felt any pressure to do an assembly in a similar way. But I always wanted to make sure that what came across was a very integrated way of working. (Teacher, Carey)

That the example Ivy gave in assemblies did become a means of learning for others was demonstrated when a teacher recalled:

Being daring is part of it, isn't it? I remember Ivy's Pied Piper assembly! Nobody would ever have done that! Were you in? It was an absolute hoot! She had the whole class dressed as rats. It was really good and it wasn't rehearsed! That kind of thing does spark you, definitely, into thinking, 'Wow! They love doing that'. (Teacher, Carey)

Teachers did not learn only from those who deliberately acted as models for them. They also paid close attention to the work of all their colleagues, so far as circumstances enabled them to do so. They walked in and out of one another's classrooms on their way to the staffroom, looked at corridor and hall displays, eagerly took opportunities to go into classrooms when their colleagues were teaching. As one teacher said:

I am always learning from other teachers around the place, just by looking round. That's another brilliant thing about being able to get release from a class and have a look at what's going on in other areas, I suddenly think of ideas. I look at something that somebody's doing. That'll spark me off thinking about things. (Teacher, Fenton)

Practice

Teachers also learned by doing and especially by taking part in activities which enabled them to acquire new knowledge and skills. For example, the staff at Fenton identified a need to learn about the possible uses of clay in the classroom and set aside an in-service training day for that purpose. Throughout the day they were actively engaged in playing and modelling with clay. Only a month later their learning was apparent in the work produced by their children:

> There was a lot of evidence in assembly this morning of clay work. It clearly derived from the INSET day... Some children from Kathryn's class showed that they'd made monsters that were brightly coloured... Dawn's class too showed some clay work. Dawn told the school that the task for the children had been to get the clay as thin as they possibly could and to decorate it. She explained that one child had thought his looked like a pond and so he had decorated it like that. Another child had done a purely imaginative shape, another a jungle and a cave... Barbara told me that she too has done some clay work with the children which they took home just last week. I asked her whether she'd ever done work like that before and she said, oh no, she would never have dared. The most she'd done was to do flat shapes of clay on which you scratched pictures. She clearly feels that it's a step forward for her, to have had the courage to do this kind of work with children. (Fieldnote, Fenton)

Significantly, the children's work observed on this occasion did not duplicate that of the teachers on their training day. The latter did not simply pass on what they had learned to the children but extended it. Indeed, the confidence that they had gained encouraged them to provide children with opportunities to use clay creatively.

The initiatives taken at both Ingham and Upper Norton to introduce or strengthen the use of information technology in the curriculum provide further evidence that confidence as well as knowledge grew from learning by doing. At each school there was a planned professional development programme which used expertise from within and outside the school. Sessions led by school coordinators and by advisory teachers provided plenty of practical activity. In both instances teachers felt that their active involvement, together with the opportunity to talk through their major concerns, had played a significant part in their learning. One teacher said:

> It's hands-on experience and chatting to somebody, this is where I feel you learn. (Teacher, Upper Norton)

Reflection

The final means by which teachers learnt runs through and underpins all the others, for it describes an attitude of mind. Teachers learned by talking and listening to colleagues and others, by observing the work of others whenever there was opportunity to do so, by questioning and appraising their own and others' practice, whether overtly or covertly, and by engaging in practical activities which promoted the acquisition of new knowledge and skills. None of this learning was passive. Rather they were actively involved in determining the course of their learning and, above all, in reflecting on what they heard, saw and did. Such reflection was not limited in its course, nature or timing to any particular occasion. It took place over time and within the broad framework of an individual's thinking and development, as the following comment suggests:

> There comes a point when you are moving along a certain track and something crystallizes it for you. Had I not been aware of any of the problems I don't know how much impact the 'multi-cultural' day would have made. But it clarified some things that I have been thinking about for some time. (Teacher, Upper Norton)

In each school, there appeared to be some teachers who habitually questioned their own practice within the classroom, tried to become more aware of what was happening there and, as a result, changed their behaviour. However, such self-appraisal is likely to be private, and it is necessarily within the control of the individual, since a willingness to learn from reflection upon one's own practice depends upon the desire to improve. Certainly, teachers rarely reflected aloud upon their own practice.

They were more likely to share their thoughts with others when they were working or talking with them; reflection was stimulated and facilitated by interaction. Also, our evidence suggests that the more familiar teachers became with the work of their colleagues the more likely they were to make comparisons with and assess their own. Some INSET courses also encouraged teachers to reflect on what was happening by asking them to observe and analyze behaviour and practice within their own classrooms. Thus Verity from Fenton, who was on an out-of-school early years course, spent some time observing reception (YR) and middle infants (Y1) children in the home corner and noticed that the older children interacted more in their play than the younger ones. She shared her observations with other course members and reflected on their implications for classroom practice. Similarly, Kathryn, also at Fenton, shared with her colleagues during a staff meeting what she had learned from a course activity about her own professional practice:

> She told them that it (the course) was largely devoted to thinking about how children talked to one another and that there was a need to listen to what children say. She said, 'Half the time I am saying, "Be quiet! Be quiet!" but we have got to start setting up situations that encourage children to talk, and observe them in the classrooms'. (Fieldnote, Fenton)

Favourable Conditions for Learning

The conditions under which teachers attempted, or were asked, to learn could also be more or less conducive to that learning. Conditions were favourable when they provided in three ways for teacher's needs: physically, by ensuring an appropriate context and affectively. The leadership of the headteachers and, other teachers' willingness to learn were also facilitative factors.

Providing for the Physical Needs of Teachers

The least important of teachers' needs was apparently the physical. Staff frequently accepted, appreciated, even enjoyed, learning experiences which involved them in long meetings at the end of the working day (when they were often tired) or at lunchtime (when missed or hurried meals were common) or in uncomfortable furniture (for example, where they were seated on chairs and working at tables designed for 5-year-olds). However they also recognized that such conditions reduced their capacity to learn effectively. One teacher said:

> I think you can feel very pressurised after school, at 3.30 pm at a staff meeting when you're thinking, 'I'm tired. I'm hungry. I want to go home!' You don't really give of your best. (Teacher, Ingham)

When thought was given to their physical comfort teachers appreciated it as something out of the ordinary and almost always attributed the value of any learning opportunity to some other cause. However two examples, one positive and the other negative, serve to suggest that when consideration was given to teachers' need to eat and rest, it may have contributed to their learning. In the first example Rosie is describing a course she had attended eight months earlier. In spite of having felt 'terribly ill the whole time' she found it 'very enjoyable', 'very stimulating'. Asked why this was so she replied:

> Because we learnt things that we can do with children. We actually learnt them. We did them. They were enjoyable to do personally. They organized it in such a way that you could actually do the clay and the stitching. You could make something that you personally enjoyed doing, but at the same time there were also things that you could use with your children. You are in a lovely place and the food was nice and the company was good. It is a rare luxury to get two days out of school and to be in a beautiful place. I personally find that very relaxing, to do something I like doing with no pressure and yet at the same time it's very relevant to your job. (Teacher, Ingham)

There were several reasons why Rosie found this course of value — its relevance to her daily task, the intrinsic enjoyment she derived from the activities in which she was engaged, the organization of the course, the surroundings, the food, the company of like-minded professionals, and time. Physical comfort was only one amongst several reasons that she gave for valuing the course. It was neither the most important nor sufficient on its own to ensure that learning would take place. Instead, it was valued as a luxury.

In the second example, teachers at an evening meeting exhibited few signs of enthusiasm. Tiredness and discomfort were probably not the only reasons, but were nevertheless almost certainly significant. None of the staff recalled this meeting as a valuable learning experience. It was held in the school hall and staff sat on infant chairs.

> Rita Kent from the Primary Science Team talked to the staff for an hour-and-a-quarter this evening, introducing them to the idea of a problem-solving approach to science in the early years and possible ways forward in designing a science curriculum. She had brought with her a vast range of equipment which was distributed around the hall. She told us that she had intended us to work to make a vehicle that would travel from

one side of the hall to the other, but time had run out. Instead she suggested that we should explore the resources she had brought with her. Staff did so in a fairly desultory fashion. It was the end of a long, hot, sticky day! There was some discussion of particular resources amongst small groups — what children liked and didn't like, durability and so on, but on the whole, I think, people wanted to get home and soon wandered off, though Tina told Edith that she was returning after she had had tea. I gathered from their conversation that this is the first of several after-school meetings this week. (Fieldnote, Ingham)

This example suggests that when staff are already tired and have to bolster slender reserves of energy to meet demands they know will later be made upon them, they are unlikely to learn effectively.

Providing an Appropriate Context for Learning

The immediate context of teachers' learning was also important. They needed adequate time, sufficient space and necessary materials. These three conditions were often met during mandatory in-service training days. The one spent by the staff at Fenton on clay work is one of several such examples. It was led by the Headteacher, Simon, who, as well as teaching relevant skills, was modelling a particular pedagogical approach. Teachers worked in a classroom where the tables and chairs had been arranged to ensure that there was sufficient space to move freely to fetch materials, of which there was an abundant supply, or to look at one another's work. They were able, because time was not a constraint, to work until they were satisfied. These conditions enabled Simon to create 'an atmosphere in which they could work and talk comfortably together without too great a dependence on him' (Fieldnote). Similar conditions also existed at specialist in-service centres to which teachers from Upper Norton, Ingham, Carey and Fenton went during the year.

Providing for the Emotional Needs of Teachers

More necessary even than physical comfort and respect for learning needs was emotional support. Such support enabled individuals to undertake tasks about which they felt insecure or vulnerable and to enrich one another's understanding or skills. This example is taken from the same in-service day at Fenton, on clay:

> Another major source of conversation was the work itself. We solicited help from one another by asking questions like, 'What do you think I should do about this?' We expressed admiration for each other's work by saying, 'That's nice', 'I like that', and 'How did you do that?' At one point Rob stopped what he was doing and said he was going to have a look at everyone else's work... At the end of each session the objects we'd made were gathered together on the desk and we all stood around looking at each product, admiring them and congratulating ourselves on what we'd achieved. We all used phrases like, 'Haven't we done well?' and 'Isn't this fun?' and 'We should market these for school funds'. We asked questions like, 'Whose is this one?' It was rare that anyone would say, 'That's mine', but common for others to say, 'That's so-and-so's'. There was an awareness among people of the work of those who'd been closest to them and a sharing of success. (Fieldnote, Fenton)

It highlights the emotional context of learning, especially the learners' need for security and a sense of belonging. The mutual support provided by the group allowed individuals to express their feelings during the process of learning — feelings which ranged from satisfaction and fulfilment to frustration but which culminated in a shared sense of achievement. Of course, learners' emotions were not always as comfortable as this example suggests. Helen at Upper Norton consistently experienced frustration and a sense of inadequacy as she struggled to come to terms with the computer. Yet she was supported by the group as a whole and by particular members of it.

> Nancy was describing how the new DART program could give practice in rotations and angles and scale and got various people to come up and have a go. She asked Helen up after Katherine had had a turn. After a bit of fumbling, Helen flung her things down and said, 'It's no good, I can't do it,' and went and sat down again. Everyone was very supportive and sympathetic. At intervals thereafter Wendy had little one-to-one conversations with her, saying, 'First you learn to do forwards and back', and explaining how, with the 'turtle', she

had drawn lines and got children to move from forward to back. (Fieldnote, Upper Norton)

Helen had been very full of self-doubt and Wendy had been supporting and encouraging her until they began to work as a group on the machine themselves. Then Helen leant over and said to Katherine, 'No, no, you don't do that, you do this.' Everyone laughed and said, 'There you are Helen — you can learn after all.' (Fieldnote, Upper Norton)

So, in both comfortable, or satisfying and uncomfortable, or frustrating learning situations the support of colleagues was indispensable (see also chapters 3 and 5). Moreover, when such support was available, individuals felt encouraged to take risks, to do something they had perhaps never done before, knowing that whether success or failure followed, they would be able to share the results with their colleagues. This, in turn, helped everyone to learn. Usually such ventures took place in classrooms and were shared informally. In the following example however Kate had been asked to lead a professional development day on assessment for the staff of Carey and that of the neighbouring junior school. Initially, this was something about which she felt very diffident and uncertain. At the end of that day and on their return to the infant school the Carey staff praised Kate:

There was a definite feeling that Kate had done a good job. Ella congratulated her warmly and said she'd done very well... The others were all very warm in their praise too. They said to one another, in her hearing, 'Didn't she do us proud?' It was as if Kate's handling of the day reflected on them all, as if she was their representative and they were all involved. (Fieldnote, Carey)

Kate herself believed that the support of her colleagues had contributed to the success of the day.

To be asked to do a INSET day was enough, but the fact that everybody clapped at the end of it was just joy really... So how can you fail to do your best when everybody is supportive? I think that comes right through. (Teacher, Carey)

Yet such a sense of security was not achieved easily nor maintained without cost, since it could be established only when individuals had admitted a need to learn and to be supported in their learning. They also had to be prepared to learn from one another. To be sure, the more the members of a group accepted that learning was a norm of their professional life and the more secure individuals felt within the group, the more prepared they were to take advantage of every opportunity to learn and to share that learning with their colleagues. However not all the staff provided their members with identical levels of security nor, in any one of the schools, did all individuals feel equally secure. The emotional context of curriculum development, like the learning which made the latter possible, had constantly to be nourished and tended (see chapters 3 and 5).

Leadership

Leadership is a recurring theme throughout this book (see in particular chapters 3 and 5). We have already described the activities of leaders in several places in this present chapter. Nevertheless leadership deserves specific, though brief, mention here since the presence within the schools of leaders, in particular headteachers, who behaved in ways that facilitated and promoted learning was itself one of the conditions for effective staff learning.

All the headteachers valued their own learning. Throughout their careers they had themselves actively participated in formal educational activities and they were still demonstrating their willingness to learn from many sources. At the time of our fieldwork Ella, at Carey, had recently completed an MA and was acting as supervisor to students on an Advanced Diploma course. Evelyne, at Ingham, had done an Advanced Diploma and was currently attending a long course which involved her in making visits to a number of schools around the country. Simon, at Fenton, had been involved in a major research project into teaching and currently provided in-service training in his LEA. Ron, at Orchard, had recently embarked upon an MA, while Dorothy, at Upper Norton, had just finished an Advanced Diploma.

Habitual learners themselves, these headteachers valued learning, and were willing to contribute to the growth of others, particularly to that of their colleagues. This they did in several ways. They encouraged and actively supported the interests of staff and responded to their concerns by recommending courses, other schools to visit, people to talk to or appropriate reading. They initiated developments themselves and supported the initiatives taken by others.

Teachers other than the heads also led their colleagues' learning (see chapter 5). However they took this role only when their head-teachers allowed and encouraged them to do so and in general the ways in which they promoted the learning of their colleagues mirrored those used by their heads. Usually, such teachers held posts (for example, deputy; coordinator) which in their view included a responsibility for the learning of others. But occupying such a post did not in itself ensure that teachers initiated or supported learning amongst their colleagues. For example, neither Kay Hale (responsible for art and display at Carey) nor Thelma (responsible for music at Carey) played a leadership role in those areas, though Thelma implied that when music became a focus for development she would expect to play such a part. Furthermore, there were individuals who, without holding an official position, nevertheless encouraged the development of their colleagues, as Noreen did in relation to maths at Upper Norton. In short, leadership of professional learning depended more upon personal enthusiasm and a willingness to assume responsibility than it did upon formal roles.

The Presence of Colleagues Committed to Learning

The final condition favourable to teachers' learning is also discussed again in chapter 5. This was the existence amongst colleagues within all the staff groups of a shared belief that learning should be valued, both for its own sake and for the contribution it made to the well-being and development of others. As a result, individual efforts to improve and extend their practice were supported and enriched by the presence of others who were also committed to learning. Not sur-prisingly, when heads recruited staff, they often therefore had a will-ingness to learn as one of their selection criteria. For example, at Fenton:

> (Simon said that) he wasn't concerned that staff coming in were able to do things the 'Fenton' way to begin with. He was concerned to establish, before permanent appointment, that they shared the same 'beliefs about children' and were adapt-able and ready to learn.

Moreover the staff recognized and shared Simon's priorities. One teacher said:

> He's very careful, I think, when he chooses new staff. He knows exactly what he's looking for. He tends to go for

people. . .(with) a similar philosophy, people that will listen to others.

In other words, Simon, like the other heads, used staff selection to try to ensure that there was a milieu favourable to learning within the school. Within a group where everyone wanted to learn ideas could spread rapidly from one person to another. While it was not impossible for individuals to pursue their own professional development in a school culture which did not explicitly value such learning, as Nancy and Katherine at Upper Norton had done under their previous head, it was much easier for them to do this in the context of a like-minded group.

Conclusion

In this chapter, we have argued that teachers' individual sense of responsibility for children's education and therefore for the curriculum, coupled with their heads' desire to ensure that all the staff in a school shared the same educational purposes and interpreted them in similar ways, led to a common belief in professional learning as the key to effective development. We have examined this learning under four headings: what motivated the teachers in the project schools to learn; the opportunities that existed for them to learn; the means by which they learnt; and the conditions which facilitated their learning.

Much of what we have written suggests that although the motivation to learn necessarily comes from within individual teachers yet a good deal of their learning takes place through and as a result of interaction with their colleagues and other adults. Within schools in which teachers are learning and so are making changes to their classroom practice, and to the curriculum, the individual and the group are interdependent. This interdependence cannot be better summarized than by quoting one of the teachers from Fenton for whom individual learning and the task of implementing what was learned in one's own classroom were inextricably interwoven with being a group member.

To be a part of a happy, sharing, communicating staff means that you are automatically learning at all levels at all times. You are learning about people. You can be learning about subject matter. You're learning how you can help and you then, actively, through your enthusiasm, want to go away and apply it.

Whilst it does not follow that when interaction occurs between members of a group, individuals will necessarily learn, activities which promote interaction seem to encourage three relevant developments. The first is of a group whose members approve of, and are enthusiastic about, learning. Closely linked to this is the second: emotional support and affective security encourage individuals to express their desire and need to learn and to take the risks sometimes necessary to learning. Third, are opportunities for individuals to learn from one another. In other words, activities which bring the staff purposefully into contact with one another increase the likelihood that individuals will learn and that the curriculum of the school will develop.

Such a conclusion has significant implications for the management of whole school curriculum development, for it suggests that attention must be paid to the professional development of teachers both as individuals and as members of the whole staff group. The fact that the learning of individual teachers is the key to the development of the curriculum in the classroom, and that the group context is important in promoting that learning explains the project heads' preoccupation with developing amongst the staff a sense that theirs were 'whole schools'. It is to this preoccupation that we turn in the next chapter.

Chapter Three

Developing a Sense of 'Whole School'

In chapter 1 we argued that according to the teachers in the project schools a 'whole school' had seven distinguishing features. First, each member of the staff group felt a strong sense of community. Second, staff shared the same educational beliefs and aims and interpreted them in similar ways in their actions. Third, they each exercised autonomy within their own classrooms, felt able to play an individual role within the school and readily called upon one another's expertise. Fourth, the members of the group related well to one another. Fifth, they worked together. Sixth, their knowledge of the school was not limited to matters of immediate concern to themselves or their own classes but encompassed the concerns, practice and classes of their colleagues. Seventh, they valued the leadership of their headteacher. Common to many of these characteristics is the idea of collaboration. Primary teachers' traditional emphasis upon individuality and auton-omy is offset by their awareness that a school is potentially a com-munity of adults and by their desire for mutual professional support. These teachers expected to have the freedom to meet their curricular and pedagogical responsibilities in the ways they judged right and to act in the light of circumstances in their individual classrooms. Yet they also acknowledged that the right to make individual decisions was not 'a licence to do as one pleased' (Teacher, Orchard). In other words, they were conscious that acting together and accepting inter-dependence were constraints which they had to accept if they wished to become participating members of educational communities, and that these 'whole schools' when they existed would, in turn, enhance and support their work as individuals.

Staff, especially the heads, regarded the process of developing a 'whole school' as gradual rather than rapid: 'We are edging towards that way of working' said one head (Ingham). Indeed, all staff spoke about a whole school as an ideal; an aspiration rather than an achievement, as this comment taken from a conversation with the Head of Orchard suggests:

'Do you think you have got a whole school?'
'No', said Ron and he paused before saying, 'We have got a semblance of one', and paused again. 'We will have one, we will have one again.' (Fieldnote, Orchard)

A 'whole school' was not something the staff of the project schools felt they had realized. Rather, in each school they were working towards accomplishing it. Therefore, in this chapter we do not consider how 'whole schools' were actually developed, since no one claimed that this could be done. Instead, we will focus on how the staff developed, to varying degrees in each school, a sense of 'whole school'. Yet these were partially, not wholly, cohesive educational communities. In all of them educational beliefs were more or less shared and greater and lesser degrees of social and professional interaction took place.

The heads and teachers also acknowledged that developing a 'whole school' was a difficult enterprise. There were three reasons for this. First, working together certainly provided opportunities for closer social relations amongst the staff and greater mutual appreciation of strengths, but in the process fundamental differences in value and practice between teachers might emerge. Learning about one another's work exposed staff to differences in practice which could stimulate not just discussion but also disagreement. When the latter occurred it was doubly destructive: social relations were harmed which, in turn, showed to everyone else that the school was not a 'whole' institution.

Second, the development of a sense of community was most telling when educational beliefs were put into action in classrooms. The headteachers were assiduous in striving to see the beliefs which from discussions and agreement on school policies they thought that they shared with the staff put into operation in classrooms. Lortie (1969) has suggested that there are two 'zones of influence' in primary schools: one is the individual teacher's classroom, the other, occupied by the headteacher, covers matters of general school policy and administration. Within 'whole schools' teachers exercise a degree of autonomy in their classrooms. But the heads did not perceive this to mean that teachers' practice should be impervious to the prevailing educational beliefs in the school. For sure, individuals were allowed to

interpret policies in their own ways and so differences could sometimes be regarded as divergence rather than deviance. Indeed, the
latitude and scope given to, and expected by, teachers in interpreting
shared educational beliefs in their own ways prevented these schools
from becoming oppressive or authoritarian institutions. But this latitude was limited by the headteachers' authority and by the fact that
they worked to turn beliefs into action in both zones of influence.
Allowances were made for individuals, but 'individuality' and 'autonomy' did not mean that staff could do as they liked. Rather, within a
'whole school' teacher independence and interdependence had to be
balanced against one another (see chapter 1):

> In a sense I wonder whether successful whole school develop-
> ment doesn't actually require a degree of autonomy for it to be
> successful in the first place. I'm not talking about uniformity
> in terms of the whole school, or conformity. I think that
> they've (staff) got to feel that they are able to make a worth-
> while and recognized contribution in the eyes of other people,
> with whom they are working, say in curriculum, and at the
> same time they've got to feel that they're able to achieve an
> individual status for themselves in the day-to-day class prac-
> tice; the two go together, I'm certain they do. I think probably
> the best of whole school development is when you actually
> blend the two. It's not saying well, it's either freedom or not
> having freedom. It's more complex than that I think. (Head,
> Orchard)

So, the heads and other leaders devoted attention to individuals,
valuing them as people and for the contributions each could make to
others. At the same time they valued interdependence both for social
reasons and for the professional teamwork it encouraged. Moreover,
as a way of showing that they valued both individuals and groups,
they encouraged individuals to work together in both staffrooms and
classrooms. These are attitudes and values that have been shown to
exist in schools with a 'culture of collaboration' (Nias *et al.*, 1989). We
return to this point in chapter 5.

However, although the heads valued and respected individuals
they also monitored the extent to which staff enacted agreed policies
in their respective classrooms. Yet classrooms are difficult places to
penetrate. The capacity of teachers to resist ideas and to react to
change with inertia is well documented (for example, Jackson, 1968;
Sarason, 1971; Lortie, 1975; Fullan, 1991). Also, teachers' territorial

instincts are strong and so too is their identification with 'their' children. The task of influencing classroom practice was therefore hard and required of the heads that, on the one hand, they were patient, sensitive to individuals and appreciative of each teacher's efforts, whilst on the other they knew what went on in classrooms, made expectations explicit and vigorously promoted their own and the school's educational aims and policies.

Third, primary schools as organizations are not necessarily steady-state institutions, but constantly changing (see also chapter 1). In particular, in the project schools, changes in personnel and responsibility altered the nature as well as the dynamic of the staff group. For example, when staff left or joined, as they did in all the schools, the character of the institution altered. Newcomers had to be induced into the school's procedures and be made aware of its underlying educational beliefs (see chapter 2). In addition, the schools had to adjust to curricular changes created by national legislation, especially the 1986 and 1988 Education Acts, at a time when some of them were still coming to terms with the loss of Scale Two posts, a structural alteration which had the effect of reducing the number of teachers with designated responsibilities. Moreover, with the introduction of Incentive Allowances some of the schools had switched responsibilities away from a curricular focus to an administrative or an in-service one. Such changes threw into relief the fact that the task of developing a socially and professionally cohesive group never comes to an end.

Developing a sense that the school was 'whole' was therefore: slow in pace; delicate, requiring differences, where they emerged, to be treated with care and sensitivity and individuality to be balanced against interdependence; and vulnerable to organizational disturbances. We have also implied that the development of a sense of 'whole school' depended upon the existence of both leadership and staff collaboration; this chapter looks in detail at both of these.

Leadership was important because a 'whole school' was, in essence, an educational community in which staff shared and acted upon the same educational beliefs. Someone, in the first instance, needed to provide, promote and sustain those beliefs. It is well recognized that industrial and commercial leaders perform this task, of articulating a vision which provides a sense of purpose and direction for the organizations that they lead (Viall, 1984; Peters and Austin, 1985; Bennis and Nanus, 1985). In education too primary heads provide a vision for 'their' school (Coulson, 1980; Holly and Southworth, 1989; Nias *et al.*, 1989). So it was in these schools. The heads believed that they had the authority to determine the educational beliefs of 'their' schools.

Moreover, because the process of developing a 'whole school' was difficult, slow and, sometimes, halting, the heads often took it upon themselves to keep the process moving and attempted to overcome obstacles to progress. To do this they needed to be in touch with what was happening in the school. We noticed this in particular when, during the spring and summer terms of our fieldwork, the heads were taken away from their schools to attend out-of-school meetings concerned with the introduction of the National Curriculum and Local Management of Schools (LMS). They voiced concern about losing touch with their schools, that is they tacitly acknowledged that headship was a 'hands-on' matter and that a sense of 'whole school' would not develop among the staff if the school was left unattended or nurtured by remote control. In short, these heads saw themselves as both central to and influential in the establishment of shared beliefs throughout the school.

Leadership, of course, is a broader notion than headship and in these schools there were other leaders than the heads. However, to provide a realistic focus we have decided to restrict our attention in this chapter to the heads. There are two reasons for this decision. First, we feel the work of the heads warrants separate treatment because of the authority and influence they wielded in relation to the educational beliefs of their schools. Second, we recognize the leadership roles performed by other staff (for example, deputies; coordinators) at other points in the book (see chapters 2 and 5, in particular). Therefore, the first part of this chapter considers the heads' part in developing a sense of 'whole school'.

In the second, we focus upon collaboration, for developing a sense of educational community also depended upon the capacity of staff to work together. We see collaboration as different from social interaction for the latter is personal rather than professional, is generally non-task related and largely informal. This is not to suggest that the distinction between the two is rigid or watertight. The Primary School Staff Relationships Project (Nias *et al.*, 1989) which throws a good deal of light upon the social aspects of primary schools as collaborative institutions showed that social interaction and professional teamwork overlapped. The same finding emerges from the present project. When staff members were in social contact with one another, their exchanges were full of humour, lightheartedness and spontaneity. Yet it was common for task related concerns (for example, the progress of children, ideas for lessons, sharing of equipment) to be woven into such conversations. Further, the discussion of personal and professional concerns often seemed to occur almost simultaneously. Although we do not focus explicitly upon the social side of life in these schools, we do not see it as irrelevant or unimportant. Collaboration by contrast, is task related. In the project schools it took a number of forms (see table 12) which we examine in greater detail in the second part of the chapter. We do this because working together is not only one of the characteristics of a 'whole school'. It is also the prime means by which many of the other characteristics are established. In part, this is because it serves two purposes: one practical, the other symbolic. In chapter 2 we showed that when the staff worked together, they had opportunities to learn from and about one another and to appreciate one another's strengths. Also, as they exchanged ideas and practices they were likely to come closer together in terms of educational beliefs and behaviour. In addition, when teachers and other staff worked with one another they demonstrated that they could, at least from time to time, do so productively. In this sense, collaboration was more important as a symbol, even a celebration, of interdependence than it was for the instrumental gains that it brought.

Finally, although we have separated our treatment of leadership from that of collaboration we are aware that they are dependent upon one another. Much of what the heads were trying to achieve involved them in encouraging interaction so that their staffs would work together and learn about one another's beliefs and practices. Equally, they could not reach their goal of building a 'whole school' through which their vision could be realized unless teachers related well to one another in a working context and learnt to value one another's contributions.

The Headteachers' Part in Developing a Sense of a 'Whole School'

The heads of the project schools had been headteachers for varying periods of time. The two most experienced heads were Ron and Ella. Ron Lacey was Head of Orchard Community Junior School. He was in his third headship, having been a head for fifteen years in total, nine of them at Orchard which he had opened. Ella Rhys, Head of Carey Infant School, had been in post for twelve years. It was her second headship, since she had been head in another infant school for four years. Simon Riley was in his first headship, although he had been Head of Fenton Primary for twelve years. Like Ron, he had opened the school. Simon left Fenton at the end of the Easter term, to become head of another, larger and longer established school. Evelyne Upton had been Head of Ingham Infant School for six years. It was her first headship. Dorothy Simon was also in her first headship at Upper Norton CE Primary, having been appointed four terms before the project commenced.

In addition to this range of experience and tenure each head worked in a different school setting and context (see Introduction). The individual personalities of the heads combined with their varied experience and contexts to account for the fact that each behaved differently. Whilst they were similar in ways which this section emphasizes, there were also contrasts between them. Not every head did everything that we describe here, but they all strongly resembled the overall picture.

One reason for the central and pivotal importance of primary heads within their schools is the considerable amount of power with which they are invested. However, because teachers generally regard this power as legitimate, it can be seen as authority (Hoyle, 1986; Nias, *et al.*, 1989). This was the case in the project schools. Neither the position nor the authority of heads was questioned:

> Most of the time (decisions are) unanimous. Some of the time it's majority, but if Ella really wanted something done, she would, I think, whether or not we were in true agreement, if she really wanted it she would expect it to be done. That's the role of a head. (Teacher, Carey)

Furthermore, staff expected their heads to have the final word on decisions and school policies and felt that they should make these decisions:

> We will work in a group and even though Evelyne's not in that group she has the final say... I believe that's the way it should be as well. It's her job. It's her responsibility, along with the governors. (Teacher, Ingham)

Because of the authority which was invested in their role, these heads, like other primary heads (Coulson, 1980; Nias *et al.*, 1989), believed that they ought to provide the underlying 'vision' of their schools. This was made up of the ideals which they held for education in general and those which related to 'their' school in particular. Thus each head's vision brought together a personal statement of belief with the beliefs around which he/she wanted the school to cohere and which were to underpin practice throughout it. In other words, the head's vision provided the basic values from which the shared educational aims of the school could grow. It also provided a framework within which all staff could work and develop common classroom practices.

The heads tried in all manner of ways to promote their educational beliefs and to ensure that theirs were 'whole schools'. Each head constantly directed the staff's attention to the values s/he held dear. Each strove to see these adopted by the staff and translated into their classroom practice. Their visions were set in school brochures and curriculum policy statements, and in their conversations and discussions with staff and others:

> No visitor to the school — researcher, parent, inspector, student, potential staff member — could long remain in doubt of the fundamental principles on which Simon's educational philosophy was founded. When they had heard the message in words then it was illustrated by a tour of the school. I experienced this preliminary induction process myself and I saw it repeated over and over again throughout the year. It was done quite consciously. (Campbell 1989a)

The heads used a vast array of tactics in pursuit of this overarching goal. Some of these were direct, some indirect; sometimes they were explicit, at others their intentions were implicit and could be perceived only from close observation and analysis. Whether they chose to act in direct or indirect ways depended to some extent on whether they were relying upon their authority or their influence (Hoyle, 1986; Nias *et al.*, 1989) to secure agreed school policies and to try to ensure that these were implemented in classrooms. When they acted in direct ways, they were often using their authority. When they were indirect, they tended to be relying upon influence. The heads' ability to use a range of tactics and to exercise their power in different ways usually, thought not always, made them hard to resist. This was the more so because, although they were driven by deeply-held convictions, they were prepared to be patient with colleagues and work gradually and steadfastly over long periods of time. In the next two sections we outline the direct and indirect ways in which the heads attempted to develop shared educational beliefs amongst their staffs and thereby to establish a sense of community and of commitment to common practice.

Direct Ways of Developing a 'Whole School'

The heads relied upon five mutually supportive tactics, when they were directly attempting to develop shared educational beliefs and to ensure that these were enacted in classrooms in similar ways. These were: the careful selection of staff, supported by a process of induction; speaking openly about their own educational beliefs; stating explicitly what they expected and wanted to see in the school and inside classrooms; being constructively critical of proposals for curriculum development and of classroom practice; and, exceptionally, making it plain to an individual that his/her practice was unacceptable.

As Southworth (1987) and Nias *et al.* (1989) also indicate, the most direct way of establishing shared beliefs was for the headteachers to appoint all 'their own' staff. Ron and Simon had done that, whilst Ella had appointed the majority of her present staff. However, selection alone was not sufficient. Although candidates were closely scrutinized before appointment, once appointed they needed to be carefully inducted into the school, a point which is more fully explored in chapter 2.

Not all the heads had been able to appoint and socialize all their colleagues. Where staff pre-dated the heads then the latter used other tactics to affect their outlook and practice. Moreover, not even the heads of Orchard and Fenton assumed that selection and socialization were sufficiently powerful by themselves to shape teachers' values. Consequently, all the heads vigorously promoted their visions. Where they saw particular values being expressed in action, they drew approving attention to this. They told stories and anecdotes which embodied and reinforced their beliefs. They encouraged talk and discussion so that ideas could spread and catch on:

> We've changed people by talking...I don't think that anybody should just say, 'Right, this is what we discussed and this is the document.' I think we should all be able to talk about it. I think there's much more value in talking about the document than there is in the actual document. Once the document is done, the value has gone out of it, because all the value was in the talking before. (Head, Upper Norton)

The heads also appreciated that beliefs were of little educational worth unless they were put into practice in classrooms. They saw this as the essential point of their work:

I've known a lot of schools where the curriculum discussion goes on in great depth and nothing much happens in the classrooms. If it's not happening in the classrooms then there's not a lot of point spending all your time talking about it. (Headteacher, Fenton)

In order to encourage common practices the heads were not averse, from time to time, to stating what they wanted. The heads spoke of this directness as 'pushing'.

Occasionally I'm a pusher on something that I think is not happening or is not quite right. I have a tendency to... highlight it so that (it's brought) to everybody's attention. (Head, Carey)

I think there is a tendency among most of them (the staff) to look to my expectations...because I tend to push what I think quite strongly. (Head, Fenton)

Sometimes they 'pushed' things because they were unhappy or uncomfortable with current practice. At Orchard, for example, Ron having discussed with the Deputy Head and Inset Coordinator how they viewed work in the school and, being concerned at the lack of consistency in marking children's work, decided personally to take the initiative and be more explicit about what he expected, and more vigorous in monitoring what happened in individual teacher's classes. At the start of a staff meeting Ron said:

There are two principles I want to establish. First is the need to mark only with the child present. Second, the principle of planning activities in appropriate sizes of groups so that marking can be done intensively, whilst children continue. (Fieldnote, Orchard)

At Ingham, Evelyne was constructively critical of teachers' proposals for curriculum change. A draft document on writing had been prepared for staff discussion. Being unable to attend the meeting but wishing to be involved, she submitted her response in writing. The document's author brought these to the notice of the meeting and:

waved an A4 piece of paper. She said, 'These are Evelyne's criticisms here, covered on both sides!' (Fieldnote, Ingham)

117

All the heads informally visited staff and talked, often extensively, to teachers on a one-to-one basis, or in small groups of twos and threes. Evelyne, however, had set up a more formal scheme for meeting staff individually.

> I'd also tried to set up, not an appraisal, but just an interview where each member of staff had an hour when we discussed what they liked about what we were doing, what they dis-liked, where they felt they had room for improvement, where I felt they had room for improvement. (Head, Ingham)

We also heard, how, in the past, some of the heads had occasionally spoken frankly to those teachers whose beliefs or behaviour differed markedly from their own. The heads had 'pushed' some staff hard and had 'moved' staff 'out' of the school. For example, at Fenton, we were told about an unsuccessful relationship between Head and Deputy where:

> Simon pushed the Deputy too hard and he (the Deputy) couldn't take the pace... The Deputy had been unhappy about what was happening and had left. (Fieldnote, Fenton)

On a separate occasion the Head said:

> There's very, very rarely been a time when I've had to have somebody in and say, 'Look, I'm not at all happy with what you're doing.' I've done it once or twice... (Head, Fenton)

Frankness of this sort made it clear to staff that there were certain standards below which they should not fall and, if they did, the heads would not be able to tolerate it. At the same time the heads' periodic interventions and the way in which they voiced dissatisfaction and praise made staff aware that they were being monitored, that the heads had minimum standards for classroom practice and were vigi-lant about them.

In each school the head's vision provided a set of educational goals and values to which all staff could aspire and to which the head sought to secure the staff's commitment and allegiance. Together the existence of minimum standards and the head's openly-stated vision created a set of parameters within which staff could establish their individuality, experiment, learn, discuss and influence one another. In being explicit and direct about the parameters within which they, as heads, hoped that all staff would operate, they sought to establish common goals and practices, the existence of which would in turn, help to create a sense of professional accord.

Indirect Ways of Developing a Whole School

The heads made use of seven tactics to influence their colleagues: example and demonstration; school assemblies; informal monitoring of classwork; making individuals feel valued; positive reinforcement; formal and informal meetings with staff to review and develop practice; micropolitical activity. These tactics overlapped and on occasions more than one tactic was deployed simultaneously.

The heads prized highly the power of example. All believed in demonstrating what they wanted and expected. They all taught in classrooms around the school. Some of them undertook planned teaching each week, others made use of the occasions when they had to cover for absent staff. Additionally, some of the heads modelled what they wanted by taking groups of children, working alongside colleagues, leading assemblies and putting up displays of children's work:

> I was doing display in the hall and wherever I could to show (the staff) what I wanted and using material and artefacts and things like that to arrange display... On the first Christmas I think I did practically the entire corridor by myself and that was exhausting. (Head, Ingham)

> I've got to be able to show (the staff) when I talk about something that I can deliver the goods with groups of children. It's no good me telling them things are possible if I can't actually demonstrate, by taking a class of children, that they are attainable with the children that we've got. It can be done. Not only that, I've always got to be credible in their eyes. There's no way that they're going to give me the support that they do at the moment unless they feel that I'm on top of it and aware of their problems. (Head, Fenton)

Assemblies were another way of exemplifying what they wanted. Indeed, assemblies were especially powerful arenas for the heads since all the staff were usually present to witness their relationships with children, to tune in to the main messages that they were transmitting and to pick up cues about how they wanted their staff to work:

> She told me that she does not miss class teaching saying, 'I feel
> I can have an influence on the school in other ways. Assembly
> is the main way I feel I influence things'. (Fieldnote, Ingham)

And this was borne out when Evelyne's assemblies were observed. The following is a description of a reasonably typical assembly, special only in the sense that it introduced children recently admitted to the school into a particular ritual of school life:

> The assemblies at Ingham are an important part of the day and
> important in the sense that Evelyne's standards are made clear
> through them. Once again this morning the children were
> very quiet. Evelyne was sitting at the front as the children
> started to come in. When they were all assembled they waited
> with an air of expectancy. Evelyne greeted all the new children
> and explained that she always said, 'Good morning', to every-
> one at the start of assembly because she couldn't say, 'good
> morning' to everyone separately and that the children always
> responded, 'Good morning Mrs. Upton'. They practised
> doing that and then Evelyne lit a candle for the New Year,
> referring to the fact that she had done this last week as well.
> They sang the New Year song together. Then Evelyne com-
> mended Errol who, she said, had been sitting so quietly at the
> start of assembly between two new children and that by his
> attitude and behaviour he had been teaching them. She
> brought him out to the front so everybody could see him and
> then she referred to a New Year book that she had made
> which was on an easel at the front. It had 'New Year Book'
> written on the front in lovely lettering. Evelyne opened it to
> the first page and wrote down that Errol had helped two new
> children by setting a good example to them in assembly. Tina,
> whose class Errol is in, whispered something to Marilyn,
> clearly approving of Evelyne's action. Evelyne continued to
> make entries of ways in which people had helped the new
> arrivals today, taking suggestions from teachers. Then she told
> everyone that she would leave a pencil on the easel and the
> New Year book open at the first page so that when teachers
> noticed children doing anything special to help one another or
> to help the new intake children, they could send them down to

the hall to write it into the book. As Evelyne drew this part of the assembly to a close, Tina and I exchanged glances and smiles and Tina nodded. I felt again that she was approving of what Evelyne was doing. Evelyne then read the story of a boy and his baby sister and how the boy had helped his mother in looking after the baby. They sang before leaving the hall. (Fieldnote, Ingham)

Assemblies also offered all the staff the chance to acknowledge the achievement of colleagues and to share ideas. Hence 'showing' assemblies figured prominently in some of the schools and in the minds of their heads:

> I think assembly is the main meeting place. That I think has been the success, people are aware of what other people are doing and are sharing ideas, we don't have the opportunity to work as a team and brainstorm on the same topic for the same age group like you could in a two-form entry but we've got assembly...(Head, Upper Norton)

> We had already applauded the children for their work, so Ron suggested that those children whose parents and relatives were present should go and show them their work, which the children happily did. Ron brought over to me the six small pieces of artwork the children had done, paintings of flowers and bees. He brought them over for me to admire. He said some very complimentary things about them to me...and he said, 'When we talked about curriculum and children the other day I have to say that this assembly today almost shows it all. There's some lovely work here', and as he said it, he moved his weight from one foot to another and back again, hopping about, almost, with a sense of delight. (Fieldnote, Orchard)

'Showing' assemblies were one way for the heads to observe and monitor what was happening around the school, but they also had other ways of finding out what was occurring in classrooms. They visited classrooms and teaching areas frequently. Sometimes they had to call into a classroom for some reason other than interest in teaching, often to pass on a piece of specific information. When they did this, they used the opportunity to see what was happening. They often toured the school in order to watch what some of the children were doing or to meet all the staff in an informal, relaxed way:

> At 11.48 Ron came into Michael's class and had a chat with him about something, but his visits to the unit are always characterized by his contact with children. On this occasion there was a child using a paper cutter on the floor. As Ron went past he put his hand on her head and smiled at her. On his way out he stopped and enquired what the child was doing and made some comment, and smiled and then moved off in the direction of his office again. (Fieldnote, Orchard)

> She claimed that she saw and spoke to every staff member every day and, 'If I can't, I know I haven't and I jolly well make sure I do the next day.' (Fieldnote, Upper Norton)

Such visits helped the heads not only to know what was happening in classrooms, but also to observe the extent to which school policies were being enacted in classrooms, or to note their absence. Whilst their visits were often good natured and underscored by a genuine interest in both children and adults, the heads were nevertheless using them to evaluate classroom processes and performances. Touring the school was a form of 'benevolent surveillance' (Ball, 1987, p. 93):

> She's (the head) a sort of overseer for what's going on. (Teacher, Upper Norton)

> I think he is all the time assessing and looking at where gaps are and where things can be developed...I think he is particularly perceptive. (Teacher, Orchard)

The information that the heads gathered during these visits provided them with material to discuss with staff. Usually these encounters were on a one-to-one basis after school but sometimes they took place before and during school. Heads used these occasions to influence their staff. Ideas could be exchanged, progress noted, encouragement given. These 'chats' were intended, over time, to gentle and nudge staff in particular directions:

> It's really the one-to-one chats that I have with the staff, just giving them the confidence to do what they should be doing or by suggesting alternatives. (Head, Ingham)

Being in close contact with staff, the heads often offered them advice which was valued because their exemplary behaviour and their active interest in teaching gave them credibility. They gave advice on project plans, educational visits, individual children or curriculum developments. Sometimes it served several purposes at once:

> Simon came back a bit later with a folder full of photographs of classes of children presumably from years past. He also gave Kathryn a tape which had been recorded during the Domesday Project of a grandmother talking about what Fenton used to be like. He suggested other people that Kathryn could go and talk to about the changes that had taken place in the village. In so doing he was not only being practically supportive, but was also reinforcing the importance of using first-hand evidence in the teaching and learning process. (Fieldnote, Fenton)

In addition the heads gave practical help which in turn enhanced their influence. This took many forms and for their part staff members felt free to ask for it. The heads joined in working party curriculum discussions. They did their share of mundane chores. They solved problems in resourcing, helped set up displays and exhibitions, contacted people outside the school, set up scenery and found props. In all of this they exemplified principles of participation and interdependence and thereby helped to build 'whole schools'. As they joined in and helped out they fostered a climate in which staff could relate well to one another and individuals could learn to value and to call upon one another's expertise. By their own example, they emphasized the fact that they wanted the staff to work together, to share, to cooperate and participate with others. These heads, in sporting parlance, were player-managers, members of the team as well as managers of it, players of the game as well as being evaluators of the team's performance. Furthermore, as player-managers the heads were closely involved with their staffs and the team often had an 'extra' player. If these heads had all the time confined themselves to their offices, the school, to some degree, would have 'lost' a teacher. Being willing to join in and help out enabled the heads to be aware of staff needs, whilst also supplementing and enhancing the size of the staff 'squad'. Having more players plainly made a difference.

As the heads watched what was happening, joined in and became involved with their staffs they had the chance to notice the achievements of teachers and their classes and to recognize and celebrate them. All the heads regularly used positive reinforcement. They praised individuals and recognized their efforts, either openly, or vicariously by drawing attention to 'their' children's work.

As a result, staff felt valued:

> Evelyne has given us more and more responsibility...she has
> allowed us to put forward views and I certainly felt that more
> (this) year that our views were very much valued. (Teacher,
> Ingham)

When heads openly praised individual teachers in the presence of their
colleagues, the staff knew that these individuals were being held up as
models. The heads were 'seeding' examples of 'good practice' which
colleagues might nurture and transplant into their own teaching.
Assembly was the obvious occasion for this, but so too were staff
meetings, year group meetings and informal gatherings. In fact,
wherever and whenever staff congregated, the heads were to be
found, encouraging individuals and sowing ideas for others to
cultivate.

The heads tended to play a leading role in formal meetings
usually by chairing them and also by making major contributions to
the discussion. Yet they also appreciated the significance of informal
meetings and discussions and the impact of these on teachers' actions.
They knew too that they could influence individuals by taking an
interest in their work:

> Certainly the formal curriculum meetings are important but
> perhaps more so, I think, is the time spent talking to indi-
> vidual teachers and to individual children about what they're
> doing. I think if I had to identify one key area of, if you want
> to call it, curriculum influence, it would be time spent between
> half past three and five o'clock or half past five, almost every
> day, in talking to individual teachers or groups of teachers,
> about what they're doing and how things have been going.
> (Head, Orchard)

As she came into the staffroom at break Noreen caught
Dorothy at the sink and said, 'You know when you were
working with my class last week you suggested afterwards
that they might...' and then there was something about, 'read
each other the instructions'. 'Well, I did that and it was
wonderful and it worked extremely well and V. did this and so'
and she was quite excited about it. She went to get the book
they had been working from and she and Dorothy sat by the
wall in the staffroom and talked to each other all the way

through the break, despite the wider conversation that was going on about assembly and the last reverberation of the school journey. (Fieldnote, Upper Norton)

Another way in which the heads influenced colleagues was through micropolitical activity. Several staff alerted us to the presence of micropolitics and to the heads' involvement in it:

> It's like the Firebird, Dorothy must have had a picture of that in her head and knew exactly what she wanted to slot into what, but nobody else could see it and she didn't tell us. She was masterminding it, we just did our own bits. (Teacher, Upper Norton)

> He (the head) knows what he wants and gets it. (Teacher, Orchard)

Another way of putting this is to suggest that the heads were sometimes manipulative, as indeed they were because they had to deal with the competing interests of individuals and/or groups. Faced with divergent opinions and preferences amongst members of staff the heads sometimes chose to deal with differences by negotiating with individuals and establishing compromises (see chapter 5). Although there were some issues or policies on which they took an unequivocal stand, and felt confident in doing so, on other matters (for example, the implementation of policies, approaches to teaching) they relied upon their ability to strike open or implicit deals with individuals in order to create the impression that staff shared and adhered to the same educational beliefs.

This was not a matter of hypocrisy or weakness. Rather, they realized that the road leading to a 'whole school' was a long one which could wind down as well as up. There would therefore be times when, for whatever reason, differences occurred within the staff group which might, if confronted, threaten the unity of that group. Since its members too wished to have a sense of belonging to a cohesive educational community, they were often ready to compromise. Micropolitical activity was not a reflection of the heads' desire to have their own way on all matters of policy and practice, but a result of everyone's wish to nurture a shared sense that theirs were 'whole schools', even at times when this clearly was not the case. Such compromises occurred in all the schools at some point during the year, and at Orchard for much of it. That they were not damaging to the short-term unity of the respective schools is due to two facts. First, in each school there were matters on which the head would not strike deals; everyone realized that issues affecting the fundamental beliefs of the institution might be temporarily ignored but would, if they persisted, be confronted. Second, the parameters within which the staff normally operated were not so tightly drawn nor narrowly defined that individuals lacked scope to interpret school policies in their own ways. Even at the best of times the heads sought unity, not uniformity. The success of the micropolitical activity in which heads and some staff members engaged rested upon the fact that all parties wished to maintain a temporary semblance of common purpose, in the knowledge that achieving such a purpose was the long-term aim of them all.

Another way of expressing this apparently contradictory state of affairs is to suggest that the heads sought to establish and maintain a 'working consensus' (Pollard, 1985) with their staff which embodied some accommodation of each other's interests. As Nias *et al.* (1989) also argued, the success of this policy depended upon the political skills of both heads and teachers. We return to this point in chapter 5.

There is one further general point to make about the indirect tactics that these heads used in seeking to develop 'whole schools'. Headteachers often make classroom visits, monitor the teachers' and children's work, spend time with teachers, discuss and negotiate, tour the school and lead school assemblies. These activities have been generally interpreted in terms of the contribution that they make to a healthy network of communications or intelligence gathering (Wolcott, 1973; Blumberg and Greenfield, 1986; Whitaker, 1983; Day *et al.*, 1985; Holly and Southworth, 1989). We see in them another purpose as well. The heads in the project schools were certainly interested in sustaining communication and collecting intelligence, but at the same time the tasks they undertook created opportunities for them to influence members of staff. Indeed, the very familiarity of the tactics that the heads used can be misleading, because it masks the potential capacity of mundane or routine activities to influence individuals and to bind them together in a framework of common beliefs and actions. The influence of these heads was pervasive. It was difficult for staff to remain untouched by it or immune from its effects:

> I think he operates in quite a subtle way...he's got that role of leader, but it's not too obvious and it's not an authoritarian approach at all. He kind of guides people through things and seems to sort of steer the school, keep the school together and

on course in a very subtle way without making things too obvious. Often, at the beginning of the term, he has particular views about things and talks to everybody and says, 'Right, I'm not very happy about this area or what you're doing', and he can get everybody motivated because he gives you a pep talk, but then the rest of the time he just seems to lead people along. But people tend to work the way he wants them to work just naturally, without there being any confrontation... He had quite a forceful personality I suppose...in a persuasive sense. He was a very easy person in the sense that he never came and demanded. Everything was done in a very gentle approach, very considerate. If he wanted you to do anything different it would be handled in a way that wasn't upsetting in any way. (Teacher, Fenton)

However, influence and sometimes manipulation were two-way processes. Because the micropolitics of each school were subtle, and often transacted in one-to-one encounters, we did not find it easy to record instances of teachers successfully manipulating their heads, though attempts to do this were certainly made. Influence was easier to document, especially in relation to specific curricular areas. For example, Wendy at Upper Norton stimulated her head and colleagues into an active and continuing concern for information technology, as Edith and Tina did at Ingham over mathematics.

The heads, then, made two main contributions to the development among their staffs of a sense that theirs were 'whole schools'. They provided a set of educational beliefs and values to which staff in their schools were expected to subscribe; and they encouraged them to put the beliefs into action in their classrooms in similar ways. In pursuit of both these policies they used a range of direct and indirect tactics, relying sometimes on their authority and sometimes on their capacity to influence others.

Professional Attributes of the Headteachers

In addition, although the heads differed from one another in many personal ways, they all had certain professional attributes in common. Underlying all of them is the fact that they were educators. Whilst they still sometimes taught children they were now in some respects also teaching their teachers. A substantial part of their work was in one way or another concerned with staff development (see chapter 2).

As teachers, they believed first-hand experience was a powerful way of learning. So they sought to develop and change teachers' beliefs and practices by showing them what was expected of them. They supported this process of modelling with advice, positive reinforcement, and formal and informal discussions. They also played a facilitating role in encouraging staff to learn from one another or to undertake in-service activities.

That they had retained many of their skills and qualities as teachers is obvious from their first attribute: the capacity to balance. Nias (1989a) noted this as a distinguishing characteristic of effective classroom teachers; these heads possessed it to a notable degree. They had plenty of reason to exercise it. For example, they needed to balance the extent to which they would be direct or indirect, authoritarian or influential. They needed to reconcile the wishes of individuals with those of the group. They had simultaneously to manage the development of shared educational beliefs across the staff group with the translation of those beliefs into action within each classroom or teaching area. In this context, a balance needed to be struck between rhetoric and practice. Of course, other aspects of the heads' responsibilities had to be balanced as well. For example, we noted that the expectations of 'outsiders' (for example, governors, parents, the LEA, central government) were not always compatible with those of the 'insiders' (for example, the staff and heads). As the heads responded to a range of expectations and interests and chose what they thought were the most appropriate ways of reconciling differences amongst individuals and groups they were continually engaged in balancing, in the interests of building shared perspectives, common practice and a sense of community.

Their second attribute was patience. We have already claimed that developing a sense of 'whole school' was a difficult, slow and gradual process. Indeed, some saw it as unceasing: there was 'no end to development', said the head of Orchard. Sometimes too, schools could become less 'whole' as Orchard did during our year of fieldwork, because of staff changes and widening differences within the group. It was not, therefore, surprising to find that these heads were professionally patient, even if they did not see themselves as patient people. The time span that they adopted for any piece of whole school curriculum development was a matter of years not months (see chapter 4) and they took a long term view of change in individuals.

They also needed to be tenacious, since the development of their educational communities could not be left unattended or to chance.

Rather, movement towards a sense of 'whole school' had to be led and guided. So they 'pushed' their staffs along, sometimes overtly, sometimes covertly, helping to build and then to maintain a cohesive group of teachers. They were assiduous and indefatigable in their efforts. Their doggedness, often in the face of competing demands, interests and values, did much to shape the outlooks and actions of others. Relentlessly, they promoted and reiterated their own beliefs and reminded the staff of them and of the vision they wanted every-one to share. Their persistence was remarkable.

They also possessed a capacity, which Woods (1987) also attri-butes to skilful teachers, to synthesize or link ideas and information. For example, they frequently drew attention in staffroom discussions to instances, examples and illustrations of classroom practice. Through informal conversations they made others aware of what was happening in particular classrooms. Because they were able to see more of the school than any other teacher could, they could select from their knowledge of what was happening and bring it to the attention of others. 'Showing' assemblies reinforced and repeated this process, albeit on a larger scale. Staff meetings too sometimes in-volved the sharing of children's work and of teachers' plans. In other words they were constantly 'weaving' together the work of indi-viduals, making connections amongst the teachers between beliefs and action. They were like a running thread stitching the fabric of the individual parts of the schools together and making it 'whole'.

Professional Interaction

At the start of this chapter we noted that the teachers in the project schools identified seven characteristics of a 'whole school'. In sum-mary they are: a sense of community; staff who shared the same beliefs and interpreted them in similar ways in their actions; individual self-esteem and a measure of teacher autonomy; staff who related well to one another; and who worked together; teachers who were aware of the perspectives and practices of colleagues; staff who valued the leadership of the head. In the previous section we showed that the heads played a leading role in providing a vision for their schools and in encouraging staff to put that vision into practice. In other words, they were largely responsible for establishing the beliefs of the school and for checking that these were carried into action in ways that were similar from one classroom to another, but allowed individuals some freedom of interpretation and action. Yet there is clearly more to creating a sense of 'whole school' than seeking agreed aims and monitoring their implementation. The heads worked partly at the level of beliefs, but they could not turn those beliefs into action without the teachers. Their work was necessary but not sufficient in the building of 'whole schools'. In addition, their beliefs could not be shared among the staff unless the latter interacted with one another. Further, interaction provided teachers and non-teaching staff with the opportunity to work together and value one another and to establish that they could relate well to one another in a working context.

In this section we therefore focus upon the work-related or professional interactions that took place in the schools, though in the knowledge that these overlapped with and were to some extent dependent upon the existence of productive social relationships (see chapter 5). We have maintained a loose distinction between professional interaction, that is, contact of any sort between staff members which was work-related, and collaboration, that is, any type of work consciously undertaken in cooperation with others in pursuit of a common goal. The second involves a closer relationship with colleagues than the first, because it can take place only when they have, or are willing to find, a shared aim.

Professional interaction took a number of forms. We have grouped them into seven categories (see table 12). Individually and together these forms of interaction provided opportunities for staff: to collaborate; to share, challenge and extend one another's aims and values (see also chapters 2 and 4); to exchange ideas and practices and to modify these when they saw fit (see also chapters 2 and 4); to play an individual role within a team and to be valued for it; to lead and accept responsibility for others. Also, when the staff jointly planned and performed particular collective events such as concerts and plays, all the adults and children were normally involved. So, such activities helped to build both a sense of the school as an organizational entity and a knowledge that the staff's shared success and achievement was due to their teamwork. All in all, frequent, regular and, sometimes, long-lasting interaction with their colleagues helped to build and maintain among teaching and ancillary staff alike a sense that their's was a 'whole school'.

Two wider aspects of this complex process stand out. The pervasive nature of interpersonal contact in all the schools made it difficult, though not impossible, for individuals to avoid being members of their staff group. In particular, each and every form of professional interaction with others served to remind individuals that they were inescapably part of the school. Whether or not they shared educational

Table 12: Forms of professional interaction

---

1 Practical, 'domestic' tasks: (for example, tidying up library books; organizing equipment; sorting out resources, stock cupboards).

2 Organizing and undertaking 'events', such as school journeys and holidays (for example, local visits, excursions to Isle of Wight, Holland); large displays in public areas of the school (for example, foyer, hall); exhibitions; sports days, festivals, fetes; fund raising; parents' evenings.

3 Organizing and putting on a performance: (for example, Christmas concerts, musical and dramatic productions; assemblies).

4 Participating in the formulation of policy: (for example, staff meetings; working parties; writing documents; sharing in decision-making).

5 INSET: school-based (for example, staff development days and workshops; paired observation); attending offsite courses and conferences with colleague/s and disseminating what was covered upon returning to school.

6 Sharing knowledge about children, such as case histories, background knowledge, previous experience, special needs, progress and development of individual children; sharing records at time of class transfer.

7 Teaching together: (for example, planning and carrying out classwork with colleagues); sharing responsibility for a class (for example, job shares; teacher and nursery nurse); team teaching; pairing up for specific initiatives, to share interests or expertise.

---

beliefs and methods with their colleagues, they were nevertheless linked to them. Moreover, because such interaction was task-related, it easily became collaboration. Singly and together, the many ways in which staff collaborated symbolized to the members of each school that working together was a principle of procedure. The medium, working with others, was also the message.

Moreover, no form of collaboration was problem-free. There were six main reasons for this. First, individual teachers' sense of responsibility for 'their' children's learning resulted in the feeling that they should control what went on in their own classrooms (see chapter 1). Yet there was a continuing and inescapable tension between this and the fact that in a 'whole school' responsibility and therefore control is shared with others. Although we noted teachers, and ancillary staff, interacting and working together in a myriad ways, we encountered few instances when within their classrooms, teachers substituted joint for individual responsibility. One teacher always felt responsible for children's learning or welfare, and s/he normally remained in control of their activities with other adults acting in a subordinate capacity. This contrasts with activities (for example, curriculum planning) during which staff worked together outside teaching situations. On these occasions they often shared control of the activity in which they were jointly involved. The reluctance shown by most of the teachers in the project schools to part with control over 'their' children's curriculum may account in part for the fact that they did not claim that their schools were yet 'whole'. It certainly contributed to the difficulties and tensions that they encountered in moving towards this goal.

Second, on most occasions during which adults worked with one another, whether inside teaching situations or outside them, they were involved in a degree of professional disclosure and self-exposure (for example, when staff shared with colleagues descriptions or examples of children's work in staff meetings, curriculum review meetings or 'showing' assemblies; when they organized children in choirs and orchestras or directed children's dance and movement or dramatic performances). The potential discomfort of such disclosure did not come so much from making one's work public to one's colleagues as from doing so in a context in which professional judgments would be made about it.

The teachers in these schools were aware that their headteachers were monitoring their work. Moreover increased attention to the idea of teacher appraisal (Day *et al.*, 1987; Bradley 1991) and its introduction into all schools (DES, 1989b) increasingly makes it plain to teachers that schools are evaluative settings. However, it is a relatively new experience for many teachers to expose their practice, inside or outside the classroom, to the critical gaze and judgment of their colleagues.

In other words collaboration was potentially threatening for many of the teachers in the project schools. As a result, those who lacked confidence in their practice or who had low self-esteem often found working with others difficult. They might be reluctant to be involved in such ventures, because they perceived their colleagues as generally more able or more experienced than they were and felt that their efforts, by comparison, were inadequate. Of course, the opposite sometimes also happened: displaying and sharing one's work with other members of staff could result in praise, increased confidence and a sense of self-worth. This was particularly likely because people often used positive reinforcement in their dealings with one another, thus contributing to an atmosphere of shared trust which counterbalanced individual feelings of exposure, inadequacy or threat (see chapter 5).

For example, at Orchard two teachers combined to put on a third year (Y5) assembly for the rest of the school. One of the teachers, Graham, was a probationer and it was the first time his class had participated in a 'showing' assembly. Helen was a teacher from another unit. She was excited by the children's work but was also aware of Graham's need for encouragement. It was she who offered him support and encouragement:

Third year 'showing' assembly: the third year's topic was movement and we saw a variety of work. Some children had done graphs to record which children moved quickest on a range of exercises, from press-ups against a wall to thrusts and various other arm exercises. There were various zoetropes for animation, which moved one sheet over another. There were spinners and double spinners, revolving cards and even a mechanical device using cogs; all of them give the impression of animated movement. There was also work on hinges, balls and sockets and human bodies; drawings of skeletons and attempts to make the skeletons move; string puppets, card puppets and string-pull puppets; cartoons and some turning pictures and enlargements; poems about moving quickly. The children, from both classes, ended with a song, plus percussion and recorders, of 'Them Bones'. For forty-five minutes the assembly went on, and it was a most impressive array of work. At one point Helen moved to the back of the hall in order to be able to see the work more clearly. At the end of the assembly, as she walked past Graham, she said, 'Well done' to him and touched him on the shoulder. Graham looked pleased. (Fieldnote, Orchard)

The third reason why working together was not problem free also relates to self-disclosure. Where teaching or ancillary staff did not share the same practices, but notwithstanding, opened up the latter to their colleagues, they laid themselves open to the judgments of others with dissimilar values and methods. When marked contrasts were revealed, all the staff were made aware of the differences which existed between them, and so of the fact that their school was not 'whole'.

Fourth, the occupational traditions of primary teachers favour independence rather than interdependence (see chapter 1). The territorial instincts of primary teachers are strong and this can make them reluctant to accept responsibility beyond their own classrooms, unready to work with others, or indisposed to participate with them.

Fifth, other barriers, some of them interacting with territoriality and the risks of self-disclosure, also played a part. The design of the schools emphasized individuality, either because it was cellular (for example, Carey, Ingham, Upper Norton) or because, though open plan, it provided individual teachers with a specific location as part of a 'unit' (for example, Orchard) or a class 'base' (for example, Fenton). At Fenton and Upper Norton, the use of mobile classrooms added to this problem.

Sixth, staffing ratios in all the schools meant that each teacher, except for a few part-time teachers and the headteachers, had a class responsibility. Consequently, it was difficult for teachers to work together during the school day. Unless they doubled-up classes or one, or more, teacher was freed from class teaching responsibilities by the head or a part-time teacher, they seldom saw one another in action.

In table 12 we listed the seven main forms of professional interaction that we identified. Rather than illustrate in detail each of these, and in particular each of the ways in which teachers collaborated, we have chosen to give three long case examples. There are two reasons for this decision. We wanted to show, first, how a single instance of collaboration could help to establish more than one characteristic of a 'whole school' and second, that working together was not always a brief process but sometimes extended over a protracted period.

Taken together the three case examples show that it was possible for many types of collaboration to encourage the development among the staff of the project schools of a sense of 'whole school'. A similar range of collaborative activities occurred in all the schools. For example, each school undertook at least one across-school concert or dramatic production and all the schools held assemblies at which all staff were present. In all of them regular and frequent staff meetings took place and extensive use was made of smaller working parties. In short, no school relied upon a single form of collaboration. Rather, they all made use of a rich mixture of them.

We have selected examples which highlight different aspects of working together and which contributed in varied ways to the development of a sense of 'whole school'. They are: producing a school concert; preparing and carrying out a curriculum workshop for parents as part of a larger process of whole school curriculum development (see chapter 4); and teaching within a 'unit'.

Starship Silver Grey: A School Concert

The first of the case examples describes what happened at Ingham when the staff agreed to put on a production of *Starship Silver Grey* for parents, at the end of the autumn term. It was not unusual for them to undertake a production of this sort. The account shows how all the staff and children participated in the process of producing this concert. It has been reconstructed from fieldnotes taken over the course of several days. The production was jointly planned and organized and involved the children in singing, dancing and acting. Staff, children and parents made costumes and props and put up around the school displays of work. There was a widespread feeling of excitement and stimulation amongst both the adults and the children.

Initially many of the staff felt a little daunted at the prospect of such a seemingly ambitious production. Some were also concerned at the pace and intensity of the schedule. Mutual support and the practical help given by the head eased both these concerns. Also, careful organization of particular tasks, resources and equipment gave everyone a part to play, devolved responsibility to individuals and small groups and provided a sense of corporate action. As preparations gathered pace a sense of unity developed and after the event everyone was left with the feeling that 'the school' had produced a successful event. In terms of developing a sense of 'whole school', the whole staff and sub-groups worked together, people learnt more about one another's strengths and talents, everyone was valued for his/her particular contribution to others and they all appreciated the leadership of the head. Perhaps most important, their sense of collective purpose was strengthened and this helped all the participants to feel that they belonged to a community.

The eighth item on the agenda was Christmas. Evelyne told the staff that she'd found tapes of space music and a play over the half-term holiday. She had three copies which she asked the staff to look at. The copies were distributed. Evelyne said, 'It lends itself to your planets, Theresa'. She suggested that they spend half an hour one lunchtime allocating responsibilities to staff. There were general discussions as staff decided who was going to read which copy tonight...

At a subsequent staff meeting Evelyne asked the staff how they'd felt about the idea of *Starship Silver Grey*. They responded that they'd been overwhelmed by it, but that there was plenty of music in it. She asked how they thought they should set about producing the play, given that there was only three weeks to the performances. Kirsten said she was very concerned about this, but the others all assured her that there was no problem, that they'd done similar things in as short a period of time in the past... Evelyne suggested that they have space displays in the hall and the corridors and Christmas displays in the classrooms... Beth asked what they were going to do about silver since they would clearly need a lot of it... Evelyne agreed to contact some local companies to see whether they had any aluminium foil left over from making bottle tops. She suggested that the people with classrooms in particular corridors should get together to decide on their corridor displays...and said that perhaps they could organize things as they had done in the past, each member of staff taking a particular part of the play to work on with their class. Lori asked how many groups would be needed... Tina worked out the groups on a piece of paper and said there were seven. Evelyne also said that she did not think it was necessary to put it all together until the last moment. 'It won't be so bad doing four performances. The children won't be bored with it'... Lori wondered whether it would be difficult to find a role for everyone, if they didn't have a part to play in the singing... Elaine said everyone would need copies of the play and she'd see to that. Rosie asked whether anyone had a preference for groups and said that she wanted to be a 'gobbledegook'. Lori said she wanted to be a 'gobbledegook' too, so Evelyne suggested they do it together. They began to make arrangements across the staffroom. Other people began to negotiate their roles at the same time. Evelyne said they could add material into the play if they wanted to — a planet's dance or a star's dance or a space monster's dance — and there were jokes about X-rays and skeletons and type casting.

People talked with their partners about what they were going to do. Some of them changed seats so that they could do this more easily. Elaine said she wanted to be something covered from head to foot and Evelyne told her she could be the person to whoosh the rocket across... Evelyne asked, were people assuming that she would be the captain, because that was all that was left now that everybody else had agreed what they were going to do? Elaine said, 'Well, everyone else is typecast so why not you?'... Karen suggested that Natalie should be a shooting star and Natalie talked about the possibility of using roller skates. Rosie said they could even have Superted in it... Karen said she was happy to play the piano... Someone suggested having an electronic keyboard to add to the space theme.

Four days later and assemblies were being used to learn the songs:

Much of the conversation at break centred round the Christmas production, comments about how much the staff had enjoyed learning the song this morning in assembly, how one of the children had gone up to Marilyn several times since then to tell her that he thought the songs were lovely and that the play was going to be very good. Lori had bought some masks with long noses from Tesco over the weekend and these were for the Gobbledegooks. They would need fifty of these, she said. They would need fifty robots too.

Tina told me that Evelyne, Beth and Natalie were marvellous with the special effects for any production and that Evelyne was particularly gifted at pulling everything together. 'We're very lucky', she said, 'to have someone like her'. . .

I went into Theresa's classroom and there in front of me was a rocket, three or four feet high, three dimensional, brightly coloured orange with a silver paper cone at the top. On the side was the rocket's name — 'Rocket Starship Bright'.

Once the register was taken we all went across the playground to the corridor which was jam-packed with children waiting to get into the hall. Some delay was caused by the fact that the children were being seated in the hall in the places where they'll be for the performance. . . In the hall we learned a new song and practised some that the children already knew. . . They were clearly enjoying themselves and as they were leaving the hall began spontaneously to sing yet another song that Karen was playing on the piano. We went back to the classroom via the far corridor so that Theresa could show the children a rocket that Kirsten's class had made with paper plates for portholes, with children's faces drawn on them. 'We're going to do a rocket like that to go with our poem', Theresa told them. Outside Karen's classroom were robots made out of egg cartons and toilet rolls. Theresa lifted one of these and said, 'We're going to make some robots too, but we need lots and lots of toilet rolls so it would be helpful if you brought some from home.' Mr. Hammond (the caretaker) was passing and he said he had lots of toilet roll centres. He brought a big box of them across to her classroom later. . .

The dress rehearsal went largely without problems though the children were a little distracted by the costumes and, as it was only the second time they had put all the separate parts together, they wanted to watch what was happening. . . The story is simple. Some earthling children get caught up in a spaceship so that they can be studied by the spaceship's crew. They travel through the universe stopping at

Planet Roboticus to choose a new robot for the spaceship, and at the planet where the 'gobbledegooks' live. The skeletons come into it because the professor invents some X-ray glasses. He also invents a time machine that eventually returns the children to their own planet and time, where they wonder whether their adventures have all been part of a dream. The story is told mainly in song, but there are connecting pieces led by Evelyne (the Captain of the crew). All the staff take part with their children. The lighting, costumes, sound effects, singing and the huge silver rocket that travelled from one side of the hall to the other were magnificent. (Fieldnotes, Ingham)

Developing Mathematics at Carey:
A Curriculum Workshop for Parents

The second case example shows how staff at Carey worked together to increase the amount of investigative and problem solving activities which the children undertook in mathematics. It highlights two aspects of this process. One is the general wish of the staff to increase their practical understanding and teaching of mathematical investigations throughout the school, a development which had been under-way before our period of fieldwork began and continued beyond the time covered in this extract. The second is the many ways in which they worked together, not least to organize a mathematics evening for the parents so that the latter could experience and learn at first hand the educational benefits of investigative approaches.

The decision to develop this aspect of mathematics in the school coincided with other calls upon the teachers' time. The school was involved in pilot work on pupil assessment, at the invitation of the LEA, and this in particular placed heavy extra demands upon the staff. Some teachers began to experience feelings of pressure, believing they had taken on too many tasks. However, after a deputation of staff had sought the head's opinion on the issue, their decision to continue with the parents' evening was upheld by the rest of the teachers. The outcome was an occasion which the staff regarded as very successful.

Within this broad and lengthy process of curriculum development staff worked together in a number of different ways. They undertook paired visits to other schools and made use of 'critical friends' and teaching partnerships. They organized resources together and there was much evidence of corporate planning which took place in informal discussions, working parties and staff meetings. In terms of developing a sense of a 'whole school', this case example shows the staff acting as a community of professionals who shared the same beliefs about the nature and teaching of mathematics and wanted to ensure that they all incorporated a problem-solving approach into their practice. As they worked together to achieve these ends, they deepened and extended their sense of community through discussion and shared practical activity and by involving parents as a wider audience. They were reminded of one another's strengths and capacity for leadership and of the areas in which, individually and collectively they needed support. They celebrated the former and worked together to compensate for the latter. They learnt more about one another's practice and perspectives, particularly within their classroom pairs, they enjoyed one another's company, despite the pressures under which they were all working. Throughout all this, they had occasion to be grateful for the experienced leadership of their head and for her grasp upon the educational principles which they were seeking to develop and to implement.

This account is reconstructed from observations and interviews gathered during an even longer period of time than that covered by Starship Silver Grey. At the start of the academic year mathematics was the focus of staff discussion as part of a pre-term, in-service training day:

> Ivy (the Deputy, and Maths Coordinator) began the pro-
> gramme. Very briefly she reviewed the past, referred to visits
> carried out by pairs of teachers to other schools to look at
> problem-solving in maths in practice elsewhere. She also refer-
> red to the 'critical friendships' and teaching in pairs in the
> classrooms. Very soon the initiative was taken from her as
> Thelma and Kay Hale began to talk about the visit they'd paid
> to another school... Ivy brought the discussion back to maths
> by mentioning two other initiatives they'd had last year —
> teaching together and having parents into school to look at
> problem-solving activities among the children. They discussed
> some of the difficulties... Kate said they needed to remember
> that it actually had been very successful... Ivy suggested that
> they should build a bank of ideas of things to do in problem-
> solving. Ella, giving an example, referred to an activity Ivy
> had done with her class last year in the playground and said
> that it had been a jolly good idea. Everyone, including Ivy,
> nodded. It's clearly perfectly acceptable to commend good
> ideas and to accept that commendation without any sense of

embarrassment. Ivy said there were many resources in the school, but they needed some sort of organization. She also suggested that they should hold an evening where the parents could be involved in problem-solving activities.

Kay Hale told Ivy she thought the parent's evening was a great idea. Ivy responded, 'So do I!'. . . They began to talk about practical difficulties. Ivy suggested that a theme be adopted. It could be used in all the suggestions — working together, parents visits into school to see their children problem-solving and an evening of problem-solving for the parents. Kate suggested that the theme might be something that would include computation because she was concerned about parental expectations. Various suggestions were made. They decided that they would leave the decision until another occasion. Ella suggested that ideas for activities should be recorded somewhere centrally. Ivy said it was possible to spend hours cataloguing ideas, but they get 'stuffed away up there' on the staffroom shelves. She emphasized that it is discussing and doing which actually means that ideas are passed on and used. Ella summarized what they needed to do — make a decision about the theme, try out some tasks among themselves, arrange staff meetings to plan the activities.

This discussion set the scene for development activities over the next few weeks, and is fairly typical of staff discussions on the curriculum. Later, the idea of 'critical friendships' and paired teaching, used so successfully during the past year, was employed again.

Ivy suggested that they should spend some time on investigative maths with their partners this term. Ella suggested that the teachers should change 'friends' and Ivy agreed with her, because this gave the staff as a whole further opportunities for sharing their experiences. . . Ella pointed out that they would need to rely on herself and Christine to release teachers to go into their partner's classroom and work for an hour or half a day on some sort of problem-solving maths with that class. . . They decided to change 'friends'. Last time partnerships had been cross-age. This time they decided to keep them within age groups. They decided on one hour sessions sometime during this half-term with return visits, if possible, after half-term. . . Ivy emphasized that all this would contribute to future discussions, eventually leading to a maths document.

Each partnership differed in the ways in which it organized and directed the activities for these sessions. This was so even when pairs undertook similar tasks or when one member of a partnership also worked in another pair.

> As we walked across to Thelma's classroom (which is in the mobile outside), I asked Christine how they had decided what to do. She said that they had discussed it together and tried to choose things that were based on the children's experience so far... Thelma had organized the class into groups of four. She and Christine were going to work with two different groups each, a parent and myself were to take the remaining two groups. One group was going to work with logiblocks, some were going to use conkers for estimating, counting and weighing, some were going to sort buttons, some were going to use multi-link to measure with, some were going to play the game 'What's in a square?' I was given a sorting task to do...

Each partnership informally evaluated what had happened.

> We talked about the fact that it had been a very intensive time, that the children had the attention of the teacher in a very small group, leaving them no time to sit back and reflect... Christine and Thelma both said they felt very tired themselves and they were sure the children were tired too. Christine said that she thought she would like to think about it tonight and talk to Thelma in more depth about it after she'd had time to reflect. Thelma said she thought the activity had gone well and that they ought to do it every week. Christine offered to do it again, saying now was the opportunity, while the reception classes are still small enough to be combined. Thelma accepted her offer.

The maths evening for parents was an important early event. Ivy coordinated it, but the planning was a corporate activity.

> There has been a good response from parents to the letter inviting them to the maths evening. They think they will be packed out.... Christine asked whether or not they were planning to aim activities at an adult or children's level. Kay Hale said she thought they should be challenging to adults... Ivy

said she'd make a list of their suggestions and of the equipment they had available in school, such as construction toys, that could be out during the evening. Thelma suggested some games that parents could play and this started all the staff off making suggestions which Ivy scribbled down... Ella pointed out that it was important to extend the parents' thinking so that they weren't just involved in various different activities, but that they understood the rationale behind them in terms of teaching and learning... Ella summarized the suggestions made so far. Ivy said that perhaps they should deliberately plan some activities that could not be done alone so that parents would have to ask other people to join with them. She also said that every activity should be accompanied by a list of instructions so that parents would fully understand what was expected of them... Ella offered to prepare these.

The day of the maths evening was a very hectic one for the staff. It coincided with the filming of a video related to Kate's involvement with the LEA Working Group on Assessment and fell during a particularly busy period for all the staff.

Ella told me that at one stage a group of the teachers had got together and come to say to her that there was really too much going on and they were under too much stress... She had said, 'Well, if you're feeling under too much stress, let's drop one of the things we're involved in'. In fact, the staff decided to go ahead with the parents' evening and had said something like, 'Well, we might as well get it all over and done with at once.'

Despite these tensions, activities for the evening were organized without any apparent fuss and were assembled in a surprisingly short amount of time at the end of the school day. The apparent ease of this final stage of the organization was probably due to preliminary preparation on the part of all the staff.

The reward was a successful, well attended evening for which many parents expressed their appreciation.

The parents began to arrive, collecting a fairly informal, friendly, introductory letter at the entrance together with a copy of the map of the proposed National Curriculum for mathematics. The parents who spoke to me acknowledged the hard work of the staff and seemed to appreciate the worth of what was being done in the school.

Partway through the evening I found myself next to Ivy. She said, 'Isn't it going well?' She talked about the fact that often over the last fortnight she'd been unable to sleep at night or had awoken in the middle of the night thinking about the evening. She had felt an enormous responsibility for its success... Kate told me that she felt the importance of the evening had been in the teachers being open with the parents.

A week later at a staff meeting the staff, fairly informally, evaluated the evening.

Ella said how well she thought the maths evening had gone last week and how hard everyone had worked and how much she appreciated that. Kay Harvey said the parents she had spoken to had thoroughly enjoyed the evening. She said she felt they had been a bit inhibited. She explained that by saying that their own educational experiences hadn't led them to be active in the way that the tasks required of them... Naomi said that several parents had said to her that they wished maths had been like that when they were at school. Ella said that she rather thought that most of the old battles about maths were over now. Kate said that many of the parents had been amazed at the depth and breadth of the work and that many had expressed surprise at the large numbers the children were dealing with.

Reflecting on the evening later in the year, the teachers found that its value had extended beyond their primary intention of informing parents. As one teacher said:

That maths evening was very successful...that was a really good way of sharing... The whole thing was developed over a while...from going in pairs to look at schools, to coming back and working in each other's classrooms, to planning activities for parents to be involved in, to that maths evening. I was very pleased with that. I thought that worked very well... I felt by us planning together as a staff activities that we'd all have to do, we shared things that different people did in different classrooms and different approaches. (Fieldnotes, Carey)

A Day with the Third Year Unit at Orchard: Teaching Together

The two previous examples have focussed upon projects involving all the staff at Ingham and Carey, schools at which the teachers also at times worked in overlapping twos and threes. By contrast this example looks at a pair of teachers, Sarah and Graham, at Orchard, who worked together because they had joint responsibility for the third year junior (Y5) unit. However, although responsibility for the unit was shared it was not equal. At Orchard it was customary for there to be an asymmetrical distribution of responsibility within unit pairs; in each partnership one teacher was designated as the 'unit leader'. In this case it was Sarah who was charged with an oversight of all the children's work in the unit and of curriculum planning, as well as with helping, supporting and offering guidance to her partner. Her latter role was especially prominent in this case, because Graham was in his probationary year.

Since we have several times drawn attention to the fact that during our year of fieldwork, Orchard was not, in the view of its head and staff, a 'whole school', the inclusion of this case example deserves explanation. We have selected it for several reasons. It shows how a pair of teachers may help to build a sense of community when this has ceased to exist within a school. Throughout their day together Sarah and Graham were developing their own partnership and were demonstrating to others that collaboration could be professionally productive.

It also illustrates the public nature of their teaching and the fact that the teachers still had the habit of taking an interest in what their colleagues were doing and so of learning more about it. Similarly, despite the fact that the staff as a whole did not share a sense of interdependence during the year, this extract shows that the norms of teamwork and mutual support persisted, albeit in pairs rather than larger groups. It demonstrates the pervasive nature of the head's leadership and of the educational and social principles that he embodied, even though, in this extract, he was acting at second-hand, through Sarah, through Dave the Deputy, and through Sarah and Graham's joint awareness of their imminent 'showing' assembly. Both Sarah and Dave obviously felt a strong sense of delegated responsibility for Graham's work and did not allow him a completely free hand. Notwithstanding, Graham was free to act with some individuality and independence within his own classroom, as was Sarah. It is also clear that these two teachers related well to one another and to the others who came and went from the unit during the day. Despite Graham's inexperience, he was not threatened by his colleagues' interest, perhaps because he was aware that Sarah valued his enthusiasm and good nature. Lastly, this extract indicates that collaboration can take place within a teaching situation without the need for a formal team-teaching arrangement.

What follows is a detailed description of part of a day's teaching in the unit. Sarah's formative, advance planning helped to structure in detail the morning's activities. At lunchtime Sarah and Graham discussed and decided upon the afternoon's work, for which Graham had made preparations on this particular day. The two sets of children in the unit did not work together. Even though they were kept separate, Sarah was conscious of the need for them all to experience a similar range of topics and activities. Both teachers were also mindful that the next day it was their 'showing' assembly. They would need to have ready for this some children's work which was sufficiently presentable to share with their colleagues and the other children in the school. Therefore, whilst they provided activities which gave the children experience of process learning in science, they were also aware of the need to generate some products that they could set before the rest of the school. Despite this tension, most of the afternoon session for Graham's class was given over to their active investigations of 'surface tension'.

Around 8.35 I was in the third year unit. Sarah was checking some overnight experiments she had set up, looking at capillary action. She still had her coat on but there were children beside her. They were looking at the experiments and the results. They all seemed pleased, including Sarah.

'Can I help today?' I said, 'Oh yes', she said. 'It's music first, but after play it's maths. We'll be doing lots of measuring, weights, lengths, number work connected with that, the four rules of number. It'll be great to have an extra pair of hands for that. Graham's going to be doing time on his side, too. Then this afternoon we're going to be doing some water experiments, I think Graham's going to do more than us, actually. An extra pair of hands would really help.' I saw some of Sarah's new displays, one was entitled 'Floating and Sinking' the other 'Experiments with Water'.

At the end of the maths session, during which neither Sarah nor Graham had any contact with one another, Graham came over as the children left for lunch and there was a lunchtime planning meeting between Graham, Sarah and myself. It was an impromptu discussion about what we'd do this afternoon.

'Well, we need to do some syphoning' said Sarah, although 'we' meant she and her class. 'And I'll have to follow this work up on capillary action. I think maybe I'll talk the children through it. They don't all need to do it'. Then she seemed to change her mind and thought maybe they did. 'They also need to finish off their collages. That could take ages. I don't think we're going to get it all done.'

Graham said he wanted to do some work on surface tensions and wanted to get on to the bubble work he'd planned. He'd prepared a bucket of what appeared to be 'Graham's Magic Mixture'. It contained washing powder and sugar which had been left to steep for three days and which he now thought would make very good bubbles. It seemed quite a large quantity.

Sarah and Graham were also aware that tomorrow was their 'showing' assembly. They wanted to show the experiments they'd done, but they hadn't done very much writing about the experiments. 'There's more to work in primary schools than always writing about everything', said Sarah. 'That's true', said Graham, 'especially when we haven't done the writing!' Graham, though, seemed pre-occupied with his bubble bucket. He showed us how it worked and blew bubbles. We began to think of some artwork that might be done using the bubbles.

In the afternoon I worked on Graham's side. On each table equipment was set out, a couple of yoghurt pots, a jamjar and a tray for holding water and there was a worksheet alongside, too. The worksheets presented a range of tasks under the heading of 'A stretchy skin'.

Between 1.35 and 2.00 Graham talked to the class. He was checking who had done which tasks and what were their understandings. It was a fairly straightforward question and answer session.

On her side of the unit Sarah was doing the same, but it was based on activities her class had done. They'd not studied surface tension. She was talking about capillary action and she was making use of the pieces of cloth that had been set up overnight. Elsewhere the same principle had been established using celery, which had been left overnight in some cartons. Later, Sarah took the celery over to show the class.

Graham now showed the children the bucket of bubble-making liquid. The children gathered round in a cluster. 'Everyone will be given some, in a jar, and you'll have a plastic glove to wear. You can make them by blowing it through your fingers, but you must wear the gloves'. He emphasized some safety reasons for that.

Graham's class began the experiments. Since quantities of water were needed for each trio of children working together, some spillages and slopping occurred, but the children were very actively engaged and concentrated hard although there was little recording, which was perhaps as well, given the volumes of water that were being splashed around in some places. Gradually, as the children progressed, more and more moved on to the bubble experiments. The children regarded these as particularly exciting. 'Great! Good fun', they said. Sarah's class were working on collages although some were also finishing off some written work. It was interesting to see all the activity on Graham's side with the experiments and the bubbles flying around and Sarah's side with the children all seated and working reasonably well, given the potential distractions in the unit. Sarah looked across from her side of the unit from time to time and smiled at Graham and me, but we were also kept busy servicing each trio, helping them change water, asking them questions.

Marie came in to borrow something. She stopped to enquire of some children what was going on and she smiled at Graham and at some of the children as she left. When the excitement was perhaps at its height, Dave came by and looked at the unit. He leant against one of the entrance way walls and pulled a face as if to say, 'What a mess!' Graham noticed him, but seemed to take very little direct action as a result of Dave's grimace.

By now there were quite a few wet towels on the floor particularly in the wet area and there were some rather damp tables too. Around the sink it was particularly messy. Some time later, Dave returned and said to me, 'I think I'd better keep Len (the caretaker) away from all this.' Dave looked rather concerned and I thought Graham noticed that this time. However, for another five minutes the children continued, playing with the bubbles, seeing what sizes they could make, looking at the surfaces. Then, at about ten to three, Graham asked the children to tidy up and clear everything away. I helped out as well, and within ten minutes the whole class was shipshape again. In a couple of places the carpet was damp, but nothing was sodden and everything was soon tidied away. Graham said to me, 'That's almost a model clearing away session.' He sounded relieved by it.

Then the children settled to their storytime and Sarah and I tidied up quite a number of bookshelves. Sarah said she thought Graham's lesson went well. 'He's ever so good and so patient.' She had said earlier in the day, that next week, for two days, she and Graham were swapping classes. I asked what that meant and she explained: the intention was so that each group of children could have a glimpse of what the others had been doing on their side. 'We'll do the experiments. They've done a lot of these in the last two weeks, all to do with water. We've been doing solutions, dissolving, flowing, that kind of thing.' She also repeated that writing up each experiment could sometimes take for ever. 'In any case, it's the doing which is important', she said.

At the end of the afternoon Graham came over to Sarah's side again and they began to talk about their 'showing' assembly tomorrow. 'What will we show? Which children will be asked to be present?' And they negotiated as they went along. 'Do you want that to go in?' 'Are you happy with this?' 'I think we've already shown that.' 'That's a good one to show.' 'Oh yes, he can talk about that very well.' 'That's a good idea.' 'You cleared up really well', said Sarah, at the end of looking through some of the materials for the 'showing' assembly. 'Mmm', said Graham, in a rather pleased way. (Fieldnotes, Orchard)

Conclusion

In this chapter we have shown that both leadership and professional interaction, and especially working together, or collaboration, were both central to developing a sense of 'whole school'. The leadership of the headteachers was important because they provided an educational vision for their schools. They all worked hard in a variety of ways to secure their staffs' allegiance to their particular visions and to ensure that the educational beliefs and values on which these rested were put into practice in classrooms. Sometimes the heads relied upon their authority and were direct in their efforts to establish a common set of educational beliefs among their teachers. At other times they were indirect, relying upon influence rather than authority. Their ability to control their staff through these two types of power was supplemented by their possession of certain professional attributes: at heart they were educators; they could strike a balance amongst competing demands and tensions in the school; they were patient and persistent; they had a marked capacity to perceive and make connections between the work of staff members.

We have distinguished working together, itself one of the characteristics of a 'whole school', from social interaction and have argued that the former was the second major way in which the staff of the project schools developed a sense of collective identity and came to feel that they belonged to an educational community. We listed seven main forms of activity which brought staff together in work-related situations and which often resulted in collaboration among them. When the latter took place, it provided opportunities for beliefs, values and practices to spread amongst the staff and for the latter to learn from and about one another; for individuals to come to realize that they could get on well together in a task-related context and to show that they valued and respected one another's talents and strengths; and, as a result of all of this, for a growing sense of institutional unity. Yet, whatever form collaboration took, it left individuals some autonomy and the freedom to be themselves, within the constraints set by the task and by the educational, social and moral principles for which the school stood.

Collaboration is not however a panacea which will heal all divided staff groups. In particular it means that individuals must open up their professional practice to the scrutiny of their colleagues and take the risk of exposing their work to the evaluative judgment of their peers. The greater the pressure on individuals to become part of a 'whole school', the more their potential need for support, reinforcement and encouragement. Yet this can be provided on a school-wide scale only within a 'whole school'. For heads the question then becomes one of knowing when and how to break into this 'chicken and egg' cycle so that the staff can begin to work together without discomfort and fear and can experience the satisfactions of belonging to an educational community whose members actively seek the same ends.

The rewards of working in a 'whole school' are more immediately obvious for heads than they are for teachers, since it is only through their staff that heads can realize their educational visions. Yet they too face risks, for if they force collaboration upon a recalcitrant staff or upon individuals with irreconcilable beliefs and values, they may open up divisions which will destroy even the semblance of unity. It is small wonder that the heads in the project schools moved slowly, patiently and with a due concern for micropolitical activity towards their goals and that they continued to use with their staff, as well as their pupils, their professional skill as educators.

In the next chapter we put together our claim that the professional learning of individual teachers is the key to curriculum development with the arguments, advanced in this chapter, that 'whole schools' do not grow naturally but have to be carefully shaped and tended by both their leaders and their members. The development of the curriculum within a 'whole school' is an even more complex, delicate and time-consuming affair than is the development of the 'whole school' itself.

Chapter Four

Developing a Whole School Curriculum

This chapter has two main parts. In the first we suggest that the notion of 'whole school curriculum development' is more than a sum of 'whole school' and 'curriculum development' and attempt a definition of the term.

In the second, we look in detail at the processes of whole school curriculum development, though always in the knowledge that the teachers in the project schools saw the 'wholeness' of their schools as an aspiration rather than a reality. We distinguish between the ways in which beliefs and values are spread and those in which people learn to translate them into action. In chapter 2 we examined why and how teachers learn, but not the content of that learning. Here, we argue that as staff members and others acquire the educational perspectives and principles on which the head's vision for their school rests, they are learning 'what'. Since, however, these principles become part of a 'whole school' only when they are realized in action, teaching and ancillary staff must also be able to carry them out in classrooms. That is, they must also learn 'how'. We then show the ways in which the same school events and structures are used to bring these two processes together and to extend them into a third form of learning which we see as 'whole school curriculum development'.

Detailed case-examples are used to illustrate each of these processes. We have drawn in particular upon Carey, Fenton and Ingham, making less explicit reference to Upper Norton though, if space had allowed, we could have drawn examples from this school too. We have not used evidence from Orchard in this chapter because during the year of our fieldwork, it was not, in the view of its members and of ourselves, a cohesive institution. We saw curriculum development taking place, but this was individual or specific to particular groups or unit teams. We have suggested reasons in the Introduction and in chapter 5 why this situation unexpectedly existed in a school which had a clear and well-documented history of whole school curriculum development in the long-term and recent past.

Whole School Curriculum Development: A Definition

In earlier chapters we have demonstrated that the curriculum in the project schools was in a constant state of development, in the sense that the teachers whose felt responsibility it was to educate their pupils habitually, though often individually, pursued their own learning. We have also suggested that learning was highly valued in all the schools and that this propitious climate stimulated the development of appropriate motivation, opportunities, conditions and methods, aspects of the learning process which were interlinked and acted upon one another.

However, the curricular learning which we observed and which staff identified as taking place in their schools was not always directed towards the fulfilment of corporate goals. Nor was individual development always shared with others in ways which fostered collective growth. Indeed, some development was openly undertaken for reasons of personal satisfaction or need and not because it contributed to colleagues' learning or to the spread or attainment of collective aims.

We have also argued that the staff in the project schools could describe what they meant by a 'whole school' and that they saw this as an ideal towards which, in general, they wished to move. They perceived 'whole schools' as communities with respected leaders whose members shared the same educational beliefs and intentions and in which the majority, at the least, attempted to put these beliefs into action in broadly similar ways. In such schools people knew a good deal about the actions and purposes of others, and felt a sufficient degree of 'likemindedness' to work well together. Yet they also felt free to make many individual decisions, were conscious of a considerable measure of classroom autonomy and of being valued for their particular contributions to the school community. As with staff learning, each of these characteristics interacted with, and was dependent on, all the others, so that the process of building a 'whole school' could begin with the development or encouragement of any one of them. Each was essential to a sense of 'wholeness', but growth which took place in any of them could stimulate or enhance the others.

At first sight the two notions of 'curriculum development' which emphasizes individual learning and personal endeavour and 'whole school' with its stress upon collaboration and consensus do not appear to have much in common. Indeed, as we argue in chapter 6, they are in many ways in tension with one another, since the first stresses individual and the second corporate goals and activities.

The teachers in the project schools were aware of this tension:

> I think each teacher here can contribute their own particular stamp on the school and the curriculum. I don't think we are that dogmatic as a staff that you've got to do things in such a way. Having said that I think if anybody came here who was much happier to shut the door and get on in their own way, completely on their own, they would probably find that difficult because we do quite a lot of things together. They would definitely need to be able to work with other people. (Teacher, Ingham)

> I think where the tensions exist you've got to find ways of getting through it. I've learned a lot about myself, as well as other things... Life isn't really about...being alike and sharing the same attitudes. Tension is part of collaborative working. (Teacher, Orchard)

Even those teachers who initiated curricular developments did not necessarily have a view of the curriculum offered to other pupils than their own nor a desire to change the practice of their colleagues. Involvement in curriculum development was often an egocentric activity, in the sense that individuals' main motives were the improvement of their own practice or the acquisition of more or better resources for their pupils. As the whole-school topic at Upper Norton demonstrated, the teachers' willingness to centre much of their work on a common theme for a term did not indicate that they intended to shape their own plans by reference to what others were doing, nor that they sought to influence one another. Indeed, the uncomplicated plan to obtain a central stock of reference books from the authority library which could be used by every child broke down partly because some of the teachers saw these resources as being for their classes' learning alone. Furthermore, it was clear in all the schools that particular teachers who thought beyond their own classrooms in relation to one issue (for example, the introduction of a child safety programme (Kidscape) to the curriculum of both Ingham and its feeder junior school) did not do so in all matters. As one of the chief proponents of the Upper Norton whole-school topic said, 'It's the head's job to make the whole school dominate the territorial instinct of the class teacher. Class teachers will subconsciously subvert that at all times and the head has got to pull them out.'

Yet although tensions such as these keep the complementary elements of 'whole school curriculum development' apart, they are brought together in 'whole schools' at two levels: that of beliefs and values, and that of action. We have repeatedly stressed the ideological nature of primary schools whose members seek to establish a sense of educational community. Policies in such schools derive from beliefs — about the nature of human societies and moral behaviour within them, about knowledge, teaching and learning. They embody values which derive from these beliefs and the staff's shared adherence to these in turn helps to secure agreement on educational goals. As the curriculum is discussed and developed and beliefs and values are articulated and progressively realized, it becomes increasingly difficult for individuals to pursue their own goals, especially if these run counter to those of the rest of the staff. In 'whole schools' curriculum development necessarily involves some degree of consensus, and normally therefore also of compromise over values and aspirations. Of course, if the compromise is voluntarily espoused, the resulting sense of collective aspiration strengthens and enriches staff members by giving them a sense of common purpose. But it is false to suppose that membership of educational communities which are rooted in values can be achieved or sustained without imposing some constraint upon individuals.

Further, the values with which 'whole schools' are imbued are not rhetorical. The notions of 'whole school' and 'curriculum development' also come together through action. Most obviously, neither can be realized without purposeful activity. 'Whole schools' are not built on shared intentions, important though these are, but on individuals' efforts to realize through their actions the beliefs and values that they share with their colleagues. Similarly, teachers engage in curriculum development not so that they can talk with greater knowledge, but so that they can behave in ways which will increase or enhance their pupils' learning. Being a member of a 'whole school' involves doing, as well as believing, valuing and intending.

One of the means by which 'whole school' and 'curriculum development' are brought together is through learning. We have suggested (chapters 1 and 2) that a concern for their own professional improvement is central to teachers' understanding of curriculum development, while within a 'whole school' there is pressure upon individuals to move closer towards the beliefs and practices of their colleagues (chapter 3). So, both notions have embedded within them the ideas of growth and change and so of learning. Furthermore, the development among a staff of a sense that their school is, or is becoming 'whole' influences the nature, direction and pace of individual learning, be it of values or classroom norms. In a 'whole school' each person's learning takes place within a communal setting, by which it is influenced and to which it contributes. Every member's development makes an impact on that of others, for it takes place within the context of beliefs to which everyone subscribes, of aspirations towards which everyone has contributed and of practice which everyone shares.

The emphasis upon learning is important because the very existence of a shared belief system and a high level of mutual influence over practice raises the question of how dynamic 'whole schools' are. Indeed, it could be argued that such schools have the threat of stagnation embedded within them, for the goal of 'wholeness' is achieved through consensus about purposes and a degree of conformity in practice. This is not to suggest that no staff development goes on within 'whole schools'; at the least, newcomers are inducted and socialized into the values and norms of the school culture (see chapter 2). But the fulfilment of a staff's agreed goals may trap them into self-justifying complacency and may limit the growth of the schools. Activity does not lead to development, unless it is also accompanied by a continuing commitment to individual and collective learning.

There is another sense too in which the idea of learning brings together the individual and the collective elements of whole school curriculum development. Teachers who are committed to their own professional development sooner or later realize that their learning, like children's, cannot be isolated within a single classroom. Nias (1989a) claimed that most of the teachers whom she interviewed in a longitudinal study wanted to work in schools in which there were agreed aims and policies and in which people felt that they could build upon one another's work. As one of her interviewees said, 'My greatest satisfaction was the feeling that I had clicked in and become part of an organization which was doing something worthwhile. It gives you a sense that your own work isn't wasted' (*ibid*, p. 162). Primary teachers who are committed to the achievement of high professional standards soon realize, she argued, that children's learning in any area of the curriculum is strengthened and enriched when pupils experience a measure of consistency as they move between classes and when collective attention is paid to curriculum development.

Further, by mid-career many of her interviewees had become what she describes as 'bounded professionals', that is

> They have whole-school perspectives and an interest in collaboration and collegiality, but are largely atheoretical and school-bounded in their approach to other educational issues. Like 'extended professionals' they derive satisfaction from school-wide problem-solving activities and from an enhanced sense of control over their work situation, but like 'restricted professionals' they also find great rewards in successful classroom practice. (*ibid*, p. 167)

These 'bounded professionals' had discovered that a continuing interest in children's learning, and therefore in their own development, inexorably led them into an awareness of their schools. They could not separate a concern for their own classroom practice from an interest in school-wide policies and in the impact of these upon their pupils' total experience of school.

In each of the project schools there were a few teachers whom we could identify as 'bounded professionals'; they were aware of the interdependence of the classroom and the institution and were interested in both. Furthermore, during our year of fieldwork the introduction of the National Curriculum forced other teachers, whose preoccupations were still mainly with their own professional practice and the activities of their pupils, to become conscious of their colleagues' work and of the need to develop curriculum policies which affected them all.

So, whole school curriculum development carries within it a persistent and continuing tension between the individual's sense of professional responsibility and the staff's commitment to common purposes. These two elements are held together by compromise, by the daily imperative to act and by the fact that learning plays a part in both of them. Yet the equilibrium which is reached in these ways between individual and collective aims and practices is a dynamic one, precisely because learning plays such a large part in it. Accordingly, neither individual teachers nor the school community to which they all belong can stand still. When curriculum development takes place within a 'whole school' context, it does not result in the mere confirmation of existing assumptions and habits. Instead, it changes, however subtly, the beliefs and values that the staff share and the ways in which these are realized in practice.

To sum up: Whole school curriculum development is a dynamic, even restless, process in which beliefs and values are translated into action, but in which a common commitment to learning also means that both principles and practices are continuously reviewed and reinterpreted. Put another way, it can be defined as a set of individual and collective learning activities which is inspired by, and takes place within, a framework of common educational beliefs, values, intentions and actions, but which also enriches or extends the scope and shared understanding of that framework.

The Case of 'Progression'

We illustrate this definition by exploring the way in which a single issue — that of progression in children's learning — was understood, applied and extended in the project schools and in Fenton, in particular.

Over the past decade school-wide issues relating to children's learning, especially those of 'continuity' and 'progression' have received increasing attention from groups such as HMI, the DES and the National Curriculum Council (for example, DES, 1980, 1984a, 1984b, 1985b, 1987 and 1990b; ILEA, 1985; NCC, 1989). There is little agreement over the meaning of the first term, few attempts have been made to explore its practical implications in classrooms or schools and it was seldom explicitly mentioned in the project schools, except as part of a more general attempt gradually to secure a consistent approach to teaching and learning from one classroom to another.

There is rather more agreement among educationalists about the meaning of 'progression'. This term is used to imply both that staff will ensure that pupils do not repeat curricular content as they move from one class or school to another (for example, DES, 1980, 1984a and 1984b; NCC, 1989 and 1990; SEAC, 1990) and that they will sequence children's learning of skills and concepts so that understanding and attainment becomes progressively more abstract and complex as they move through the school (for example, DES, 1985b and 1990b; NCC, 1989). Both understandings of the term impose some restrictions upon teachers' freedom of choice in relation to curriculum content. Yet although all of the staff in the project schools assumed the right to make choices about what they taught, most of them consciously sought to avoid repeating subject matter to which their current pupils had recently been exposed. They did not perceive this restraint as an infringement on their autonomy, because, as we have suggested in chapter 1, they had internalized it and made it part of their own thinking.

They were also aware of their responsibility to sequence children's learning, especially of skills, so that it represented clear progress towards increasingly complex and difficult goals. They talked, in the context of their own classes, of 'knowing what standards to expect', 'having a plan of where the children should go next', needing to establish early on in the year 'what gaps there are in the children's knowledge and what they can do', 'understanding where they should have got to by July', 'having ladders in my head', 'slotting individual children onto these ladders'. They all felt a responsibility to ensure that children made progress while they were in their classes. In one teacher's words, her task was 'to build on what the children know when they come to me' (Upper Norton).

In Ingham, Orchard and Upper Norton, however, many teachers did not appear to feel responsible for the learning of pupils other than their own. In this sense 'progression' was a matter for individual, rather than school-wide, concern. This is not surprising; we have repeatedly argued that to take on an other, rather than a self-centred perspective on teaching is a characteristic of mature professional development and that it is difficult, because of the demands of the job itself. Moreover, it is consistent with an individualistic view of the curriculum that teachers should take cognizance in their planning of what children have already learnt, but will see as restrictive any suggestion that they should shape their choice of content according to what children will learn in the future. School curricular policies which embody a sequential view of children's attainments are relatively uncommon, perhaps because they seem to many teachers to allow the requirements of the oldest or most able pupils to determine the curriculum and to place artificial limits on the expectations held of younger or slower learners.

In this context Fenton and, to a lesser extent, Carey pose a puzzle, for in both schools the staff accepted as a matter of common policy that children's learning should be viewed sequentially over the full period of their time in the school, even when this dictated what individuals did or did not teach to their own classes. Yet as teachers they were no less individualistic in their perspectives on the curriculum than were their colleagues in the other schools.

The answer to this apparent inconsistency lies, we suggest, in the fact that the teachers in both schools believed that children were capable of producing work of a very high quality, but that to make this possible, the appropriate content and skills must be carefully thought through and taught in sequence. They expressed their belief in the value of sequential learning in speech and written policy documents and in their day-to-day behaviour in relation, for example, to choice of subject matter, provision and allocation of resources, school-based INSET. It was so much part of their shared thinking that it permeated their approach to curricular changes and innovations, such as those resulting from the introduction of the National Curriculum.

However, at Carey the fact that the teachers were concerned with sequential learning was obscured, because they normally took a class through from entrance to the school to departure from it; individual practitioners assumed responsibility for school-wide progression through their work with their own classes. During our year of fieldwork 'progression' surfaced as a school issue only when classes had, a-typically, to be regrouped in the summer term.

By contrast, at Fenton the need to sequence children's learning throughout their time in the school frequently featured in staff conversations and discussions, in relation to many curriculum areas. The Head showed an active concern for this issue (for example, when he led a school in-service day on the use of clay). Indeed, there is evidence from his behaviour on that day and from the oral history of earlier curriculum development within the school that a belief that every teacher should be concerned with progression stemmed from him. In particular it seems to have arisen from his deep and openly expressed conviction that children should achieve the highest possible quality in all their work. A practising artist himself, he had chosen some years before to use two and three-dimensional art work as a means of showing children and staff alike the standards of which the former were capable, and how, by careful sequencing of content and skills, these could be achieved. His commitment to quality in children's work and to progression as a means to this end were clear. It is declared in formal documents:

We must be striving for the highest possible standards for all children in all areas of the curriculum. This is a tall order but we cannot and must not accept second best for our children...
We set the standard for the school by the work displayed...
We are working along the right lines and, with a united staff

with a shared belief in children, we can lift the school on to another level where we can all share a pride in the achievements of our children. (Curriculum Policy Statement, Fenton)

It was manifest to visitors:

The new local inspector was clearly impressed...by the sequence of development that was evident from the reception class through to the top class. (Fieldnote, Fenton)

Progression featured in staff conversation in relation to many curricular areas:

Last term we had (a visiting speaker), for example, who came in for the day. Well, you can't pass up an opportunity like that. You then get a lot of work out of that input...stories, research and some artwork as well. But again, it has to be at the sort of skills levels that we've, as a school, identified for third (Y5) and fourth year (Y6) children... There's some progressions that we've laid down, though I don't personally think we've laid enough down, for it to be immediately obvious to everybody, especially for a new person coming in. I know from past experience...what sort of levels are expected, where they will have got to by third and fourth year and where I've got to take them to. (Teacher)

Verity explained the use of CLARDS (comprehension, language and reading development exercises)... They concluded that they needed to bring some•of the Oxford English materials down lower (chronologically in the school) and the Ginn 360 materials up higher. (Fieldnote)

So highly was sequential learning valued that when the staff began to develop a new curriculum area — craft, design and technology, referred to from now on by its National Curriculum name of 'technology' — it was one of their first concerns, individually and collectively. The coordinator addressed it at an early stage:

There are certain things that have happened this year that I would love to see repeated so that children go through a like experience, perhaps on a two yearly cycle. It doesn't matter if you're making a boat or a car or an aeroplane, there are certain key things that young children need to be taught... We need to make time as a staff to sit down and talk through steps that children could go through. (Teacher, Fenton)

A teacher with less than a year in the school and no previous experience of technology had already internalized the importance of progression, in relation to the development of that curriculum area:

I want to know what comes next. I'm thinking what I can do with the top infants next year. I've taken the middles right through. Now I'm already scheming the next stages up. It's exciting to get the progress right and then have a school policy to get it right for the future children coming through. (Teacher, Fenton)

The staff as a whole also felt that their school policy for the area should 'get the progress right'. They accepted that this would not be simple or straightforward; it would not be an easy task to agree and organize the sequential teaching of content and skills in a subject which was new to them. Moreover their use of the term 'progression' suggested that they saw it in broad and widely-focussed terms. For example, the staff meeting described below covered: the nature of technology as part of the primary school curriculum; children's thinking at different ages and how it might be extended; the potential value and limitations of commercial and craft materials; timetabling and classroom organizations; assessment and recording.

At 12 o'clock the discussion went on to the document on technology. Once again, Rob talked about this. He said it was based on a staff meeting held last year when the staff had talked together, plus a DES document and LEA documents. Simon (the Head) mentioned Rob's decision to set aside a time each week for his class to do technology and invited Rob to talk about why. Rebecca recalled a stated intention last year to link the infants and the juniors so that there was the opportunity for skills to be passed on from one to the other. This was met by general approval... Simon picked up her suggestion and made it clear that he too approved of the idea. The INSET day before half-term is being spent on technology and the hope was expressed that this would give the impetus for developing it in terms of the skills that ought to be encouraged. Rob admitted that he had some difficulties with the idea of technology for infants, but Simon said that it was really a matter of building on things that already happen. For example, when children are making boxes, that could be extended to problem-solving about wheels and axles and so on. The school has new materials, several of which were listed in the document. One in particular was emphasized, it had work sheets. Simon suggested that these should be worked through consistently because they are in a developmental sequence, and they could then be reviewed at the end of the year. Tamsin told the group about a construction kit called 'Play School'. . . There was some discussion, particularly on the part of Simon and Rob about structured, task-oriented play. Rob talked about the use of plasticene, blu-tak and rubber bands rather than glue in the lower part of the school. Simon advocated avoiding plasticene and blu-tak because they weren't used in real technological problem-solving. Susan raised the problem of getting the trolley containing the tools into the mobile classrooms; Simon suggested that these classrooms should have a basic kit of their own. He also referred to the design folder being used as a record, as suggested on page 2 of Rob's document. Rob emphasized that this was not merely a record of achievement, but a record that the children should refer back to themselves, in the same way that designers did, rejecting and then picking up on designs. He also emphasized that the proper names of tools should be used consistently from the start and that their correct names were contained in a section in the LEA document. There was some discussion about children's reluctance to lose what they had constructed. Simon said that the school camera was kept in his room and that photographs could be kept as a record of the children's constructions. (Fieldnotes)

As the staff explored technology in the light of their shared belief in 'progression', they also extended their understanding of the ideas and practices to which it referred. For example, two staff took up the head's suggestion about the use of the school camera and developed a new means of recording children's progress which was to prove of value to everyone:

Verity and I are producing a sort of infant booklet. We have taken photographs so we're going to have a photographic record of the sort of areas we've covered. We will probably make a list of the skills we've covered as well.

In the meantime, every teacher was exploring the capabilities of the children and experimenting with ways of teaching them:

> Everybody's very aware that technology is now part of our curriculum and that we have to deliver it... Everybody's trying hard to gain some expertise themselves and to work with children to see what works and what doesn't and sharing ideas and sharing knowledge to make technology important.

In due course, individual and collective understandings merged. At the time when our fieldwork ended, the staff were about to embark on another stage of the long journey towards a school policy for technology which embodied their belief in sequential learning. They accepted that this would take time but they also knew that it was a creative activity in the course of which 'progression' would once again be interpreted in the light of 'our experiences and our ideas' and would emerge in a modified form as 'our thing':

> It's going to be better now because everybody, to some extent, has had experience of working it with their classes so everybody's got a contribution they can make. We are at the point now where we get our own ideas. We can make it our thing, our science and CDT progressions.

In this example we have shown how the staff of Fenton approached a new curriculum area which they knew would be mandatory under the National Curriculum and made it part of their own thinking and practice. Their endeavour was many-faceted. Part of it was individual, part collective. Each influenced the other. Much of it appeared to be purely practical; the Head and the staff taught, experimented with materials and designs, organized resources, held and attended workshops, made and shared displays, discussed, wrote documents. But their activity was shaped and given purpose by a strong and long-established framework of educational beliefs, in this instance related particularly to the importance of sequencing children's learning as a means of helping them to achieve high standards. Accordingly, as the staff, in their own classrooms and together, developed technology as part of every child's curriculum, one of their main emphases was upon 'progression' — what it meant, which areas of children's learning it affected, how to achieve and record it. However, their interpretation of this term was not a static one. As they worked out the practical implications of 'progression' in the context of a curriculum area which was new to them, their understanding of its extent and potential was modified. Later in this chapter we use technology at Fenton to illustrate the complex processes of whole school curriculum development. Here we have demonstrated that these processes were themselves underpinned and given meaning by educational beliefs and values which were shared by all the staff, but which were also shaped and interpreted by them, through both their individual practice and the activities that they undertook together.

It is worth stressing that only at Fenton, and to a much less obvious extent at Carey, was 'progression' a collective staff concern, even though we saw whole school curriculum development with different emphases taking place in Ingham and Upper Norton. We suggest that this is because in these two schools the heads had, over a long period, helped their teachers to see the standards of which children were capable and the resulting importance of sequencing and building upon their learning. As a result, as the staff worked by themselves and together to plan and implement each curriculum area, they perceived the learning of the children in their school as a continuous process and felt responsible for all of it. In other words, a respect for sequential learning had become part of the 'whole school' thinking of the staff of these schools, because they believed that it was vitally important that it should be. It does not follow that this will be the case in all schools. Whole school curriculum development does not necessarily result in a collective desire to achieve progression in children's learning as they move through the school.

The Processes of Whole School Curriculum Development

So far, we have argued that in the project schools whole school curriculum development was more than the sum of its opposing parts. The development and implementation of a curriculum which affected the practice of all the staff in a school differed in kind, not simply in degree, from the professional development of individual teachers and from the growth among them of a sense of educational community.

The key to this fact is learning. First, teachers in these schools were interested in their own professional development and often vigorously pursued it. Second, during the year most were becoming familiar with, or being confirmed in, the beliefs and values which underpinned their school's work. Third, they acquired, or sought to acquire, the knowledge, skills and attitudes which they needed in order to put these beliefs into action. Fourth, in the process of undertaking all these other forms of learning, individually and together, they reflected upon and modified the framework of principle and practice which itself determined the nature of their learning.

We considered in chapter 2 the processes by which the first of these types of professional learning took place. In the rest of this chapter we examine the other three. We have given the name 'learning what' to the process by which beliefs and values were spread amongst those associated with the schools. 'Learning how' describes the ways in which teachers and others acquired appropriate practical expertise. Whole school curriculum development itself occurred when a combination of learning 'what' and learning 'how' resulted in an extension of them both.

Although later in this chapter we consider these processes separately, they are woven so closely together that to pull them apart is to risk damaging the rich, densely-woven fabric which they combine to create. Whole school curriculum development is an intricate and complex process which Campbell (1989b), in her introduction to the case study of one of the project schools, likened to lace-making:

> Anyone who has seen a lacemaker at work will know how impossible it seems that all those threads and all those bobbins with their coloured beads should be united in a process that results in the production of delicately patterned lace. Making lace may be an inadequate picture of life at Carey, but it allows me to make two points. Firstly, the processes of curriculum development were inextricably woven together with each other and with other aspects of school life... Secondly, there was a continuous pattern to curriculum development, stretching back into the past.

In addition, as Campbell suggests, to examine single examples of curriculum development in isolation is further to oversimplify the complex nature of the total process. In all of the schools, many curricular initiatives were taking place simultaneously throughout the year. In removing individual cases from their contexts in order to highlight their developmental characteristics, we have reduced the self-evident complexity of a messy, subtly-changing, many-faceted and long drawn-out reality.

It is also difficult to disentangle the processes of 'learning what' and 'learning how' because they both took place by means of the same structures and events (see also chapter 3). For example, open evenings, 'showing' assemblies and school productions often served to encourage and promote the learning of individuals. They provided a forum for colleagues to share with one another parts of their own curriculum and pedagogy and an opportunity to see others working with children of different ages and abilities. However, such occasions also helped to develop among the staff a corporate sense of purpose and belonging, that is to feel that theirs was a 'whole school'. Occasions such as these enabled the heads to emphasize and model those aspects of learning, teaching and curriculum content which they regarded as central to the school, provided reasons why the school community should come together and should celebrate the individual and collective achievements of its members, encouraged teachers to collaborate and feel interdependent in pursuit of common goals. They could also be used to confirm and deepen the common values and purposes of the staff, and sometimes too of the children, their parents, and the governors, while simultaneously demonstrating and extending the ways in which these aspirations were realized in the day-to-day activities of teaching and learning.

Similarly, meetings and small group activities, whether formal or informal, served multiple purposes. For example, a group set up to examine a specific aspect of the National Curriculum in English, a staff discussion on the school's teaching of mathematics, a pair of teachers engaged in reciprocal observation or shared teaching could enhance individuals' professional learning, develop their sense of interdependence and likemindedness and help to ensure that they understood or accepted the framework of belief and action within which everyone worked. Such events also provided opportunities for the exchange of perspectives, knowledge and skills, thus ensuring that individuals learnt more about one another's practice. They gave them a chance to discover or reaffirm, through laughter and mutual support, that they liked one another or valued one another's contributions to the whole and so provided a secure context for challenge, debate and mutual critique.

Written documents too served many ends (for example, to launch an initiative, to encourage the development of deeper understandings, to develop shared thinking once new practices had begun to take root in a number of classrooms, to make a permanent record of that development for later reference, to help newcomers learn more about agreed policies). Writing itself was seen as part of both 'learning what' and 'learning how'. Indeed, in a few cases (for example, the new mathematics document at Carey) the very process of writing was a communal one. In general, the approach in all the schools was pragmatic: a written statement was produced when it would promote the process of development and not as an end in itself. Writing and the discussion of what had been written overlapped in a complex sequence, the details and timing of which were unique to each school.

Talk too was central to all these activities, and to others like them. It preceded, accompanied and fostered the introduction, growth and implementation of all the policies and changes which we observed. Development in these primary schools had practical foundations but floated on an oral tide. However, since talk is treated in greater detail in several other places in this book (especially chapters 2, 3 and 5), we do not explore it any further at this point.

The processes of whole school curriculum development shared two further, related characteristics. Both relied first on people's willingness to take initiatives and then on purposeful leadership. The mere existence within a school of structures which could be used to promote development did not by itself result in such development. Rather, such structures had to be purposefully used to spread active, critical ownership of the school's guiding beliefs, values and intentions and to extend practical mastery of them. Since leadership is more fully discussed in chapters 3 and 5 we do not further explore it here. We do, however, consider who took initiatives and their reasons for doing so.

Taking Initiatives

In all the project schools, each move towards the development of a whole school curriculum could be traced to some source which had given an individual, a pair, or a small group of teachers the desire or the incentive to make a start. Such sources differed widely in kind and included, for example, the development of the initiator's own classroom practice, raising an issue for formal or informal staffroom discussion, attending a course, calling in a curriculum expert from outside the school, acquiring or organizing resources. The resulting development was almost always, however, small-scale. Only when its value had been proved, through its impact on children's learning and the initiator's own practice, was it shared more widely with others.

Initiators were themselves responding to pressures, the four most powerful of which were: (i) external forces, particularly the National Curriculum, assessment, other requirements of the 1988 Education Act and the perceived expectations of parents; (ii) in-service courses, particularly those outside the school, which fuelled or supported an immediate curricular concern and/or stimulated educational thinking; (iii) headteachers, themselves partly, but not exclusively, influenced by legislative requirements and by course attendance, especially in the past; (iv) personal felt-needs (for example, to solve a classroom problem; to justify holding an allowance; for promotion; to make better use of existing resources). None of these sources was independent of the others, as three examples, taken from many, suggest. At Ingham, concern over a child's apparent racism led a teacher to consult her Head. The latter recommended a course at a local college. Stimulated by this course, the teacher talked to her colleagues, three of whom joined a group under her leadership and themselves went for similar training. A combination of all these influences subsequently led the staff to adopt and begin to implement a multicultural policy for the school. At Upper Norton, the requirements of a National Curriculum training course led a teacher to gather information on children's oracy from her colleagues. This sparked among them a practical interest in an area with which the Head was already known to be concerned and which she then actively fostered throughout the school. At Carey long-term developments in reading had been set in train some time before by the Head's dissatisfaction with existing resources, and had been fuelled by her attendance at two advanced courses. But they were carried forward by the staff's growing awareness that their existing methods were unsatisfactory in terms of children's attainment and understanding and by their own subsequent course attendance.

We have suggested (chapter 2) that the project schools were full of curricular initiatives. Sometimes these faltered or remained very localized within the school, for reasons which we explore in chapter 5. At others they were taken up, fostered and developed, becoming in time part of the thinking and practice of the school and, in turn, helping to alter or extend each of these. In the next two sections we examine the processes of learning 'what' and learning 'how' by which small-scale curricular initiatives were sometimes transformed into whole school curriculum development.

Learning What: Spreading the 'Ownership' of Curricular Beliefs

If the beliefs, values and ideas central to any development are to move beyond its initiators, to become part of the majority's thinking and practice, they must be dispersed in a way that enables individuals to 'own' them, while ensuring a reasonable degree of 'fidelity' (Fullan, 1982) to the spirit of the innovation. For if teachers are required to alter their practice without conviction or understanding, that is, they change but do not learn, there is a strong likelihood that they will subsequently reject the innovation. Conversely, if they assimilate the innovation so that it does not change their behaviour, they cannot be said to have learnt at all. A balance must be struck between the initiator's drive and the inertia which results from others' experience and conviction.

In the project schools, the key to this balance lay in a slow, widening pattern of interaction between those who 'owned' the new ideas and those who did not. In visual terms this pattern resembled a series of widening circles with one fixed point in common. It had four characteristics. First, whatever the time span, the same person or small group, sometimes augmented by other people, carried implicit or explicit responsibility for spreading the ideas and for ensuring acceptance of the beliefs and values which underlay them. Second, the ideas were brought, over a period of time, to the attention of different groups of people, often in a sequence which started with the initiator's immediate pupils and colleagues and worked outwards to parents, governors and the community at large. Third, the innovation was always shared with the members of these varying groups in ways which required the latter's active involvement, and which encouraged modification or development of the practical implications of the central ideas. Fourth, after each such period of active dissemination, responsibility for moving the modified ideas onwards to other audiences returned to the initiators, with or without the addition of one or two other interested people.

Details of time, place and personnel differed according to the institutional circumstances of each school, but the pattern was essentially the same in them all. New curricular understandings moved gradually, yet repeatedly, outward from a small, committed group and then returned to them, after being altered or extended by the active participation of others. Put another way, the ideas central to an innovation were taken by one or more persons to a group who discussed or worked with these ideas before delegating or implicitly entrusting further development of them to the original instigator(s), working on their own or with newly-recruited supporters. In due course, the revised ideas were brought to a fresh audience for further processing. These people in turn delegated responsibility for the next stage of development back to one or more of the initiators who worked on it until the time was ripe to involve a further group. And so the circles widened, encompassing more people at each turn, but always coming back to a nucleus of teachers who felt responsible for both the central ideas of the innovation and its onward movement (see figure 1). To illustrate this pattern, and at the same time to emphasize that the image of circles with a coincident point itself distorts reality by over-simplifying it, we tell a story, using as much first-hand evidence as is possible in the space available. It has been difficult to narrow the choice to one example, because the pattern was so prevalent in Carey, Fenton, Ingham and Upper Norton. Our choice is the slow spread of fresh ideas about mathematics among the staff at Ingham, but we could have selected other instances, in different curriculum areas, from any of these four schools.

Mathematics: Ingham

To summarize, this slow-moving, widening series of circles had as its 'fixed point' two teachers, Edith and Tina, each of whom had a continuing interest in mathematics. Inspired and later supported by course attendance and by a reference group of mathematics coordinators from outside their school, they actively involved their pupils, then Evelyne, the Head, and gradually all the rest of the staff, parents and community members. They broadened everyone's understanding of the term 'mathematics', seeking to ensure that all the children in the school had increased practical experience of it and that it was integrated into other curriculum areas. After each phase of dissemination, responsibility for developing further implications of these principles and for following through what had so far been agreed came back to Edith and Tina, though on most occasions others too became or remained involved. At the end of five years, all the staff felt that they had made ideas, which at first had been understood by only two of their number, into part of their own thinking. It was also clear that many of them had changed or developed their practice in line with their modified beliefs about the nature of mathematics and about appropriate teaching and learning activities.

Four years before our research began, Edith and Tina had attended a course on infant mathematics. As a result they had both become members of a national research and development group and subsequently, during the year of our fieldwork, of a group of primary maths coordinators:

> I like going on courses because...usually they are putting forward something new (as well as) something that you probably already know. It gives you some impetus to go back

Figure 1

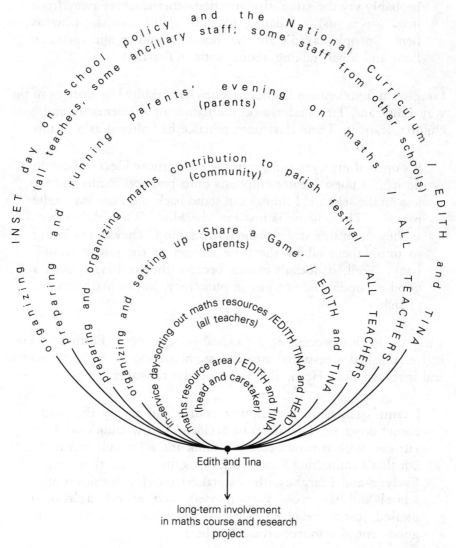

Edith and Tina

↓

long-term involvement
in maths course and research
project

Note: The circles are drawn so that they expand chronologically, rather than in terms of a widening audience.

Key: Capital letters denote who was responsible for activity. Brackets show who was newly involved in activity, or as a result of it.

again and look at things in a fresh way... I think Edith would probably say the same, that meeting other teachers away from here (gives us) a chance to talk about maths, whereas here...people haven't got the time to sit down and spend an hour and a half talking about maths. (Teacher)

Long-term involvement in these groups had resulted in changes in the way Edith and Tina understood the nature of mathematics and how children learn it. Their classroom practice had altered as a result:

It's opened my eyes and given me many more ideas of how to do it.... I put a greater emphasis onto practical maths and far less on the scheme. I think I can stand back and I can say to the parents, 'The scheme is just our checklist'. When they panic, as they do at this stage of the term, saying 'They're not going to finish them all by the time we get to the junior school' I say, 'Well, it doesn't matter because they're having such a good grounding...not just in numeracy, but in mathematics. (Teacher)

Early on in this process of individual development, Edith and Tina had established a resource area for mathematics, an initiative which had involved their Head, Evelyne, and the caretaker:

I came back from a computer course and set up the maths corner down there (almost) by accident... I wouldn't say I am satisfied with it now because I think it's a bit dull and dark, but that's something I can work on again... Together we got Evelyne and Fearghus (the caretaker) moving furniture after school and we were very pleased, and everybody's been pleased, just to create another corner in school...(with a) jolly good central resource area. (Teacher)

Spurred on by their continuing involvement in the mathematics research project, Edith and Tina had then made up boxes and packs of resources for particular maths topics. They either used these themselves or stored them in the central area so that they were available for use by other teachers. Some time later, with the active backing of the Head, they had organized an in-service day, part of which had been spent sorting out all the maths resources in the school:

We had a whole Saturday on maths... It was a lovely, informal day. We insisted that they took everything over from
their cupboards that was anything at all to do with maths and
put it in the hall, which was quite exhausting... We did that
on Friday...and set it all out in the hall and then on Saturday
we spent the day, first of all, looking at everything, then
deciding what each class needed in their classroom. All
together we drew up a list of everything we felt each class
ought to have as basic number apparatus, then we drew up a
separate list of what each unit of three classes could work
within, and then we had another list of what ought to be kept
in a central area. By the end of the day, exhaustingly, we were
staggering back to our classrooms with either our own particular equipment or the unit's...

The second part of the day had involved the staff not in practical
activity, but in sharing insights from their own practice, and as an
extension of this, in discussion of their beliefs about the nature and
teaching of mathematics:

On that same day, we had just half-an-hour or so when we
went around the group and had a quick brainstorm of an idea
of a number activity that we did... It was good because you
listened to people's reasonings and you could understand why
they liked it, and why they used it because they told you how
they used it. Yes, that was a profitable day. (Teacher)

At about this time Edith and Tina also involved parents. They developed an initiative called 'Share-a-Game' which encouraged parents
and children to engage in mathematical games together at home:

We discussed the thought of actually having workshops for
parents...but on the whole we felt that that could make it
more difficult in some respects, because parents might have
wanted to take the more formal aspects of mathematics and
forget about the practical side. So we plumped for 'Share-a-
Game'. There was one school (nearby) that had actually
started, and so before we began, we went and had a look to
see what they had done. We came back with their ideas and
got a grant from the PTA to buy some games... From there
on we got some mums interested in running it and they

adapted the way they were going to organize it... It's gone from strength to strength. (Teacher)

Later still, when the school was asked to contribute to a flower festival at the local parish church, the whole staff decided to develop their contribution from a mathematics theme. More recently, an open evening jointly organized by all the teachers, had introduced parents to the maths resources used in the school. Edith and Tina had worked together to support these ventures:

> The parents did ask this year if they could have a maths talk and, I think because last term was so short, Evelyne felt that it was too much to expect. But she came up with the idea that perhaps the open evening, which we normally hold in March, could be maths orientated, which seemed a bit daunting at first but actually wasn't too difficult... That's when we had the nursery rhymes and the whole school was number orientated. (Teacher)

Meanwhile, dissemination of their ideas continued within the school. After discussion with their reference group of coordinators, Edith and Tina spent a day together matching the school's maths curriculum with the National Curriculum. Supported once again by Evelyne, they developed their thinking and then shared it with their colleagues:

> Working with the other coordinators gave us confidence that we could bring back to share with the rest of the staff and say, 'Look! It's not so bad.' That in itself has been certainly the important thing...being able to bring your joint expertise back and actually share with other people... Then Edith and I found out that we couldn't actually spend the time that was needed...so Evelyne gave us a day together to sit down and complete it, because we had spent a couple of evenings doing it. So we completed that within school (time) and then we shared what we had found out with the rest of the staff. (Teacher)

Finally they helped to organize an in-service day at a nearby Maths Centre, on the implications of the National Curriculum, in which all the teaching and some of the ancillary staff participated. Teachers from other schools were also present and shared in their learning:

> It was led by a advisory teacher (from outside the school) who
> introduced a number of documents and then suggested that
> groups of staff should share their expertise in order to choose
> and plan a topic... The teachers organized themselves into
> groups according to the age group of the children they would
> be teaching the following year. Discussions were extensive and
> prolonged. In the afternoon they were introduced to some
> investigative activities and a variety of resources. (Fieldnote)

By the end of our year of fieldwork, although no new mathematics
policy had been formally agreed or written, there was plentiful evidence throughout the school of a broad, active and investigative
approach to the teaching of mathematics which, according to the staff,
had not existed five years earlier. As one teacher said:

> I think we are, as a school, much more aware now of maths as
> a cross curricular involvement. (Teacher)

A changed view of the subject and how it should be taught to young
children had been brought into the school five years before by two
enthusiastic teachers. They had gradually involved not just their own
pupils but also their headteacher, their colleagues, the other pupils in
the school, parents, community members, in working actively with
these new ideas, modifying them and making them their own. When
each new group was securely involved, this pair resumed their unspoken responsibility for spreading their own developing understanding of mathematics and mathematics teaching to another audience so
that they could in due course turn the ideas through another, wider
circle. The staff themselves summed the process up:

> Sometimes (curriculum development) is like the maths, it
> is...a filtration of ideas. (Teacher)

Learning How: Extending Practical Mastery of Shared Beliefs

Before teachers can make new ideas part of both their own idiosyncra-
tic approach to the curriculum and the belief system which they share,
or are coming to share with their colleagues, they need to feel confident about handling them in practice. Also, in a 'whole school' all

the staff must translate their beliefs in relation to any area of the curriculum into action in broadly similar ways, for beliefs, values and intentions which remain at the level of words make little impact on children's learning. So, whole school curriculum development involves not only learning 'what' but learning 'how'. Individual teachers, and sometimes ancillary staff, must acquire appropriate knowledge, skills and attitudes and ensure that the ways in which they behave towards children are compatible with those of their colleagues.

However, 'whole schools' are also characterized by a respect for individuality and for the unique contribution of each member. Accordingly, such learning also has to take place in a context which preserves individuals' right to interpret in their own ways the understandings and practices which they are coming to share with others. Learning 'how', like learning 'what', is an interactive process not a passively receptive one.

There is another similarity between them. In the project schools, learning 'how', like learning 'what', was a cyclical process in which increasing numbers of staff participated. Times, places and arrangements varied from school to school, but the three main components of the cycle — opportunity, support and demonstration — remained the same and occurred in the same order. First, opportunities existed for one or more people to acquire new knowledge, skills or attitudes. Second, their learning was supported. Third, they were provided with the incentive, which was usually perceived as an obligation, to demonstrate what they had learnt and were offered, implicitly or explicitly, the chance to share their new expertise with others. That is, their learning could not remain private. They had to make it public and to be openly accountable both for it and to those who had provided them with opportunity and support. In turn, their colleagues, stimulated by what they had seen, were offered the opportunity themselves to learn. If they chose to take this up, they too were given first support and encouragement, and later the opportunity to share their efforts and achievements with a wider audience.

We illustrate this pattern with the example of teachers at Carey learning how to teach science to young children. This story illustrates yet again the complexity and many-faceted nature of the development process, for it is not always easy to distinguish learning 'what' (for example, the belief that children learn best when they are actively involved in their work, or that effective teaching requires good classroom organization and management) from learning 'how' (for example to introduce 5–7-year-olds to the idea of 'fair tests'; to assess the development of scientific thinking).

Science: Carey

To summarize, Naomi was given the opportunity to learn more about teaching science to young children. She was supported in her learning and then encouraged to demonstrate to others, through her pupils and in other ways, what she had learnt. Encouraged and enthused by her example, others followed suit, learning from her and from other sources, supported by their Head, by Naomi herself and by their colleagues, and in their turn, showing others what they had achieved. By the end of the year all the staff had begun consciously to teach science in ways that were new to them, and were growing in confidence as they did so.

In the past the teachers at Carey had discussed science in connection with the development of topic work. It had appeared in the curriculum mainly in response to teachers' perceptions of children's interests and learning needs. No serious collective thought had been given to its development as a distinctive curriculum area with its own vocabulary until Ella, the Head, with the National Curriculum in view, recognized the need for the staff to address it as a subject in its own right. She asked Naomi to take on the responsibility of science coordinator because she was the one member of staff with any qualification in this area of the curriculum. She knew Naomi was naturally reticent and would probably need support. Since there were no others on the staff who were qualified to work with her in a team, Ella offered to give her some help herself, even though she was very aware of her own ignorance and lack of expertise. Together they worked out Naomi's job description and decided on her attendance, supported by Ella, at a long course on 'Science and Technology in the Infant School'. This course gave Naomi opportunities to visit other schools and encouraged her to introduce her class to an active approach to learning science. As she said,

> So I thought, I'm the Science Coordinator, I'd better have a go and see if it really works in a practical sense in the classroom... When we did batteries and bulbs at Christmas... I linked it with the fact that we had coloured lights at Christmas and that you could make different colours by using the batteries and the bulbs and they experimented with the batteries and bulbs by making circuits. (Teacher)

As she introduced this integrated and experiential approach to science into her own classroom, Naomi discovered some of the difficulties:

> It's time consuming and you often need another adult helper to
> be with (the group that's working practically). Or else you've
> got to be with them and get the other children working on
> something fairly simple that won't involve you too much. But
> it has worked. (Teacher)

She began to show to other pupils and to her colleagues, through
assembly, some of the activities the children had undertaken in her
classroom:

> This morning it was Naomi's assembly which was on light
> and colour. She told us that the work had begun when they'd
> put up the Christmas lights in their classroom. This had
> prompted them to think about light. She showed us some
> experiments they had done with coloured acetates held in front
> of torches. She talked about light travelling in straight lines,
> and demonstrated that if you put a mirror at different angles
> in front of it, it is reflected in different directions. She talked
> about prisms and the colours of the rainbow. Considering the
> colours of the rainbow had led them on to colour mixing.
> (Fieldnote)

She was able to demonstrate her growth in practical expertise in
another way too, because her attendance on the science course entitled
her to supply cover, in order that she could work alongside at least
one of her colleagues:

> Naomi, Thelma and Christine met after school one day last
> week. Naomi had prepared various activities which she sug-
> gested were appropriate. They discussed these, suggested addi-
> tional ideas and decided on a final programme. Naomi and
> Thelma then met yesterday afternoon and collected together
> all the materials they needed. Course funds had provided
> supply cover for half a day to work with another colleague and
> for half a day to spend in preparation... They decided that an
> adult would take responsibility for each activity. They had
> organized six activities, but one was cancelled because the
> parent who had been coming to help was unable to do so...
> Before break the adults were Naomi, Thelma, Christine, Mrs.
> Shane and myself. After break Ella joined us instead of Mrs.
> Shane. (Fieldnote)

Sometimes Naomi also used casual staffroom conversation to share what she was learning and thinking.

> Naomi talked a little about science attainment targets, saying that there was nothing in them about infants researching from books, rather, they were based on knowledge and skills. She'd been on her course yesterday and had taken the opportunity to express her surprise about this. The person leading the course had agreed with her that this seemed to be a gap and that infants could indeed be expected to use books to obtain information. (Fieldnote)

In addition, she took advantage of more formal occasions to share her growing insights with her colleagues. For example, a staff meeting discussion on assessment led to other people becoming involved in providing the resources needed for an active approach to science teaching.

> They talked about the difficulty of finding resources. Naomi and Thelma agreed that it had taken them a long time to gather all they had needed. Ella suggested that an idea could be to have resources on a trolley, accessible to everyone. An easy way of organizing this would be for each teacher to collect resources for one scientific activity. (Fieldnote)

Further, Naomi's formal responsibility for science made her persistent in claiming time in staff meetings for discussion of that curriculum area, sometimes in the face of digressions and rival claims:

> Ivy suggested that they sort out the arrangements for the INSET day at the beginning of next term. Naomi said 'Well it ought to be on science'... Naomi asked again about what science input she was expected to make... Later Naomi said, 'Well, I need at least an hour.' They needed, she said, to look at a map of the different areas and give some time to considering assessment too. (Fieldnote)

As a result of her persistence, the staff later participated in a school-based INSET day on science in the National Curriculum at which Naomi was able to demonstrate, yet again, what she had learnt on her course and from her own teaching, and to offer guidance to others.

Naomi's next opportunity to continue and extend her own new-found learning was also supported by Ella. Together, during the early part of the spring term, they produced curriculum guidelines for science:

> She's much braver now, in that she'll come to me and say, 'Well you know, you can't have that. That's wrong.' It's marvellous, because I am no scientific thinker. (Headteacher)

The staff contributed relatively little to the fulfilment of this task, perhaps because they had a limited knowledge and understanding of science in general and the National Curriculum science proposals in particular. However, they carefully discussed at a meeting the document produced by Naomi and Ella, were concerned that it should accurately represent their views and constantly related it to their own practice:

> Having spent the INSET day talking about science and the National Curriculum, the staff had floated a lot of ideas about classroom practice. Following that meeting, Ella and Naomi had met to talk about the actual curriculum document. Today the staff intended to talk through the first two parts, before giving it to Nerys to type... Ella went through the skills one by one and, in discussion, they were slightly modified or were illustrated with reference to common classroom practice...
> The staff took a long time getting the wording of the document exactly as they wanted it. In fact Ella eventually passed the piece of paper to Kay Harvey and Thelma, while (the rest of them talked) about the colour of children's eyes. When Kay and Thelma had settled the wording to their own satisfaction, they passed it back to Ella. Everyone agreed with what had been written. (Fieldnote)

Naomi did not think that this meeting directly affected what her colleagues did in the classroom. However, she felt that subsequent staff discussion, and the fact that she could confidently use her own increased knowledge to guide and illuminate it, had had an effect upon them:

> On the last day of our course they suggested ways of finding out in our school what people's worries were, about any areas

of the curriculum... In the last two staff meetings we've been through each area and read specifically what is in the National Curriculum and talked about how you'd actually do it in the classroom. That's the only way they've come to terms with what attainment targets are. (Teacher)

She felt that these two later meetings were particularly productive because she had gone through the National Curriculum very carefully to make sure that if any problems arose she could have an answer or that she would be able to say 'I'm sorry. I can't answer that. We need some extra, external help.' (Fieldnote)

As a result of the example set by Naomi and because of the practical support she offered in meetings and through ordering and organizing resources, the other staff began to feel more confident.

It's all there now. It's all labelled. We've actually got the electrical equipment in our classrooms... It's that sort of activity that's valuable to teachers, not producing great volumes of written documents. It's putting the thermometers somewhere near in a labelled box. (Teacher)

Their self-confidence and Naomi's continuing enthusiasm for the subject had in the meantime begun to stimulate others into learning. Thelma, alongside whom she had worked, looked to formal in-service education:

Thelma's got motivated...and she's put herself down for a science course next term. Maybe (Naomi's activity) has given her the confidence to go ahead and get some more help and advice, so that she can try something on her own in her room. (Teacher)

Others learnt by doing, as they introduced, with Naomi's encouragement, more consciously scientific elements into their curricula:

We were all doing a little bit of science somewhere in our topics, but I think we've all become far more conscious of including more science, that there's got to be more done. (Teacher)

> Before, a little bit of science might come into something, but I think people are thinking more as scientists... When we were doing that 'water', the sinking and floating and things, I think perhaps I was thinking more scientifically about it than I would have before, and I think everybody else does too. (Teacher)

These teachers too started as Naomi had done, to make their growing expertise public through their classroom work, and especially in their displays:

> On a display was the question, 'Which colour do insects prefer?' Underneath was written, 'We put coloured paper outside on the grass. Which colours catch the most insects? Each piece had to be the same size, in the same sunshine for the same amount of time or it wouldn't be fair. This is what happened. In thirty minutes the red attracted three insects'. Below this were rectangles of coloured paper. On the red rectangle were written, 'three insects', on the black rectangle was written 'one insect' and so on. The last rectangle was white and carried the caption 'So many we could not count. We estimated thirty'. This display included photographs of different insects. (Field-note)

As the teachers' confidence and ability to teach science increased, they were simultaneously supported and spurred on by the availability of appropriate resources. Moreover, the public use of such resources reinforced everyone's sense of accountability for the development of the science curriculum.

> Particularly in the area of science, everybody's looking for ideas and making sure they are going in the right direction and making sure they understand what's required... Even on open evening — I had a twenty minute gap between my parent appointments, I came to the staff room to make a coffee and there was a teacher in there. She also had a gap to fill and she was busily looking up something to do with 'energy' because that had come up as a topic in our staff discussion this week. As soon as I walked in, she said, 'Oh, come and look at this. I've found this book and it lists all kinds of energy. We could have done with this on Monday', and then she said, 'I

must go now, but I'm going to take this home and read it.'
(Teacher)

Next it was Christine's turn to learn, by attending a course called 'Science Topics for Classroom Teachers'. She too made public the fruits of her learning. She talked in the staffroom about the work she was doing with her children as a result of this course and the robot, incorporating electrical circuits, that she and her class had made together was later displayed in the entrance hall.

By the end of the year, this repeated pattern of opportunity, support and demonstration had come full circle. Other teachers had begun to give Naomi ideas to enrich her own classroom practice.

In the discussion we had on Monday I had to say 'I don't know. I think it means that a child should be able to explain how a simple toy works that stores energy'. I could think of clockwork toys. I could think of rubber band type aeroplanes where you could let go and you could actually see the move-ment. The others were able to say, 'You could use steam engines'... They were bringing ideas. Kay Harvey said she had done an experiment when they talked about materials, and, to understand about how rocks can crumble away, she had actually done an experiment with chalk... I hadn't thought about that. Talking about it (with the other staff) you can think of other things to do. (Teacher)

Moreover, the learning pattern seemed set to continue. By the end of the year Naomi was conscious that her role had changed. Neverthe-less, she expected that she would continue to be involved, though in different ways, in others' professional development:

Now it's to help the others to feel more confident that they can do it... I think the only way is to do some workshop type staff meetings. When they are scared of putting the wires together for the battery circuit they bring it along and we all make one. (Teacher)

During the year, all the teachers in this infant school had begun to feel confident about teaching a curriculum area which, in its National Curriculum form, was new to them. Their development had started with the learning of one teacher, supported by the Head and by her attendance at a long in-service course. After a time she had made her learning public, by sharing it in many different ways with her colleagues. These activities had in their turn triggered others' appetite for learning and their confidence that they could do so. One by one, the rest of the staff were given opportunities to acquire appropriate knowledge and skills. While they were learning, they were supported, by Naomi, by the Head, by each other and through further local authority in-service provision, until they too were ready to demonstrate to one another and to one another's pupils their growing confidence, understanding and practical expertise.

Whole School Curriculum Development: Reflection and Extension

In the first part of this chapter we offered a definition of whole school curriculum development as: a set of learning activities, individual and collective, which is inspired by, and takes place within, a framework of common educational beliefs, values and intentions, but which also enriches or extends the scope and shared understanding of that framework. In the second part we examined that learning in greater detail, as it related to understanding shared beliefs and values and to knowing how to act consistently with them. We argued that beliefs and values spread among those associated with a school by means of a process that we have described in visual terms as a series of widening circles with a fixed point; and that appropriate behaviour is promoted by means of a repeated learning cycle which enables increasing numbers of staff to realize these beliefs in similar practical ways. Throughout, we have also suggested that although individuals acquire the same kinds of new curricular understandings and capacities through their involvement in these processes, they all put their own stamp upon them, creating a pool of interpretations and practical ideas upon which everyone can draw. Moreover, this pool is an enlarging one; as the staffs' curricular understandings and their practice evolve, their grasp upon their schools' guiding beliefs and values becomes deeper and, paradoxically, more personal. In other words, the development of the curriculum within a 'whole school' includes a third type of learning which occurs as staff members extend their understanding of their shared beliefs and values and their ability to translate these into practice. So whole school curriculum development is a continuing and not a finite process, which enriches, stimulates and extends everyone who participates in it. It also makes the school itself more 'whole', by focussing the staff's attention upon the educational, social or moral purposes which give them a sense of community and upon the practical implications of these purposes; and by sharpening their need to interact with one another on immediate professional concerns (see chapter 3). When a 'whole school' develops part of its curriculum it is itself developed in the process.

When earlier in this chapter we used stories from Ingham and Carey to explicate learning 'what' and learning 'how', we were guilty of a double over-simplification. First, for three main reasons, the patterns that we described were not always as easy to separate from one another as we may have suggested. Leaders and participants used the same structures and events both to spread the ownership of ideas and to foster practical learning. Both processes often occurred at the same time; and both depended for their success upon the active involvement of participants who did not make the distinction that we have done between learning 'what' and learning 'how'. Second, although these stories made it clear that curriculum development is complex, they did not draw explicit attention to its challenging and open-ended nature. Yet these too are distinguishing features of whole school curriculum development.

We now therefore give one further story, selected from several, in order to illustrate at one and the same time: the complicated and the unfinished nature of the development process within the project schools; the way in which a small-scale initiative, sympathetically and enthusiastically tended, could become a major development focus for the entire staff group; the enriching quality of members' interactions with one another and the productive effect of their collaboration upon the thinking and practice of both individuals and the group as a whole.

This story describes how the head and staff of a school came to understand, internalize and teach an area of curriculum content which was new to them all; how they did this within the context of their established beliefs, using the subject to serve the agreed educational purposes of the school; how they challenged and extended one another's curricular thinking and pedagogical practice; and how they forged fresh understandings and acquired and applied new practical insights and skills at one and the same time and often by the same means. As a story, it runs concurrently with that which we told earlier in this chapter, about the development of 'progression' as one of the most important of this school's educational purposes. You may find it productive to re-read that section, before or after reading this one.

Because all the events in both stories were taking place simultaneously, by means of the same structures and events, we have found it impossible to unravel the threads without destroying the fabric. Accordingly, we have told this story — of the development of technology at Fenton — as far as we can in the way in which it occurred, in all richness and its complexity. We invite you as a reader to search for the two learning patterns as they interweave and overlap, and for the ways in which the 'whole school' and the individuals within it both moved forward.

Technology: Fenton

To summarize: Staff learning began some years before our fieldwork started, when Rob, the Deputy Head, became interested in technology. Supported by Simon, the Head, he used a variety of means to increase his own knowledge and understanding of the subject. He then took a leading part in spreading opportunities and support for learning throughout the school and in encouraging individuals to show one another in an increasingly open forum what they had learnt. That is, it was Rob who was initially responsible for helping his colleagues to learn 'how', but they carried his initiative forward, increasing their own knowledge and expertise, supporting one another and publicly demonstrating the fruits of their learning. At the same time Simon, working first with Rob and then with another teacher, Barbara, as well, was helping the staff to learn 'what'. He set in train a number of activities which deepened individual and collective understanding of the curricular and pedagogical principles which underlay the teaching of technology as part of the primary school curriculum and of the ways in which these could serve the school's established ends. These activities involved children, staff (teaching and ancillary), and the many parents who worked in classrooms and attended assemblies. Over two years, all these people and had recurrent, varied opportunities to become familiar with technology and to shape the way it was organized and taught to the school's own goals and circumstances. Throughout all this time it fell to Simon and Rob, joined later by Barbara, to keep the process of dissemination moving and to ensure that participants were actively involved.

In short, over several years various kinds of learning were going on simultaneously within the school and amongst those most closely associated with it. Teachers in particular encountered new curricular content and ideas, had the opportunity to identify those parts of their practice in which change seemed necessary, tried out different ways of teaching this new curricular area and of organizing it at school level, shared what they had learnt and their reflections on their learning, and deepened their own and one another's understanding of the school's values. As a result all the staff, teaching and ancillary, gradually came to approach in similar ways children's learning of technology and these ways were consistent with the school's established educational principles. At the same time all the staff were assimilating technology into their common framework of beliefs and practices. As they did so, they reflected on this framework, deepened their understanding of it and extended it.

Put another way, what happened over a long period was more than the addition of another subject to the school's curriculum or a matter of individual learning, though both of these occurred. Rather, the thinking and practice of all the staff moved forward in ways which were consistent with their existing beliefs but which also involved some extension of them. The curriculum, in its broadest sense, of this 'whole school' gradually altered and, as it did so, the basis on which the staff's 'wholeness' rested also developed. The educational foundations of the school subtly shifted, the staff's practice changed and the ties between its members were strengthened, as they worked together to master, individually and collectively, a new aspect of their children's learning.

In the year before our fieldwork began, technology was the concern of Rob who was both the Deputy Head and a full-time classteacher. Several things contributed to his growing awareness that it was an area of the curriculum that needed to be developed within the school:

> I became aware of it because of the National Curriculum...
> There was a lot of talk about technology. I'd always been interested in that side of things anyway and it gave me a push to do something and start thinking through some ideas. Then Simon came back with one or two ideas he had seen in other schools and I started to read more about it. I joined the Science Association and they send a primary journal through every month and I got a lot of ideas out of that. (Teacher)

He began to put these ideas into practice in his own classroom:

> I started putting that into my class and testing it out and seeing how it was going. (Teacher)

His interest was encouraged by Simon:

> It's important that people are given their own head to do these things...after consultation and after we've all had a chance to think about it and talk about it. I think if you don't give people the opportunities to develop things they stagnate. (Headteacher)

In due course Rob and Simon together made the decision to raise awareness amongst the rest of the staff, through the provision of some in-service training. This they supported with appropriate resources:

> Then Simon and I made a conscious decision to push what was happening in technology, to push it amongst the juniors to start with. So I did one or two in-service things. I did a morning for the whole staff and also the afternoon was taken up with Lego Technic. That gave the staff a bit of a push. Now, not a lot happened from that initial day. I forget how long ago it was — a couple of years perhaps. Not much happened from that, because people were still mulling it over in their minds. It was something that was bubbling up a bit but they'd got other things to do. (Teacher)

That day was followed by further in-service work, organized and led by Rob. These meetings slowly began to capture the staff's interest and to encourage them to increase their own relevant knowledge and skills:

> I had probably about 1 per cent knowledge of technology in the past... One of the courses we had was at a staff meeting on one of the INSET days... We did technical Lego, pulleys and systems like that. Well, that didn't inspire me at all. That was a complete switch off. I thought, 'I hate this...' Then the next (INSET staff meeting) we had on technology which was in the evening, was on axles and wheels and cutting and sawing and all that sort of thing. That actually appealed to me. From then, I've been on lots of different courses with different people from the authority who have run marvellous courses. (Teacher)

In the meantime, Simon and Rob bought further resources of various kinds, suitable for all age groups in the school and encouraged their use, informally and by demonstration and discussion in staff meetings.

There was a further, focussed discussion on the principles and practice of technology when the staff examined a document, one of several that Rob and Simon had prepared, at an in-service day at which all the teachers were present. The resulting debate covered a number of topics ranging from the practicalities of resource management to how the subject could be taught to all ages in a way which was consistent with the staff's shared beliefs (for example, that children learn from direct experience and the solving of problems real to them; that it is important to provide a structure for children's learning, from the earliest stages).

Meanwhile, his colleagues' expertise and confidence were increasing, Rob continued to develop in his own classroom the kind of technology that he wanted to see being taught throughout the school. He consciously shared the results of the children's ideas and endeavours with teaching and non-teaching staff, with parents and visitors, using display, and 'showing' assemblies.

> I set up a trolley and I ordered a lot of things and shortly after that I did quite a big thing with my class on making cars and bodywork, and testing. I made a big thing of sharing that in assembly and made a big display and we talked about it a lot. I made a point of talking about it a lot to staff...just showing them what the children had done. People started saying things like, 'That's very good. How did you do this? How did you do that?' and from that I spread it down into the other junior classes and got Kathryn and Susan doing it a little bit. (Teacher)

Rob continued to make sure that resources were available and encouraged staff to get involved in in-service training courses, as well as sometimes providing them himself. As one teacher said,

> We have been on courses collectively and individually... Everybody's trying hard to gain some expertise themselves and to work with the children to see what works and what doesn't. We're sharing ideas and sharing knowledge to make technology important, because most of us have never done any.

Meanwhile, at regular staff meetings throughout the two years Rob and Simon encouraged further discussion about the nature of this new curriculum area and how best to teach it in ways consistent with the school's established principles:

> I suggested to him right at the beginning that it would be a good idea if he started at the top and worked down, rather than start from the bottom and work up. So what he's done is work with his own children, which has demonstrated that they can do quite exciting things. He's also demonstrated that there are possibilities there for younger children, and made that even clearer to the staff by getting them to do things with their own children... So what he's done really is said, 'Look, all these things are quite simple. Let's get started. Let's not do anything complicated.' He's deliberately avoided getting too much in the way of pre-packaged stuff, and said, 'Let's stick to the simple'. He's got most people interested and involved in doing things and it's worked really well. And again, it's being done in a way which is cooperative, everybody committed to the idea that if we do this at our level then it's going to enable children to do far more later on. (Headteacher)

A significant step forward occurred when Simon, after consultation with Rob, asked Barbara to take on responsibility for lower school science (YR, 1 and 2). One of the first things that she did was to start working out with her lower school colleagues and with Rob a systematic development of technological concepts and skills through the school, a concern which reflected the value placed by the staff on high achievement and on progression in children's learning. In due course, at meetings, they shared these ideas with other staff members and invited discussion and modification of them.

Barbara's active involvement in the subject also quickened and stimulated the learning of the other teachers, a development which Rob was keen and ready to support:

> Then Simon and I made another conscious decision, to involve Barbara on that side of things. As soon as she got involved in it, her enthusiasm took the rest on, because they could see from her where it fitted in. (Teacher)

Meanwhile, Rob himself continued to teach and influence his colleagues, using whatever means he could devise:

> I see my job (at this stage) as contributing lots of ideas for how we can get free materials and putting out pleas for all sorts. Once those start coming in, people feel duty bound to use them and so it snowballs from there. We also had a Science 'cluster day' in October where (a polytechnic lecturer) did a day... He was brilliant... It was extremely accessible and that gave the staff another buzz and another push on, because it was somebody else... It gave them some more ideas. It gave them a bit of enthusiasm for the whole thing.

Throughout all this, Simon and Rob, working individually, together, and with others, were pursuing three aims: (i) to spread understanding of the principles underlying technology; (ii) to ensure that the staff assimilated these in ways which simultaneously promoted and extended the school's purposes; and (iii) to encourage and support the growth of appropriate practice:

> (At an INSET meeting) the major part of the evening was given over to talking about science and technology. Rob led the discussion. He mentioned a book called *Springboards* which is an Australian publication, saying that this provided a sequence and continuity that was linked with cognitive development. It had a similar approach to that agreed in the school's curriculum statement on Science and CDT. Simon said, 'It's all to do with integrated learning, which is what we've said we want'. He also said that the philosophy behind it was not only similar to that within the school, but also of Science 5–13. There was an awareness in the discussion of the need for accountability and therefore the need to develop a means of record keeping. There were references to the fact that there is now a workbench in the reception area so that even the youngest children can be taught how to use tools properly. (Fieldnote)

> (The in-service work) was essential because the trouble is you don't get enough time in school to spread these ideas and make sure that people feel happy about them. You can talk about them in an odd ten/five minutes to people but you're not

actually taking them on any further... What you need to do is set the thing up and give them something they can take away and they can do, even for a short spell. Then, of course, there's the problem of resourcing it. It had to be things that I knew we had resources for, because otherwise it's pointless... Now I keep getting pressurized about not enough tools and not enough of this, that and everything else! That's all because people have had enough time to start feeling really happy about it as a process. It's still nowhere near perfect and we need more time... to sit down and talk it over as a staff. But the big thing about it is that everybody, to some extent, has had experience of working it with their classes so everybody's got a contribution they can make. (Teacher)

At a staff meeting there was quite a lot of discussion on the various construction kits in the school, and a commitment to buying some more, particularly for Susan's classroom (in the mobile). Particular attention was paid to 'Constructs' which was especially admired because some of Barbara's class had shown models made of this in assembly that morning. Simon emphasized that the children should be encouraged not simply to use the kits, but also to use other materials that they needed to adapt to their own purposes. (Fieldnote)

As other teachers became more closely involved in the development of technology throughout the school, they too took on an increasingly active role. They worked to extend their own knowledge and pedagogical skill and they devised fresh initiatives involving their colleagues.

I went on another (course) on hydraulics and pneumatics and making things move in the infant classroom which was a whole throw up of ideas and different ways to use materials. We actually sat down with the children and made it work. From there I have taken the inspiration on... I go to the library and find the relevant books and I go out of my way to find information from various areas and get it all together and make it work. It does rub off on the children. All mine now are quite confident with making frames axles, and the ideas they get from it are just amazing... If it wasn't for Rob running the courses initially I probably wouldn't have got started, nor would the others. It would have just been, 'I'll fit a bit in if I've got to because of the National Curriculum next year' and that would have been it. As it is it's really taken off... Verity and I are...going to have a photographic record of areas we've covered. (Teacher)

By the end of the summer term, many teachers were trying out in practice with their classes some of the understandings that they had gained during the year. In addition, most had added ideas of their own. As they took these initial steps, they supported one another and showed their colleagues what they and their classes had achieved.

Barbara and Marguerite both showed me with pride the musical instruments they'd been making this morning... It was clear that Barbara was really pleased with the ingenuity that the children had demonstrated in making their instruments... They'd developed from (the starting points). Some had made shakers with straws and bottle tops, which was an idea entirely their own. Others had modified the ideas that they were given by punching holes in things to find out how they could make different sounds, and so on. (Fieldnote)

A boy showed a birdhouse that he'd made out of one of the construction kits in the classroom... Verity said, 'Don't tell them what it is! Let them guess'. When the children had guessed Verity said to him, 'It's bigger than the one you made before, isn't it?' Then she asked him where he would put the food and suggested that perhaps he might find some way of making a platform where the birds could eat their food before going inside to sleep. The boy nodded enthusiastically and looked quite excited at this suggestion. (Fieldnote)

When the infants were out for afternoon play, some of them came to the doorway of the little room where I was sitting with a group of juniors. They wanted to show me what they had made. They'd all designed little figures with syringes as part of the figures. Some had put these in the chest of their figures, some in their eyes, some in their noses. From the back of each syringe a long plastic tube led to the plunger, and there was a little plastic dart at the end of the syringe. The children pushed the plunger down and the dart came flying out of the creature's nose or eye or tummy. The designs were intricate and beautifully crafted and the children were proud of their work. On the back of each figure was written, in an adult's

hand, the words 'pneumatic power'. One of the children seeing me look at this, said 'It's spelt with a "p". It's a silent "p"!'
(Fieldnote)

Moreover, as our fieldwork ended, the development of both the
understanding and the practice of technology in the school seemed
set to continue:

At the end of assembly... Kathryn was talking to the juniors
about a boat competition. Last week some of the infants had
shown their boats in assembly and Kathryn had proposed that
they have a school competition. One junior boy had gone
home and made a boat out of various waterproof materials,
polystyrene, tape, plastic and so on, and had brought it in to
show her. She now showed it to the rest of the children and
praised him for his enthusiasm... 'We might make (the competition) the whole length of the swimming pool. It depends
how it goes', said Kathryn. 'We'll see. We'll decide later'.
Susan asked what the deadline was for the completion of the
boats. 'Well, sometime in the last week of term I should
think', replied Kathryn. (Fieldnote)

In this case-example, one member of staff and his headteacher initiated
a series of collective activities which gradually, as they moved out
from this pair in a series of widening circles, enabled the staff and the
parents who worked in their classrooms to understand the principles
underlying technology as part of the primary school curriculum.
These activities also helped those who participated in them to see that
technology did not threaten the school's agreed educational goals.
Instead, it could be made to serve them. Moreover, in the process of
discovering this, individuals' own grasp on these goals was deepened.
At the same time as these understandings were spreading through and
beyond the school, the same staff member, supported by his head,
started to increase his own ability to teach technology, publicly shared
what he had learnt and then involved others in similar cycles of
opportunity, support and demonstration. Throughout all this, meetings, focussed discussions, in-service days, courses, displays of work,
assemblies, informal conversations and the spontaneous sharing of
classroom experiences served multiple purposes. The cumulative
effect of all this was to make the development of this new curriculum
area part of 'whole school' thinking, to modify that thinking, to provide the means for appropriate practical learning and to leave the way
open for further development.

Conclusion

In this chapter, we have attempted a definition of whole school curriculum development, stressing that it was a set of overlapping learning activities which engaged individuals and groups at the level of their beliefs and of their actions. We have also analyzed and examined the processes through which this learning took place. Since our argument has in places been complex, we have summarized it at intervals throughout the chapter and do not do so again at this point.

Instead we do two things. We relate our analysis to the introduction of the National Curriculum and we highlight a number of points which draw attention to the lived reality of whole school curriculum development, as it is experienced by those inside or closely associated with schools.

All three of the pieces of curriculum development which we have examined in this chapter arose partly in response to the requirements of the National Curriculum, though in each case relevant curriculum review was already underway or was on the school's agenda for future discussion. The stories of technology at Fenton and science at Carey, and to a lesser extent that of mathematics at Ingham which predated the 1988 Education Act by several years, show how the staff of these schools used an external initiative which they might have seen as a constraint to serve their own educational purposes. In the process they came to feel both that it was part of their own curricular thinking and that they were in control of it. That is, by the time that our fieldwork ended the staff in these schools felt that they 'owned' the relevant parts of the National Curriculum.

Now the head of one of these schools, in her explication of the term 'whole school', talked of a 'community of people who have come together with a common vocational purpose...in which... there is a lot of love'. Her desire to establish and develop a purposeful educational community derived, as did that of her staff, from a sense of concern and responsibility for children and of accountability to parents. In chapter 1 we showed that teachers' urge to 'own' the curriculum sprang from the same sense of responsibility and of accountability. It is primary teachers' and headteachers' strong sense of moral commitment to their pupils and not an innate, inflexible conservatism which urges them towards control of the curriculum. The proactive stance towards the National Curriculum taken by the teachers in the project schools is representative of the same drive. Individually they felt that they could not fulfil their deeply held responsibilities for children unless they were masters, not servants, of what they taught and had made this internal rather then external to them. Similarly, only if the National Curriculum becomes part of the shared belief system of a staff can it help them to realize their collective educational aspirations for their pupils.

Our study of whole school curriculum development in action, and the examples we have analyzed in this chapter, have also taught us a good deal about how it is experienced by heads and teachers. In the first place, it is stressful, not least because the notions of 'whole school' and 'curriculum development' do not fit easily together, since the emphasis of the first is collective and that of the second individual. The tension between the two can be eased by the processes of building a 'whole school' (see chapter 3) which bring the individual and the group closer together in terms of educational beliefs and values and of classroom practice. It can also be reduced by encouraging within the institution an emphasis upon individual and collective learning. For, when staff members are willing to learn, it is more likely that their perspectives will gradually draw more closely together, or that they will be able to use their differences constructively, and that staff members will see change as an opportunity for growth, whether it is initiated within the school or comes from outside. But the tension between individual teachers and the community to which they belong can never be completely removed without reducing the potential of both for development. We return in chapter 6 to the idea that whole school curriculum development is necessarily full of tension.

Our emphasis in this chapter has also been upon the ways in which staff and others associated with a school come to share and to accept the same understandings of their school's fundamental purposes and to act in ways consistent with them. We have shown that learning is central to both these developments. We have also argued that when teachers are individually and collectively willing and able to reflect upon and modify their aims and their behaviour in pursuit of 'whole school' curriculum development, then the basis on which their 'wholeness' rests also develops. Whole school curriculum development is an open-ended, restless endeavour, involvement in which places staff under continual pressure to learn and to grow. This throws a new light upon Stenhouse's (1975) famous dictum that 'there is no curriculum development without teacher development'. It makes the latter into a more challenging and dynamic process than recent official publications on school development (for example, DES, 1987; NCC, 1990) suggest that it is.

Moreover, whole school curriculum development involves repeated opportunities for teachers to learn, since the main processes by which it takes place are cyclical. Curricular principles (learning 'what') are spread by the persistent action of one or more individuals who move them through a series of widening circles, actively involving different groups of people in shaping and using these principles, yet at the end of each phase picking up responsibility for their onward movement. Similarly, curricular practices (learning 'how') pass from one teacher to another by means of a repeated cycle of opportunity, support and demonstration which has the potential to influence all staff members in turn. Individuals have the chance and the freedom to make their own contribution to both processes and as they do so they help to maintain the collective momentum of change and the continuing pressure to learn.

Further, the development of a 'whole school' curriculum, even of a small piece of it, is extremely complex. In part this is because so much is happening at once, in part because the same roles, structures and events are used for many purposes. Although in this chapter we have identified 'patterns', to its participants the reality of whole school curriculum development is complicated, untidy and often organizationally confused. We return to this point too in chapter 6.

Indeed, it is because we may have given the impression in this chapter that the processes of curriculum development are easy to set in motion and smooth in operation that in the next one we examine some of the obstacles to development which existed in the project schools and identify the conditions which helped to promote it. The success of such restless, finely-poised, intricate institutional growth should not be taken for granted nor its difficulties underestimated.

Chapter Five

Conditions Which Facilitate or Inhibit Whole School Curriculum Development

In our discussion of development — of individual teachers and therefore of the curriculum for which they felt responsible, of a sense of 'whole school', of a 'whole school' curriculum — we have focussed upon evidence from the project schools which have presented an almost uniformly positive and productive picture of such developments and of the ways in which they came about. Yet in all the schools whole school curriculum development proceeded fitfully, at an uneven pace and in the face of obstacles which sometimes brought it almost to a halt. In this section we consider the organizational, professional and interpersonal conditions which appeared to facilitate the staffs' attempts to find and implement approaches or policies which influenced the thinking and behaviour of them all. We also look at conditions which seemed to impede or inhibit such developments. We treat the two together because they appear in most cases to be the obverse of one another. So, certain conditions encouraged growth and change, but in the absence of any one of them, there was little development and changes which were already under way slowed down or disappeared.

Four sets of conditions bore powerfully upon curriculum development. The first sprang from institutional values and from the normative effect of these on individual predispositions to behave, or refrain from behaving, in particular ways. The second derived from the manner in which the schools were structured, formally and informally, in particular in relation to interaction between individuals and groups, to communication and to participation in decision-making. A third set of conditions related to the availability of resources, especially teacher time and commitment, and materials and equipment. Finally, effective leadership permeated and underscored all the other conditions and was itself one of them.

In this chapter we examine each of these four sets of conditions in turn, suggesting ways in which their presence encouraged whole school curriculum development and their absence held it back. None of them appeared by itself sufficient. However, each was necessary so that in the absence of any one of them development often faltered and initiatives were stillborn.

Some are described in greater detail than others; when we have discussed in an earlier chapter the importance of, for example, a particular institutional value it receives only summary treatment here. Moreover these conditions were interdependent. The boundaries between them were not clear cut and elements in one affected aspects of another.

This is not to argue that development cannot begin until all the appropriate conditions are in place. Rather, an initiative which launched one or more people onto one activity often appeared to facilitate or stimulate the growth of others. This in turn could help the emergence of conditions which were later to prove favorable to development, even though at the time this did not appear to be the case. The complexity of the matter is well-illustrated by Upper Norton where, in the summer term, a plethora of changes to routine sapped the staff's energy and distracted their attention from the curriculum. But these very changes contributed to their growing awareness that they were a community with shared educational beliefs and that they could work productively together, a state of affairs which in the long run was to prove beneficial to their pursuit of whole school curriculum development. Or, to cite other examples, a single teacher, or, more powerfully, a pair, their enthusiasm for a curriculum issue or area sharpened by course attendance, could urge their colleagues into staffroom discussion or collective in-service activity. Similarly, children's work shown in assembly could arouse or focus a shared interest in an area of the curriculum by demonstrating what children were capable of achieving. This interest might, in turn, encourage peer interaction, peer learning, course attendance, school-based in-service work, a shared desire to buy or organize resources, informal staff discussion or a common awareness of the need for a written document of some kind. Each of all of these activities might at one and the same time highlight a critical shortage of resources (for example, time) or a collective unwillingness openly to face differences and yet might encourage development by creating organizational structures (for example, working parties) or by fostering values (for example, mutual support) which in the long run proved productive.

In this context the case of Orchard is instructive. This school had a long and well-documented history of whole school curriculum development but during our year of fieldwork little took place (see chapter 4), and the school was not, in the view of its head or teachers, a 'whole' one. We puzzled over this change which had apparently taken place within a short period. Our tentative conclusion is that the wish to function as an educational community inspired by shared purposes was still present in the Head and many of the staff. However, recent changes in personnel had reduced corporate allegiance to necessary institutional values (for example, the importance of teamwork; a willingness to deal constructively with differences) and had thrown into relief particular resource shortages, especially teacher time, commitment and expertise. We find the metaphor of a rocket launch helpful. None of the staff groups appeared to need all of the conditions which we go on to describe, before it achieved 'lift off', that is, it successfully embarked upon whole school curriculum development. But all needed some of them. Each, except Orchard, found its own point of 'lift off', after which the potential within almost any activity for stimulating collective gains in altitude seemed to counteract the possibilities which also existed for bringing the rocket back to earth. At Orchard, by contrast, the fuel-mix was never quite right and although parts of the engine fired at intervals during the year, the staff as a whole were not able to launch themselves into the orbit which some of them, including the Head, still desired.

Central to our understanding of this and other complexities of whole school curriculum development is the issue of institutional values. To this we now turn.

Shared Institutional Values

We identified in the project schools five shared values which were so strongly held by the head and the majority of staff that individuals felt under normative pressure to behave in accordance with them. The first of these encouraged professional learning. The remaining four helped to create the conditions under which teachers could learn and work together and could develop a shared sense of educational purpose.

These values and the norms associated with them did not grow by themselves. In each school their valency depended to a large extent upon tenacious leadership and upon the activity of one or more stable and respected staff members who modelled appropriate behaviours and who looked beyond their own classrooms. Since awareness of the entire school and of others' potential and actual contribution to it is a relatively late professional development for most staff, we were not surprised to find that it was only a few teachers other than the head who consistently thought in school-wide terms. However, these teachers were respected by their colleagues either for their expertise and experience or for their drive and energy. Consequently, they exercised an influence on staff attitudes and behaviours disproportionate to their numbers. Chapter 3, and the section on 'leadership' in this chapter, throw further light on how they made their influence felt.

Valuing Learning

All the project schools were characterized by a commitment to the continued improvement of professional practice (see chapter 2). After an analysis of how teachers at Fenton learnt, Campbell (1989a) wrote:

> It was as though all the staff had antennae especially adapted for seeking out learning opportunities and receiving the signals from them... Their learning added to the rich flood of shared ideas which constantly flowed and eddied around the school.

Nias (1989b) described the teachers' readiness at Upper Norton to embark on new initiatives as 'bubbling like a hot spring'. Similar metaphors appear in the case studies of the other schools. As chapter 2 makes plain, they were places in which experimentation and growth were constantly encouraged; the seeds of development, whatever their origin, fell on fertile soil and were nurtured by a propitious climate. Teachers were under an implicit obligation, as members of these school staffs, constantly to seek for professional improvement and in the process to generate ideas, to share, to discuss, to work together.

Valuing Interdependence and Teamwork

Respect for and belief in the importance of learning was to some extent independent of a second value which was expressed through a particular type of organizational culture. Nias *et al.* (1989) showed that schools can develop a culture in which it is the norm for adults to work productively together outside the classroom. This 'culture of collaboration' is built upon four interacting beliefs. The first two concern ends: individuals should be valued but, because they are inseparable from the groups of which they are part, groups too should be fostered and nurtured. The second two relate to means: the most effective ways of promoting these values are through openness and the maintenance of a sense of mutual security.

In such a culture, interdependence is as much to be valued as independence, since individuals are important because of what they can contribute to others as well as in their own right. Among the members of this culture a sense develops that they make up a close knit group which they value because it gives them a sense of belonging. At the same time, by working together in a spirit of shared responsibility, they create a feeling that they are a team in which people help, encourage and substitute for one another (see chapter 3). A 'culture of collaboration' is marked by its members' awareness of and fostering of the collective as well as by the individual's sense of self-esteem and well-being.

Now, in all the project schools the staff placed a high value upon their own learning, and upon the development of the curriculum. But Carey and Fenton and, for the reasons we have explained, to a much less extent Orchard, were different from Ingham and Upper Norton in also having a tradition of collaboration among the adults in the school. They talked and worked together because they valued one another's views and expertise and also from a shared sense of attachment and loyalty to the entire staff group and to the teamwork which flowed from and strengthened their sense of corporate identity.

The desire of the staff at Carey and Fenton to maintain this tradition meant that all curriculum initiatives were seen as simultaneously corporate and individual. The teachers habitually worked out their ideas together and took on a common responsibility for one another's development. To be sure, some of the necessary work was often delegated to individuals, especially to curriculum coordinators, but on the implicit understanding that everyone would at some time share in the task of understanding and translating new ideas into practice. By contrast, at Ingham and Upper Norton the whole staff group came together at intervals to share individuals' curriculum thinking or expertise or to develop policies which affected them all, but at the start of the year they made no assumption that they were professionally interdependent. The value attached to self-reliance under the previous heads of these schools persisted, despite the current heads' efforts to encourage a greater emphasis upon collectivity.

As a result, it was easier for the staff of Fenton and Carey than it was for those of Ingham and Upper Norton to initiate and sustain developments which affected everyone in them. The prior existence in

Carey and Fenton of a 'culture of collaboration' ensured a readiness which did not exist in the other two schools to think in collective as well as individual terms. At Orchard, there was evidence that such a culture had existed in the past, but that it had not yet been recreated by its present staff.

Valuing the Open Expression of Professional Differences

The third institutional value which encouraged whole school curriculum development was also most evident in Carey and Fenton. It too appeared to be associated in those schools with the existence of a 'culture of collaboration'. It showed itself as a willingness amongst the staff to confront the existence of professional differences and to try to resolve them constructively. Collaborative cultures are characterized by beliefs about the means by which equal esteem can be shown to both the individual and the group or team, as well as by a belief in the importance of each as ends in themselves. Security is one of these means, openness the other. Security is seen as a necessary condition for the growth of openness and openness as both encouraging security and facilitating the expression of personal feelings and opinions. Individuals feel secure because others make their worth apparent to them and also because differences are openly expressed and so can be directly addressed. Equally, people's sense of interdependence encourages both a sense of collective security and a feeling that as a group, or team, they possess the resilience to deal constructively with disagreements. So, members of a collaborative culture interact with a forthright regard for their own opinions and emotions. Yet their openness is balanced by a respect for the security of one another and of the group (or team) as a whole. Candour is tempered by sensitivity and consideration, behaviour which in turn encourages a shared sense of security. Over time, the honest expression of differing ideas and feelings increases within and as a result of interactions which enable participants to feel stable and safe. By the same token, a sense of security grows in response to the open expression of views within an atmosphere of mutual respect.

Professional differences existed in all the project schools. Even the heads of Fenton and Orchard, who had originally opened new schools and had therefore been able to appoint all their staff, could not count on professional unanimity on all matters (for example, at Orchard there were differences on the teaching of mathematics and the use of computers; at Fenton the staff used the Deputy's term of acting headship to make changes in the reading resources of the school which had been delayed by their ex-Head's attitude to this area). At the other schools, where some staff had been in post since before the arrival of the current heads, there was certainly no consensus over all aspects of the curriculum. For instance at Carey, one teacher had only slowly come to terms with the staff's decision, some years before, to move away from reading schemes; at Ingham there were differences between the teachers or between the Head and teachers over how to teach reading; at Upper Norton disagreements occurred on the treatment of disruptive children and on the use of worksheets. Differences such as these necessarily occur in any profession which continues to debate both ends and means. Over time, heads can ensure, as those at Carey, Orchard and Fenton did, that most of the staff behave for most of the time, on most matters, in accordance with the school's basic educational beliefs even when they do not fully share them, but this does not eliminate diversity. Nor did any of the heads feel that it should. Within the limits set by their visions for their schools, they all valued individuality among teachers as well as children, fostered the personal talents and interests of adults, encouraged discussion and constructive disagreement.

Yet it was only at Carey and Fenton, whose organizational cultures attached importance to openness and to security, that the staff habitually tried to work out the differences which inevitably occurred between them. Indeed, when a new teacher was to be appointed at Carey, where for most of the time the staff appeared to feel very secure with one another, the personal qualities they saw as indispensable were 'openness', 'honesty', 'directness' and 'a tremendous sense of humour'.

This is not to suggest that at Ingham, Orchard and Upper Norton there was no open curricular debate. However, we did feel that on occasions in each of these schools such discussions were rendered sterile or inconclusive by unacknowledged or unspoken tensions, anxieties, uncertainties or disagreements. For example, at Ingham the head unwittingly opened up a sharp division between the staff on the teaching of spelling, in a way that left them confused and insecure, with their differences unconfronted and unresolved. At Upper Norton two of the staff had been at the school for more than twelve years and during that time had had little positive contact with each other. Although events in recent years had done much to bring them closer together and to enhance their mutual respect, memories of a past which they both remembered with some unhappiness remained. Consequently, as one of their colleagues observed, they were 'very considerate in their feelings for one another' (Teacher). As a result personal conversation and open discourse between them, and sometimes among the whole staff, were inhibited. At Orchard where in the past there had been a tradition of frank professional discussion, a different situation existed. There, disagreements among the staff had recently become more marked. The Deputy Head linked this with his sense that the school had not made much development during the year:

> It's been an odd term. I can't remember when there's been so much disharmony before. People seem to have become en-trenched and negative with it... I feel as if the school's been held almost in limbo, and most of my time has been taken up trying to work with people and get people professionally competent. Also trying to sort out relationship problems with-in the staff, which have got worse as the year's gone on and continue to do so... I don't sense a sense of direction and purpose to the school at the moment and haven't all year. (Deputy Head, Orchard)

Yet, some of the problems to which he referred arose precisely be-cause in two of the four teaching pairs in the school, teachers were trying to work independently, ignoring one of the guiding principles of the school, that unit pairs should plan and teach the curriculum collaboratively. Indeed, in one of them, the situation improved be-cause the head insisted that the two teachers persist in working out their differences together:

> Things are better... probably because Ron wouldn't let us work independently. Perhaps if I had worked independently, then they would have remained a problem, but now I like to think that, although we still have our moments, we are getting on a lot better. (Teacher, Orchard)

The willingness of the teachers at Carey and Fenton to engage in open curriculum debate was reflected in their high level of participation in corporate decision-making, for example at staff meetings. This con-trasted with Ingham, and sometimes too with Upper Norton and Orchard, where staff were not always so actively involved.

Whether or not staff choose to participate openly and directly in decision-making depended on three factors. First, there were times in most of the schools when individuals believed they had been excluded

from or neglected by the process of decision-making and so felt
alienated or resentful:

> I asked Dave how things were going on curriculum develop-
> ment. 'OK. People have started to fill in the sheet now, saying
> their preferences. In the meetings we've talked through and
> explained what we each mean by those areas of the curriculum
> we think need attention and review. Everyone has explained
> why they put their area or aspect of the curriculum on the list
> and now we've got to prioritize them individually'... Later he
> said that the trouble with prioritizing was that it wasn't too
> difficult to pick out the areas of most concern, nor was it
> difficult to deal with those that were the least important. But
> he felt it was the ones that were always in the middle, the ones
> that people felt needed some, but not a major amount of
> attention, that were the ones that were consistently over-
> looked. (Fieldnote, Orchard)

And on one occasion at Ingham,

> The possibility of discussing spelling was raised by Edith and
> Lori... Evelyne responded by saying, 'Well, not today, but
> we'll come back to it'. Lori said, 'It's concerning us all as a
> group'... She reiterated that they needed to know as a staff
> how they were going to approach the teaching of spelling.
> Evelyne said, 'that perhaps they would have time over lunch
> to look at the problem areas...' (Fieldnote, Ingham)

This was not done, with the result that,

> Things that have annoyed me personally are things like the
> spellings (which were) left hanging. I would really have loved
> to have sorted that out properly. (Teacher, Ingham)

The second main reason for teachers' indifference or hostility to
opportunities for shared decision-making was their occasional sense
that their heads were forcing them into particular courses of action.
This happened even in Fenton and Carey, where the existence of a
'culture of collaboration' had the staff accustomed to active participation in policy-making. Examples of unpopular decisions made
unilaterally by heads were: not reordering SPMG workbooks

(Upper Norton); the way in which classes would be regrouped in the summer terms (Carey); the form to be taken by the Wednesday afternoon activities, in which each teacher offered an activity for all the children in the school (Ingham); the status of the library (Fenton); the Tenth Birthday celebration (Orchard), of which a teacher later reflected: 'I think that was tackled wrongly. We needed a lot more discussion about that...'. Ironically, the resolute educational leadership offered by all the heads, described by their staff as 'strong', 'dominant', 'forceful' but 'persuasive', sometimes acted to restrict the very openness which they wanted to promote. As a teacher said,

> I feel quite strongly that a lot of things that we talk about in the staff meeting, where our opinions are asked for and noted are a lot of the time things that have already been decided. It's down to Dorothy in the end, for lots of things, to make the final decision. She says that things have to be decided amongst the staff and it has to be a majority decision, but there have been occasions where we've come away very dissatisfied, that it hasn't been a staff decision. (Teacher, Upper Norton)

A third and contrasting factor was the power of the staff group. Some teachers did not oppose collective decisions because of their attachment to the idea of unity or because the cohesion of the majority made them reluctant to voice a minority opinion. As a result, they tended to give group loyalty precedence over their own deeply held convictions or to prefer the illusion of consensus to the challenge of new ideas. For example, the staff at Carey considered themselves committed to interpersonal openness. Yet after they had faced the contentious issue of regrouping classes, one of them said:

> I don't know what you do when you feel very strongly about something and you know that somebody else disagrees with that... I think what tends to happen is that the more vocal people have their say and the quieter ones sit and don't say a great deal. It looks as if the consensus is there, but I have a feeling that sometimes the consensus is not... It's easy when we're talking about the curriculum because we think alike about most things. When it comes to talking about something like this, it has a potential for conflict and none of us like arguing.

The Head later reflected:

> They want everybody here to get on together and people have actually talked about (it) saying, 'I don't want to spoil the atmosphere. I don't want to change that.'

These three factors, — rhetorical consultation by the heads, use of their authority to make and enforce unpopular unilateral decisions, and individuals' deference to the idea of consensus and so their reluctance openly to raise their reservations or anxieties about a specific policy — all affected teachers' level of active participation in collective decision-making and their willingness to debate their differences openly. They also resulted, on particular occasions, in one or more teachers feeling that they did not 'own' specific decisions and so did not wish to become actively involved in carrying them out. This reduced the practical impact of such decisions upon curriculum developments. For example, at Ingham one teacher did not welcome the activity introduced by the head into an in-service day on English in the National Curriculum, in the course of which pairs of teachers, acting as 'critical friends', looked at one another's classroom organization.

> I found it embarrassing... I just sat there and I thought, 'I don't know what to say'... I just tried to ask questions and then I said, 'Look, I've tried to do mine more as corners, areas'... And yet, you see, the actual work she does is wonderful. (Fieldnote, Ingham)

Similarly some teachers at Orchard did not feel involved in the single staff discussion which led to the adoption of a school marking code. This is evident from fieldnotes of the discussion itself and from the lack of use which they subsequently made of the code:

> (The marking code) doesn't seem to me to be fully absorbed into the life of the school. The way Marie and Marion had difficulty in finding a copy reinforced that... Last week I asked Graham if he'd begun the marking code yet and he said no he hadn't, he was still working in his own way. Hadn't got round to it. He hoped to, some time in the future. (Fieldnote, Orchard)

Valuing Mutual Consideration and Support

A general willingness to value individuals and so to behave with mutual consideration and support also had a positive impact upon the staffs' capacity and willingness to engage in whole school curriculum development. These norms existed in the two schools with a 'culture of collaboration', but in the other schools as well. They do not, of course, necessarily indicate that the members of a school staff place a high value upon interdependence. The fact that people behave towards one another with sensitivity and kindness does not of itself reflect a strong feeling of group cohesion.

However, because such behaviour made individuals feel that others valued and respected them, it encouraged the growth at Ingham and Upper Norton of collaborative cultures. At Carey and Fenton it helped to maintain such cultures and at Orchard to keep the spark of one alive. The fact that staff members in all these schools treated one another with consideration and courtesy made it easier for them to feel secure together and reduced the tensions which resulted from individual disagreements. It encouraged their willingness to tackle directly interpersonal and interprofessional differences and to share publicly their knowledge and skills. It enabled individuals to show appreciation and respect for one another and to celebrate a sense of professional and sometimes personal interdependence. The obverse was also generally true. We seldom witnessed unfriendly, discourteous or abrasive behaviour but when such relationships existed they clearly made it more difficult for individuals to feel valued or to value one another, individually or as part of a group or team, and to work together.

For the most part in the project schools, then, the mundane transactions and interactions of school life were conducted with politeness, warmth and consideration for others. People were tolerant of each other's shortcomings and mistakes, and were quick to perceive others' needs, freely offering guidance, advice and practical help in response. Peer learning and teaching were characterized by generosity and sensitivity. At times of crisis and pressure staff worked harmoniously and responsively together and when they shared a teaching situation they did their best to fit constructively in with one another. This is not to say that the staff always liked one another nor that they chose to meet socially. On the contrary, interpersonal tensions occasionally rose to the surface in all the schools, and although teaching and non-teaching staff sometimes saw one another out of school, this was by no means invariably the case. However, in all the schools the teachers felt that for most of the time they 'got along well together' in a working context.

This fact contributed in several ways to individual learning, to the development of a sense of 'whole school' and to the effectiveness of the processes on which whole school curriculum development depended. It helped to create the self-confidence which gave minority opinions a voice. In turn this encouraged individuals to express and defend their own viewpoints, to make it plain when they did not understand or did not agree with a new idea. Moreover, humour often accompanied staff activity, in formal and informal settings. When tension was high or tempers had been raised, shared laughter frequently seemed to reduce the emotional temperature and to reaffirm symbolically the staff's readiness and ability to think and work together. Further, in the positive affective climate which resulted, individuals revealed their strengths and weaknesses to one another and, as they gained in interpersonal knowledge, were able appropriately to offer help or show appreciation to their colleagues. In turn, they came to feel valued for themselves and for their contribution to the learning of others. Their enhanced self-esteem then contributed to the maintenance of a relaxed but productive working atmosphere among the staff as a whole. In addition mutual help and consideration eased the difficulties of working lives that our observations showed to be busy, crowded and full of tension. It promoted effective teamwork and helped to encourage a corporate sense of belonging. It also served to support and encourage the professional development of individuals and to increase both the range of opportunities for school-based peer learning and the staff's willingness to take advantage of these.

We observed so many examples of friendly, considerate and helpful behaviour among the adults in the project schools that we found it hard to select among them, and in any case it might be invidious to do so because conduct of this kind was widespread and pervasive. We therefore cite only one teacher who summed up the atmosphere in all the schools, as we experienced it. She was a temporary support teacher working in six classes, who said, as she reflected on the sensitivity and practicality with which the rest of the staff eased the stress and complexity of her job,

> The staff here I find easy to get on with and easy to work with... Everybody realized that it was difficult having so many children in the school and that it was going to be a

difficult situation and so everybody was prepared to put themselves out. Everybody gets on well with everybody else, on
the whole which makes a lot of difference. Everybody is
prepared to help and direct you to things if you can't find
them or if you want help or anything... I haven't found it
difficult to fit in. (Teacher, Ingham)

The mutual support and cooperation which we so often observed and
through which members of staff often came to know, like and learn
from one another had another dimension too. Sometimes all the staff
had a focussed opportunity to 'feel together', that is to share a common emotional experience which provided a strong bond between
them (see also chapter 3). From time to time these occasions were
painful. For example, when several teachers' handbags at Upper Norton were ransacked and circumstantial evidence suggested that the
thief might be a pupil, the staff shared a deep sadness. As one teacher
said, 'If it was an outsider, then it's only the financial loss, but if it was
one of our children, then it's a betrayal.'

More often they were joyous events, frequently festivals (especially Christmas), ceremonies (particularly assemblies) or school
productions which signalled to pupils and teachers alike the staffs'
common capacity to triumph over pressure, human error, adversity
and fatigue. Such occasions also provided opportunities when everyone could share a sense of pride in the achievements of all the children
in the school.

Sometimes however events which headteachers perceived as having this potential did not have the desired effect upon their staff. The
pressure, confusion and barely suppressed bad temper which surrounded the summer musical production at Upper Norton was con-
verted into a felt-triumph of shared coping only by the teachers' joint
determination not to be defeated by the obstacles which confronted
them. The Tenth Birthday Exhibition at Orchard was not redeemed
in the same way and left behind it a legacy of dissatisfaction and
disappointment.

In much the same way the staffs appreciated it when their heads
tried to encourage collective pride in their shared achievements (for
example, successful open evenings or INSET days) by thanking or
praising them and by bringing in celebratory food or drink (see
chapter 3). However, they did not regard such actions as a substitute
for the sense of solidarity which came from their own experience of
successful collaboration. Similarly the practical teamwork on which
the success of such 'whole school' events depended could be double-

edged. While it often served to build a sense of mutual liking, inter-dependence or team pride, it could also become a substitute for the more difficult task of addressing educational differences. As one of the staff at Upper Norton said, 'Teachers don't talk about the curriculum, do they? They talk about "is the video working?" and "have you tried this book?"' In all the schools, teachers drew our attention and one another's to the friendliness of their staff group and to the readiness with which kindness and support were offered and received. Often they seemed to assume that reciprocal supportiveness outside the classroom was a reliable indicator of openness to mutual influence within it. Yet this was clearly not the case, as the behaviour of some of the unit pairs at Orchard and of many of the staff at Upper Norton at the start of the year suggested. Unless mutual support is accom-panied by a belief in the value of openness it may delay or impede the exploration of educational differences and thus the development of policies to which everyone is committed.

Valuing a Willingness to Compromise

The fifth institutional value which helped staff to work together in pursuit of shared aims resembled the fourth, in being a necessary but not a sufficient condition for the existence of a collaborative culture. Staff in all the schools valued a willingness to compromise and to resolve problems through negotiation. Of course, the members of any group of practitioners, especially primary teachers who have a long tradition of investing their own values in their work, are likely to disagree in some measures on ends or means. The culture (Nias *et al.*, 1989) of individual primary schools is not monolithic but is built and maintained by micropolitical processes (see chapter 3). Even the most homogenous school culture does not reflect all the beliefs of every staff member, but the beliefs and values of the dominant person or sub-group within it. Some individual compromise is therefore neces-sary in any culture. Furthermore, all teachers are likely to be operating from time to time within what Barnard (1938) has called their 'zone of indifference' (that is, areas of their work in which the outcome of decisions made by others are of relatively little personal importance to them). They will therefore be willing to negotiate on particular ends or means. This is a different situation from that which exists in schools where the staff as a whole are committed to teamwork and joint policy making. Under these circumstances, they are likely to view compromise not as an institutional necessity, but as a valuable way of showing their respect for others, of achieving collective agreement, of furthering the educational goals of the school to which they belong or of helping a sense of collective identity to grow or survive. To be sure, concessions may also secure some personal advantage for individuals, but in general they are made with the intention of helping the institution as a whole, or the other members of it, and not out of self-interest or indifference.

There were three main sets of circumstances under which the staff in the project schools were willing to compromise their own views or interests and willingly to give collective or majority views priority over their own. Sometimes they were swayed by a sense of collective responsibility for a decision in which they had participated, albeit with a minority voice. One teacher, reflecting on changes she had introduced into her teaching of handwriting in order to follow a new school policy, commented:

> I would personally go along with it, even if I didn't whole-heartedly agree. If (the decision) was made, I would have to abide by it, yes. (Teacher, Upper Norton)

At other times, following an agreed policy was an act of conscious self denial or was undertaken out of respect for the common good. One teacher at Carey followed her colleagues in undertaking a more open-ended, problem solving approach to mathematics than she had used in the past. Yet afterwards she reflected:

> When you've got a scheme like Fletcher or Peak it's much easier... The Fletcher scheme was very boring, but at least I knew where I was going... This is much harder. (Teacher, Carey)

At Upper Norton a term's school-based in-service work on information technology, vigorously stimulated and led by the coordinator, had raised everyone's awareness of the learning potential offered by computers. When the local authority circulated details, during the following term, of a forthcoming IT course, all the staff said they wanted to go. However, since attendance involved supply cover for which the school would have to pay, it was obvious to everyone that only one person would be able to. Everyone acquiesced, albeit ruefully, in the solution worked out by the head and the coordinator, that since the school already had an under-utilized Concept Keyboard, the interests of the most number of pupils would be served by training one person in its full and proper use.

Lastly, some collective decisions were accepted because their disadvantages were balanced by corporate gains. At Orchard, for example, both Dave and Jean found that teaching in a unit pair gave them extra work, but that it enriched the variety and quality of children's achievements and of their planning. When Fenton teachers planned a topic together, the autonomy of individuals was reduced, but the team gained in other ways:

> Verity did 'Touching', the rough plan and we added to it. She did the bulk of the work for that and I did the next one on 'Eyes'... Celia's done 'Hearing', the rough plan and we've all taken it away and added to it. It cuts your workload down by masses really. (Teacher, Fenton)

In this section, we have identified five institutional values and the norms resulting from them which strongly influenced the willingness and capacity of the staff at some or all of the project schools to become involved in whole school curriculum development. When one or more of these values existed, such development became easier to achieve and more productive. In their absence, it slowed down or, at times, stopped completely.

The first of these values — an appetite for professional learning — was present in all the schools and helped to make them, in curriculum terms, vibrant and lively places (see chapters 2 and 4). The prior existence in two of the schools of a 'culture of collaboration' (Nias *et al.*, 1989) meant that two of the remaining values — a deliberate espousal of interdependence and a willingness to face professional differences constructively — were well established in those schools. Behaviour consistent with the last two values — showing respect for other people as individuals, and therefore treating them with sensitivity, consideration and friendliness and giving them support and appreciation; and a willingness to resolve shared problems through negotiation and compromise — was evident in all the schools, and helped either to sustain or to build collaborative cultures in them. Separately or together the existence of all these values helped to create favourable conditions for whole school curriculum development by making it easier for teachers to learn and work together (see chapter 3) and to extend the boundaries of their own and others' thinking.

Organizational Structures: Learning Together, Working Together, Communication and Decision-Making

The second major set of conditions which affected the staff's ability to engage in whole school curriculum development was the presence or absence of appropriate organizational structures and individuals' capacity to use these constructively. We use the term 'structure' in its dictionary sense: 'the way in which a thing holds together, the supporting framework of any complex whole' (*Oxford English Dictionary*, 1934). In this sense, it means more than organizational arrangements. To be sure, the latter are often part of structures which provide frameworks to support different aspects of an organization's functioning (for example, personnel management; obtaining resources; communicating with potential users). But for two reasons they are not normally 'the way in which (an organization) holds together'. First, by themselves they are empty; the extent to which they become part of a structure depends on the way in which participants use them and the meanings they attach to them. Second, many organizations, and certainly primary schools, depend for their 'supporting frameworks' in respect of many vital functions such as communication upon informal structures (Nias *et al.*, 1989) and not upon organizational arrangements.

In this section we concentrate upon formal structures, including organizational arrangements, which facilitated whole school curriculum development, and particularly upon those relating to interaction, communication and decision-making. We have chosen to do this for two reasons. First we have already made extensive mention of informal structures (chapters 2, 3 and 4). Second, formal ones were in general consciously established and it is therefore particularly instructive to analyze the part which they played, or failed to play, in providing conditions favourable for whole school curriculum development.

This is not to say that we underestimate the importance of the informal (see chapter 3). Informal gatherings, such as friendship groups or after-school classroom conversations, often complemented formal meetings. Sometimes informal structures acted as a substitute for formal ones when the latter were absent or were inexpertly used. At others they fulfilled a different function, for example, by providing an unthreatening, discursive environment in which early thinking and trial encounters could be examined, expanded or dropped. Often they were essential to the development of collective goals and policies. However, precisely because they were informal, they could easily be used to promote the interests of individuals or sub-groups, especially on those occasions when seeking and valuing the common good was not a goal shared by all the staff. So, their usefulness therefore depended on the overall circumstances of the school and in particular upon the extent to which collaborative thinking and action were established staff norms.

In all the schools, there was an abundance of formal structures. Many of them brought people into contact with one another, and therefore were essential to the processes which enabled staff to learn from one another and work together. Many of them were also part of the school's communication and decision-making structures. Most of them are described and discussed in chapters 2, 3 and 4, so here we simply list the most important of them as a reminder of their range and variety: teaching and/or planning pairs or teams; 'critical friends'; small curriculum working parties; frequent and regular staff meetings; INSET meetings or days; rarely, non-contact time; school 'projects', journeys, fairs, productions and open evenings; assemblies.

There were several structures which were commonly and frequently used for curriculum planning, notably staff, year, team, or unit meetings, working parties and curriculum coordinators. Few formal structures existed for curriculum implementation, though coordinators were usually charged with a wide responsibility for the teaching of a particular curricular area. There were even fewer for evaluation and review, though teachers found their own ways, usually through informal meetings, to reflect upon their practice and especially upon innovations in which they had jointly engaged.

None of these structures served a single function. For example, staff meetings were used for the formal and informal exchange of news, views, arrangements and dates, to make decisions, to make curricular plans, to sort out minor differences between individuals, to give, receive and share ideas, to shape and sometimes to make policies, to influence the doubting or recalcitrant, to offer and receive mutual support and interest. They were often therefore confusing affairs for the observer and for the participant, since verbal and non-verbal exchanges moved swiftly and moods changed fast and subtly. They sometimes appeared to both participants and observers to be inefficient and formless, but viewed as part of a total process of development, they were invaluable because they required the presence and, usually, the participation of everyone, including at times the ancillary staff.

All in all, there was no shortage of formal structures in any of the schools. Nevertheless at some point during the year every school either lacked a structure with which to tackle a specific task or problem, failed to find an appropriate structure to meet a particular need, or used an existing structure in inappropriate ways. When any of these circumstances occurred, the efforts and ideas of individuals tended to remain undeveloped or to be under-exploited by their heads or their colleagues. There was a far higher level of expertise and of individual development in the schools than received collective attention during the year. This was partly because of other pressures upon teachers' time, but it was also, on occasion, because the means were lacking to make corporate use of such potential. We were conscious that lack of organizational support contributed to the foundering or under-development of curricular initiatives in the following areas in particular: sharing expertise (for example, the dissemination of new learning or information about courses; the productive use of visits from advisory teachers); the evaluation of existing initiatives (for example, school journeys, special needs policies); discovering what special contribution new teachers could make to the school curriculum; assessing what outside help the staff as a whole needed in particular areas and how best it could be obtained; deciding how to strike an equitable balance between the professional needs of individuals and those of the school as a whole:

For example, teachers at Upper Norton were repeatedly frustrated by the lack of opportunity to share what they had learnt on courses to which they had gone as delegates from the school:

> They attempt to have staff meetings in which people feed back after courses but this doesn't really come off, because staff meetings always have such very full agendas. If you know somebody's been on a course or has learnt something new, all you can do is to get hold of them and ask them specific questions. But learning is not shared and is constantly, therefore wasted. (Fieldnote, Upper Norton)

Similarly at Carey,

> The whole thing of Kate being on the assessment training... I read what she'd done. It didn't make a great deal of sense at the time. I'd have liked to have had more time or made myself look more closely at what Kate had done. (Teacher, Carey)

Kate herself felt that her attempts to disseminate her new knowledge among her colleagues had not been successful, because she had failed to create a structure which would involve her colleagues in their own learning:

> The idea of that building topic was to bring all the aspects of all the attainment targets and core curriculum together. The end results were there, but I don't know that the process really worked. I felt as though I was in the way, niggling at people to get little bits of work... I didn't do it very well... I should have got their ideas together to do the initial drawing of a topic chart and then they would have felt involved in it. But you live and learn! I learned a lot about communicating with other staff. (Teacher, Carey)

By contrast, the examples of the multicultural policy at Ingham and of Carey's renewed look at English in the light of the National Curriculum show how much could grow from an individual initiative when the relevant structures were in place and functioning smoothly. A similar point can be made in relation to curriculum leadership which is dealt with in greater detail later in this chapter. When leadership, whether from the head or from a curriculum coordinator, was vigorous, well-informed and clearly-focussed, development across the whole school was relatively swift and involved many teachers. By contrast, ideas sometimes failed to take off, or their impact was dissipated, when formal leadership was not available or was lacking in skill or direction.

Moreover, it was not enough for formal structures simply to exist. Heads, teachers and sometimes ancillary staff (for example, care assistants, nursery nurses) also needed to know how to make efficient use of them. They did not always appear to have this expertise. We marvelled at the skilled way in which the adults in the project schools used their informal communication channels and decision-making structures, fallible as these sometimes were. Sometimes too they handled formal structures in expert, though unorthodox ways (for example, digressions from the item under discussion and personal agendas were often constructively used in staff meetings to move collective thinking forward on particularly difficult issues). However many teachers did not seem familiar or comfortable with formal procedures, especially those associated with group discussion and decision-making. Ingham and Upper Norton were schools whose staff had grown accustomed under previous heads to a hierarchical and individualized distribution of power and responsibility. Some of the teachers there still needed time, practice and encouragement to come to terms with the more participative role in staff meetings that their current heads wanted, though at Ingham most of them took an active part in small working parties. By contrast, at Carey and Fenton and, on some occasions at Orchard, the staff were clearly accustomed to debating issues and to making collective decisions. They made good use of these opportunities.

Two areas stand out as examples where formal structures existed but were sometimes inexpertly or inappropriately used: collective decision-making and communication. For example, at staff meetings, it was not always clear whether items were for discussion or decision, agendas could be overcrowded, meetings sometimes started late and ran over time, chairpersons often allowed others to take up a disproportionate amount of time or did so themselves, sometimes they failed to notice the frustration or inattention of particular individuals, decisions were not always recorded or minutes kept. As a result of these and related shortcomings, at times meetings either seemed to have no clear objectives or failed adequately to meet those that they had. Disillusion, irritation and resentment sometimes resulted. As one teacher said,

> They're just so confusing. They're just people spouting, I think, and any decision that's made somehow gets lost in the process of making that decision. (Teacher, Orchard)

The poor functioning of formal communication structures also stood in the way of school development. For example, we recorded instances of key individuals not informed of ad hoc meetings; incoming INSET information not received or distributed; teachers not informed of changes to routine which affected their curricular plans; appointments missed; new teachers inadequately briefed or informed; headteachers made inaccessible to their staff by other claims on their time; ideas and information partially or randomly disseminated.

When formal communication failed or, in some cases, when it would have been inappropriate (for example, for ad hoc discussions of new curricular ideas), individuals had to rely heavily upon informal structures (such as the habit of meeting in the staffroom at a particular time, or a walk through the school). These were necessarily fallible and were, in addition, influenced by the architecture of the school (see also chapter 3.) Misunderstandings and inefficiencies resulted, tempers became frayed, especially in those schools where individual rather than shared responsibility was the norm. Much depended on the ability of the heads, themselves the victims of information overload, and their deputies to keep people individually informed and to act as go-betweens on matters of fact or opinion. The deputies, who often fulfil a communication role in primary schools, were all full-time class teachers, were often required to cover for heads absent on matters related to the 1988 Education Act and also held posts of curriculum responsibility. Perhaps in part as a result of these pressures, none of the deputies was as active as a communicator as our previous work on the Primary School Staff Relationships Project had led us to expect (Nias *et al.*, 1989).

At the start of this section, we suggested that structures are important within organizations because they help members to fulfil particular purposes. As we have shown in chapters 2, 3, and 4 whole school curriculum development depends on teachers learning, on staff working together, on the formulation of agreed goals and the implementation of common policies, on leadership and, as part of all of these on communication. The project schools were rich in informal and formal structures which helped to serve these functions, but the latter were not always appropriately or skilfully used.

Resources: Commitment, Time, People, Materials

No development, whether individual or corporate, could take place without resources. Lacking them, it was impeded or frustrated. When they existed and were productively used, initiatives moved forward swiftly and on a broad front. However, resources must be given a wide meaning, because heads and teachers felt the need not only for obvious items such as materials, equipment and space, but also for skilled personnel and above all for time.

We identified four main types of resource which had a clear bearing upon curriculum development, though the first two are closely linked. The most important was teachers' commitment, that is a 'readiness to allocate scarce personal resources' to work (Lortie, 1975, p. 189). Commitment was itself dependent on motivation, time, energy and the presence of other claims which individuals felt to be more immediate or more pressing than their own professional development or involvement in the concerns of others. The constant and most compelling preoccupation of the teachers in the project schools was the classes they taught; their own teaching and curricula were their chief priorities. Teachers who felt responsible for helping colleagues who lacked confidence, skills or knowledge carried additional burdens. Sometimes, when individuals were anxious about the progress or behaviour of children, when they were insecure, or lacking an appropriate skill, they found the time to learn from others (for example, by seeking advice from colleagues or going on courses). On many occasions however their felt-need to fulfil their main responsibility — to their own classes — reduced the amount of time and energy that they felt they had even for this kind of immediate problem-solving, let alone to foster their own development in wider ways. If they had any choice in the matter, most of these teachers gave the lowest priority of all to activities which appeared to have no obvious or immediate bearing upon their teaching.

As a result of all these pressures, the amount of attention which individual class teachers felt free to devote to school matters, such as writing policy documents or attending meetings outside 'directed time', fluctuated over the year and in response to other demands upon them. Shortage of material resources also affected the amount of motivation, time and energy they had to spare for activities outside the classroom. They often provided for their classes resources of their own (for example, maps, reference books), they made substitutes (for example, work cards), they begged or borrowed from the children's parents, their own family and friends and the community. But in the process, they expended effort and time which were not then available for other aspects of individual or school development.

Frequent alterations to school routine and wide-ranging changes in professional expectations also sapped their energy and, sometimes, morale, though individuals differed in their expressed need for either kind of stability. In chapters 1 and 3 we argued that change is an integral part of the primary teacher's work. We also demonstrated that this was a period during which all the schools faced a number of upheavals and additional demands upon their attention. Apart from anticipating the National Curriculum and adapting to other fundamental changes arising from the 1988 Education Act, they coped with building programmes; staff movements and absences; the presence of frequent supply teachers, often covering for teachers on National Curriculum-related courses; visitors (for example, advisory teachers), often also engaged in INSET; organizational changes and anxieties arising from staffing cuts or changes. In addition, the project schools were lively educational institutions, and 'projects' (for example, outings, productions, community involvements) abounded. Although, in general, teachers enjoyed these, they undoubtedly placed additional burdens upon them. On top of all this were personal worries and preoccupations, such as sickness, bereavement, financial problems, concerns over family matters. In addition, several teachers expressed a good deal of anxiety during the year about the likely impact of legislative changes upon their careers, their workload or the way in which they might have to teach in future. However, the point at which individual teachers allowed alternative claims upon them to interfere with their development activities was both personal and context-specific. Tolerance levels for pressure, tiredness and illness differed between individuals, were affected by events and circumstances in their personal lives, could be altered by individual enthusiasm and interest and interacted both with the morale of others in school and with organizational factors such as resource provision and effective communication.

To illustrate the level that demands over and above class teaching might place on heads and teachers, we summarize fieldnotes taken over a six week period in one school:

> (Commitments additional to class teaching were), in the daytime: liaison visits and transfer arrangements with three secondary schools; two intake afternoons for the new reception children; outings for classes 1, 2, 3, and 4; class photographs; a new vicar taking assembly on Wednesdays; a case conference; the appointment of a permanent teacher for the following year; visits by an adviser and an advisory teacher; a visiting governor; a music festival involving classes 3, 4 and 5; *The Firebird*; the Summer Fair; area sports; school sports; leavers' assembly; medicals; a tea party for parent volunteers; a teaching practice student on observation; another on a six-week practice; three work experience students; INSET courses involving four teachers (including the head), and two supply teachers. In addition, in the evenings, there were: three liaison meetings, a PTA meeting, four parents' evenings (for children of different ages), two heads' meetings, *The Firebird*, the governors' Annual Report to parents, two discos for children of different ages, drinks with the governors, and a retirement dinner for the caretaker. Furthermore, the builders were omnipresent, their noise, flaking paint, dust and spare materials filling the air, the lungs, the infants' sand tray, every flat surface and the playground. (Fieldnote, Upper Norton)

By the end of this period, three of the staff were receiving medical treatment and the rest looked and sounded exhausted. For the rest of the term they continued to give spasmodic attention to curricular initiatives intended for the next year, especially the planning of a whole-school topic and the development of paired observation in one another's classrooms. Overall, however, curriculum development, especially that involving collective discussion and decision-making did not receive much explicit attention during this period.

Yet, despite rival distractions such as those to which we have referred, many teachers in all the schools continued to show very high levels of commitment throughout the year. They poured their own time and often their money into development activities, carried along by their sense of responsibility for their pupils, by their own enthusiasm and by the enhanced self-esteem which came from success and recognition. Without their personal involvement and conscientiousness, several initiatives would probably have foundered, a point which is also strongly made by Campbell and Neill (1990) and Campbell *et al.* (1991). Personal commitment, tenacity and interest played such a marked part in individual and school development in all the schools that it would be invidious to select examples for particular attention.

That said, there were activities involving time away from individual teaching responsibilities which could be undertaken only when individuals were freed by their heads, a supply teacher, a student or occasionally, ancillary assistants. Lack of such time continued to limit and occasionally to frustrate learning and development throughout the year. Teachers frequently expressed the need for non-contact time so that they could learn in school from colleagues. Only in Orchard was any such time available. Here, by 'doubling up' for 'story' and by rotating responsibility for Monday assembly, all teachers had a small amount. Lacking non-contact time, teachers in the other schools knew that there were initiatives which they could not undertake or follow through, no matter how high their level of self-expenditure. Frustration and, more rarely, disillusionment resulted.

Related to the issue of commitment, but separate from it, was that of skilled personnel: to develop ideas, to act as teachers of both children and adults, to provide back up services such as typing and care for children with special learning needs. Not all of these people were teachers. Indeed an extremely important contribution was made by ancillary staff, such as secretaries, care assistants, nursery nurses, welfare assistants, and in some schools by parents and other volunteers. Sometimes they helped by relieving the burdens imposed on teachers by numbers, by disturbed children, by chores, such as washing paint pots or cleaning up vomit. At others they undertook essential out-of-classroom activities such as duplicating and making telephone calls. The ancillary staff actively contributed ideas, expertise, resources and personal enthusiasm to school activities (for example, productions, sports days) and to discussions of, for example, children's abilities and achievements, to displays and, less frequently, to assemblies. The role of advisory teachers who came into school explicitly to assist development and the use made of them are discussed in chapter 2. They too were an important and valued resource.

Lastly, there were physical resources. Some were essential. For example, without computers, there could be little effective development of an IT policy, proper equipment was needed for accurate pupil learning in science or mathematics, reading could not move forward without books. However, the presence of resources did not by itself guarantee either individual or school development. For example, at Upper Norton, musical instruments were exploited for everyone's benefit only when a music specialist joined the staff and taught her colleagues alongside their pupils. At Ingham, the mathematics resources available in individual cupboards were not fully or productively used until two enthusiastic teachers pressed their head and colleagues to explore what was available in the school and to sanction a centralized reorganization of it.

In summary, we suggest that a minimum level of resources, particularly of teacher commitment, of non-contact time, of skilled personnel and of specific technical equipment, is a necessary condition for whole school curriculum development. However, beyond that level, which itself varies from one school to another in response to existing provision and specific priorities, the value of resource-provision depends upon the uses to which they are put and the skill with which they are deployed. These in turn interact with other factors, in particular staff values, organizational and curricular structures, the ability of individuals to make appropriate use both of these and of the resources themselves. Issues relating to the provision and use of resources do not stand alone but are closely linked to the other conditions which we have highlighted in this section, and to the question of leadership.

Leadership

The fourth condition which influenced whole school curriculum development was leadership. We have already examined the central part played by headteachers in developing a sense of 'whole school' (see chapter 3). Here we wish to focus upon the part played by other leaders in whole school curriculum development.

There were two kinds of leaders in the schools; formal and

informal ones. Formal leadership occurred as a function of position and designated responsibilities in the school (for example, deputy heads; curriculum and INSET coordinators; unit leaders). Informal leadership could be exercised by anyone who wished to take responsibility for someone or something (for example, a newcomer to the staff; parental helpers; someone who wished to take the initiative in a specific curriculum area (for example, computers; art and craft) or activity (for example, an educational visit, a project planned for two or more classes)).

Although we do not intend to describe further the work of the heads, we need to make it clear that in all the schools they were paramount. All other formal leaders were subordinate to them. Deputies and coordinators were sponsored by their heads. They operated at the heads' behest or invitation and with their approval and backing. In turn, those who led did so in ways which supported and complemented the head's leadership. For example, the Deputy at Upper Norton saw her role as supporting the head in public. Others were conscious of keeping the head informed: INSET coordinators briefed their heads about developments taking place in the LEA and school cluster; unit leaders at Orchard made the head aware of successes and tensions in the units.

Supporting the head meant several things. It meant acting as an exemplar to colleagues. Those who led needed to demonstrate to others that their classwork reflected and embodied the head's and, where possible, the school's prevailing educational beliefs. This was particularly noticeable in the case of some of the deputies:

> She talked a little about the pressure of being the Deputy Head, the need to be an example of good practice in the school, to be particularly well-organized. (Fieldnote, Carey)

Deputies also usually modelled good practice in terms of punctuality and time-keeping and helped to generate a sense of 'whole school' by drawing colleagues' attention to school policies and rules:

> Dave talked about the rotas and timetables he was preparing and then, clearly with the Head's backing, reminded staff of a variety of good habits and disciplinary details with regard to pupils, playtimes, and lunchtimes, so that we all understood the rules and procedures. For example, whilst the weather was good all children would go out at breaks but when the weather becomes inclement children are given a choice of going out or

> staying in. If they stay in, their name must be put on the blackboard. (Fieldnote, Orchard)

Some of the deputies supported their heads by adding to the amount of praise and positive reinforcement dispensed in the school:

> Any opportunity I had to go into someone else's room, I'd always notice what was on the walls and make some sort of comment because...there's a side of me which knows that people like to know that they're being appreciated and what they're doing is valued and want to talk about it. (Deputy, Carey)

The deputies also helped to socialize staff and to maintain the underlying beliefs of the school by applying normative pressure.

Curriculum leaders helped to ensure breadth, in terms of curriculum attention and development. For example, at Ingham two teachers had joint responsibility for mathematics. As a result of their work outside the school (for example, on courses; in a maths support group) and then inside the school they felt they had given the subject 'a jolly good airing'. At Carey the allocation of curriculum responsibilities amongst the staff enabled individuals to consult with one another:

> The going to others for expertise is getting stronger and stronger now. People really know the strengths and weaknesses of everybody and they'll go and talk to the right person. (Teacher, Carey)

And:

> Now we all have posts of responsibility (there is) leadership from each one of us. (Teacher, Carey)

Elsewhere we have shown in detail how teachers undertook formal curriculum leadership (for example, chapter 3, the Maths Coordinators at Carey; chapter 4, the Deputy who was Technology Coordinator at Fenton) and accepted responsibility for organizing and leading INSET workshops in the school (see chapter 2). We do not, therefore, believe it is necessary to provide further illustrations of the coordinators' work.

However, there are three characteristics of formal leadership to which we wish to draw attention. First, since these formal leaders were generally supportive of their heads, they enhanced the latters' influence inside and outside the classrooms. Second, where their classroom practice exemplified the educational beliefs to which all staff were expected by the heads to be committed, they demonstrated the imperative nature of putting these beliefs into action. Since it was important in terms of developing a sense of 'whole school' that corporate beliefs be translated into action, it was, as a first step, essential that some staff attempt so to do. Many formal leaders fulfilled this requirement. Third, formal leadership contributed simultaneously to the development of the curriculum and to a sense of 'whole school'. Curriculum coordinators obviously played a part in developing aspects of the curriculum. However, since curriculum development rested upon teachers' learning, it was not sufficient for coordinators to alert staff to issues of curriculum content. They also needed to enable colleagues to learn (see chapter 2). Where coordinators could facilitate learning they had a more powerful impact upon the curriculum than when they could not. At the same time coordinators and deputies helped to establish some of the characteristics of 'whole schools'. Their active interest in how a particular curriculum area was being taught across the school demonstrated that teachers should not limit their knowledge of the school to their own classes. They exemplified the necessity of working together. They showed that it was possible for everyone to play an individual role within the school whilst remaining committed to collective goals. Also, they made it clear to colleagues that individuals could readily call upon one another's expertise.

Informal leaders also contributed to whole school curriculum development. Informal leadership could occur in several ways. Formal and informal leaders sometimes changed roles. For example, at Orchard Marion and Helen decided to take their classes on a visit to a local park. Marion was the unit leader on this occasion, but Helen took the lead in preparing and organizing the outing. A similar case was that of Dave and Jean in the second year unit: Dave was both the Deputy and unit leader and sometimes his attention was more taken up with the former than the latter. Consequently, on a day-to-day basis Jean assumed some of the unit leader's tasks:

Dave leaves the organization of the unit to me a lot of the time... I organized the language groups... So I think the organization (is) what I've developed this year. (Teacher, Orchard)

Occasionally, informal leaders became established through taking initiatives. At Upper Norton, the teacher of the upper junior (Y5 and 6) children, Nancy, organized the school's week-long field trip to the Isle of Wight. Although she had no formal post or allowance for this responsibility she nevertheless undertook the task with considerable energy and effort. During the spring term a preliminary evening's meeting with parents was held, during which the Head and Deputy, although present 'took a back seat; it was clearly Nancy's evening' (Fieldnote, Upper Norton). The venture involved much detailed planning and relied upon some common rules being set for all accompanying staff to follow. Again Nancy took the lead:

> Nancy started (the meeting of staff going on the journey) by saying, 'I'm not doing worksheets, the aim of the visit is that we should be recorders, they (the children) have got to learn by looking and listening and drawing and writing down.' Apparently each group or each class will be making a newspaper in the evenings. Otherwise it was what one would expect — safety, daily checkings for footwear, pocket money and so on.... We then went back to Nancy's classroom and looked at the names of the children who had been allotted to various groups. Nancy has given herself most of the potentially troublesome ones. (Fieldnote, Upper Norton)

Sometimes they emerged spontaneously. For example, Ingham was awarded by the Parish Council £300 worth of trees to plant on the school's playing field. Natalie was instrumental in overseeing the siting and planting of these trees, although she involved other members of staff. At others, leadership was bestowed upon individuals, usually where they were perceived to have a specific curriculum interest or expertise. For example, at Orchard staff spoke to Dave about computers, not because he was Deputy but because he was regarded as knowing more than them about IT. In chapter 2 there are similar examples of staff asking colleagues for help and advice.

When informal leaders gave advice and practical help they not only led colleagues, they also helped them to learn. Informal leaders contributed to teachers' development as much as formal ones, as was recognized at Fenton:

We were just saying yesterday, each person has different strengths and it's in combining those strengths that the children get the best out of us all. But it doesn't mean that because I'm good at something or someone else is good at something that we want to stay in those pockets... Here everyone wants to learn from everyone else and that's so lovely. (Teacher, Fenton)

Many teachers also led through guiding and directing the work of other adults who might be helping them in the classroom. At Upper Norton, for example, the principle was gradually established that the classteacher was in overall control under almost all circumstances (for example, with part-time teachers, students, welfare assistants, supply staff). As was the case in similar instances in the other schools, all classteachers thereby became accustomed to leading adults.

Informal leadership was important for five reasons. First, it enabled individuals to use their initiative when they assumed responsibility for something or someone. Being able to use that individual initiative in this way was a safety valve for those who might otherwise have felt stifled by a narrow adherence to corporate goals. Second, as staff took on leadership roles they increased their awareness of others. Both the leader and the led became less isolated. Third, when staff took a lead they accepted responsibility for others and thereby modelled interdependence rather than independence. Fourth, they helped to spread ideas amongst colleagues and fostered peer learning. Fifth, informal leadership provided individuals with the opportunity to try out leadership, to experience taking on additional responsibilities and to become used to working with adults rather than purely with children. For some, this was a preparation for accepting a formal leadership role either in their present school or elsewhere. However, perhaps more telling than such career development, was the fact that the more staff there were who took a lead, the more individuals there were who each, separately and together, played an active part in whole school curriculum development.

So, informal leaders supplemented the work of formal leaders. The presence of both kinds of leaders in a school signalled that leadership itself was flourishing and with it the likelihood that a sense of 'whole school' and the curriculum were also developing, since each kind of leadership contributed to both developments. Conversely, the absence of leadership meant whole school curriculum development was likely to be inhibited.

Conclusion

In previous chapters, we have examined various aspects of whole school curriculum development and the processes through which it takes place. Although we presented in the Introduction the salient features of the schools on whose work we based our conclusions, we have not directly described them in any further detail. We may therefore have given the erroneous impression that each school was equally well equipped to engage in the complex and difficult task of developing a curriculum whose principles were understood and shared by all the staff and which they implemented in similar ways. This is not the case. In this chapter we have identified the organizational, professional and interpersonal conditions which seemed to make it easier for some heads, teachers and ancillary staff, at some times, to engage in professional learning, and to develop both a 'whole school' and a 'whole school' curriculum. We have also shown that when these conditions were absent development was slower, more difficult and less sustained. We have highlighted five institutional values and have suggested that the prior existence of some of these in two schools in particular put their teachers in a good position to embark upon whole school curriculum development. These schools had a 'culture of collaboration' which ensured that the staff placed a high value upon a sense of interdependence and teamwork and were predisposed to deal openly, but with respect for one another's need for security, with their personal and professional differences and disagreements. In addition, all the schools valued individuals, a fact which staff showed by behaving towards one another with consideration, sensitivity, kindness and supportiveness; and a willingness to resolve problems and disagreements through compromise and negotiation. These two values simultaneously encouraged the growth of a 'culture of collaboration' in the schools where this culture did not already exist and made it easier for everyone to learn from others and work together with them. In other words, when a staff group had one or more of these values in common, they were more likely to engage productively in shared learning, in building together an educational community and in the processes of whole school curriculum development than when they did not. There was, in addition, a fifth important value: The staff in all the schools pursued and esteemed professional learning for its own sake and this in turn encouraged a school climate favourable to curriculum development.

These institutional values and the behaviours which grew from them were not by themselves sufficient to promote whole school curriculum development. Suitable organizational structures were also needed, especially for learning and working together (and therefore for interaction) and for communication and decision-making. Further, the staff had to know how to use them in constructive ways. When either structures or the ability to use them were lacking, initiatives sometimes foundered and developments moved slowly or with unnecessary difficulty.

Resources too were essential. Whole school curriculum development proceeded more smoothly and with greater momentum when the school had staff with appropriate expertise who were prepared to commit their own energy and resources to development, and who, most crucially, had the time to do so. Adequate material resources were also important, and so too was the presence of capable teaching and ancillary staff. However, none of these forms of resource could be utilized to its full advantage in the absence of appropriate structures and of the wish to direct them with enthusiasm to corporate ends.

Underpinning these three sets of conditions is, therefore, a fourth — the leadership provided by headteachers and those whom they sponsored, backed or approved. Effective leadership fostered values and the relationships which sprang from and reinforced them. It created structures and monitored their use, provided and arranged for the optimal use of resources. Yet leadership itself could not operate independently of institutional values, and without the support of appropriate people and forms of organization. Culture, structures, resources and leaders were interdependent and interactive, forming a complex matrix within which developments were conceived and nurtured, or stunted and aborted.

Chapter Six

Summary and Conclusions

This chapter is organized into three sections. The first section summarizes the main findings of the project. The second considers the conclusions which we feel may be drawn from them. The third looks at the implications of the conclusions for those who work in primary schools and are concerned with their development.

Summary of the Main Findings

In the Introduction we provide background information about the project and the five schools in which we worked and from which we gathered our data. In addition we draw attention to the three themes which occur throughout this book. The first concerns the beliefs held by the teachers in the five project schools about the purposes of education and how these might best be achieved. The second is the variety of ways in which teachers professionally interacted and by so doing developed, established and sustained shared beliefs about their purposes and practice. Third, teachers learned from and with one another in numerous ways and so developed the curriculum in accordance with these emerging or established beliefs. These three themes relate strongly to notions of 'whole school' and whole school curriculum development. Moreover, they intertwine and often need to be considered simultaneously.

Chapter 1 explores what the teachers in the project schools understood by the terms 'curriculum', 'curriculum development' and 'whole school', Curriculum was perceived in terms of children's learning. Yet, although the central purpose of each school was to ensure the maximum possible learning of all its pupils, teachers directly and indirectly determined much of the content of the curriculum and almost all the ways in which it was transmitted. They assumed freedom of choice in most areas of their teaching behaviour and classroom management. Thus, within a single school we noted differences in organization and teaching style. Also, teachers in their comments did not differentiate between the 'curriculum' and classroom practice. Curriculum then, was a comprehensive term covering all aspects of classroom activity for which teachers felt responsible. However, there were constraints upon teachers for whilst they assumed a measure of freedom and control over curriculum content they did not look for total autonomy. For example, they respected notions of curriculum breadth, balance and continuity. Also, in some schools more than others, notions of progression in the curriculum were prevalent and teachers planned their work with this in mind. Although there were constraints upon the teachers they nevertheless behaved as if they 'owned' the curriculum: they sought to control it and had internalized it to such an extent that they spoke as if it was part of them. Because of their sense of accountability to their pupils and for their learning these teachers felt the need to exercise control over all aspects of the curriculum.

Given the comprehensive nature of 'curriculum' and teachers' individual feelings of responsibility and control it is not surprising that 'curriculum development' emerged as both a broad concept and a personal process. Indeed, teachers' and curriculum development were inseparable. Further, development could take place in different ways. For the heads, development meant encouraging members of staff to show allegiance to the educational beliefs around which they intended the practice of the school to be built. They also sought to foster a climate in which every aspect of the school, except its fundamental educational beliefs, was open to critical enquiry and capable of being improved.

Teachers in all five schools shared seven similar beliefs about the nature of a 'whole school'. These were: first, each member of the staff group aspired to belong to a community. Second, they shared the same educational beliefs and aims and interpreted these in similar ways in their actions. Third, they worked together as a team to develop and implement policy, share decision-making and cope with crises. Fourth, they each exercised a degree of autonomy within their own classrooms, felt able to play an individual role within the school and readily called on one another's expertise. Sixth, their knowledge of the school was not limited to matters of immediate concern to themselves and their own classes but extended to the concerns and practice of colleagues and their classes. Finally, they valued the leadership of their headteacher. In addition, no teacher or headteacher claimed their's was a 'whole school'; rather, it was an ideal to pursue.

Chapter 2 shows that teachers and heads regarded professional learning as the key to the development of the curriculum. Four things helped to increase the capacity of the teachers in the project schools to engage in professional learning: they were motivated to learn; opportunities existed for them to learn both inside and outside the school; appropriate means of learning were used; and learning took place under favourable conditions.

Staff were motivated to learn because they generally accepted that it was necessary to be constantly seeking to improve, recognized good practice in the work of their colleagues and appraised their own work. Moreover, these teachers worked in schools where colleagues were learning; each individual was a member of a community of learners and so they all recognized they were not alone in their need to learn.

Opportunities to acquire knowledge and skills existed in all the schools and were of five different types. First, teachers explicitly took on the role of learners (for example, attending INSET; learning from 'experts' in the school). Second, staff were inducted into a school's norms, sometimes informally, sometimes formally (for example, 'apprenticeship schemes'). Third, opportunities to learn existed when teachers worked together, which they did in a variety of ways in all the schools. Fourth, learning took place incidentally as teachers saw and heard about colleagues' practice. Fifth, when individuals took on some new responsibility within the school they increased their own knowledge and understanding.

The success of the opportunities to learn rested, in part, on how they were carried out. Teachers made productive use of four means of learning: talk, observation, practice and reflection. Conditions for learning were favourable when they satisfied teachers' physical needs (for example, they were rested, relaxed), their affective needs (for example, emotional support) and took place in an appropriate context (for example, sufficient time, space, materials).

Chapter 3 argues that developing a sense of 'whole school' depended on the existence of both leadership and staff collaboration. The analysis of leadership in this chapter is confined to the part played by the headteachers in developing a sense of 'whole school'. They sought to establish and sustain a set of educational beliefs, their educational visions, around which they expected the school to cohere. In striving to establish and maintain an educational community in which everyone subscribed to the same values and goals the heads relied upon both their authority and their influence, being sometimes direct, sometimes indirect in the ways they helped teachers to put the beliefs into action. These heads also possessed four professional attributes: at heart they were educators; they could strike a balance amongst competing demands and tensions in the school; they were patient and persistent; they had a marked capacity to perceive and make connections between the work of staff members.

We noted seven forms of professional interaction which together also helped the staff to develop a sense that theirs were 'whole schools'. They provided opportunites for staff members: to collaborate; to share, challenge and extend one another's aims and values; to exchange ideas and practices and to modify these when they saw fit; to play an individual role within a team; and to lead and accept responsibility for others. Moreover, collective events such as concerts and plays helped to build both a sense of the school as an organizational entity and a knowledge that the staff's shared success resulted from their teamwork. However, no form of collaboration was problem free. There was an ever present tension between teachers feeling responsible and in control of what went on in their classrooms and the fact that in a 'whole school' responsibility and control are shared with others. Also, working with others involved professional self-exposure. In turn, self-exposure laid teachers open to the judgment of others who might have dissimilar values and methods. Lastly, the occupational traditions of primary teachers favour independence rather than interdependence so some of them were unaccustomed, even resistant to working with others.

Chapter 4 considers the notion of 'whole school curriculum development', regarding it as more than the sum of 'whole school' and 'curriculum development'. Whole school curriculum development is defined as a dynamic process in which beliefs and values are translated into action, but in which a common commitment to learning also means both principles and practice are continually reviewed and re-interpreted. This definition is illustrated by the way staff in one school, Fenton, tried to ensure progression in children's learning. Moreover, the development and implementation of a curriculum which affected the practice of all the staff in a school differed in kind, not simply in degree, from, on the one hand, the professional development of individual teachers and, on the other, the growth among them of a sense of educational community.

The key to this understanding of whole school curriculum development is learning. As chapter 2 shows, individual teachers in these schools pursued their own professional development. However, they were also involved in three other learning processes which often seemed to be occurring simultaneously. First, staff needed to learn about the beliefs and values which underpinned their school's work. Next, they had to acquire the knowledge and skills with which they to put these beliefs into action. Third, as they took part individually and collectively in these forms of learning they reflected upon and modified the framework of principle and practice which itself determined their learning. We have called the process by which beliefs and values are spread amongst staff members 'learning what'. 'Learning how' describes how staff acquire appropriate practical expertise. Whole school curriculum development takes place when both types of learning result in deepened understanding of a school's beliefs and of what these look like in practice.

Chapter 5 identifies four sets of conditions which facilitated or inhibited whole school curriculum development. None was, by itself, sufficient though each was necessary, since the absence of any one of them caused developments to falter or to fail to take root.

The first set of conditions was appropriate institutional values. We noted five: learning; interdependence and teamwork; the open expression of professional differences; mutual consideration and support; willingness to compromise. The last four of these are also characteristic of a 'culture of collaboration' (Nias *et al.*, 1989).

The second set of conditions which affected the staffs' ability to develop the curriculum in a holistic way was the presence or absence of organizational structures especially for professional interaction, communication, joint decision and policy making. Individuals also needed to be able to use them constructively. All the schools had many such structures, none of which served just one function. However, at some point in the year every school either lacked a structure with which to tackle a particular issue or failed to use or apply an existing structure in appropriate ways. When formal structures failed, staff relied heavily upon informal ones (for example, for communication). Indeed, these schools were as rich in informal structures as they were in formal ones and the two often complemented and supplemented one another.

The third set of conditions was resources, especially teacher commitment, time, people and materials; and the structures which enabled each of these to be used.

Leadership, both formal and informal, was the fourth condition. The leadership of the head was paramount and all other formal leaders were sponsored by their heads, operated at their behest and with their approval and backing. In turn, the formal leaders supported their heads, especially by acting as exemplars to other members of staff, offering additional positive reinforcement, and socializing newcomers into the prevailing norms and values. Curriculum leaders helped to ensure the availability of expertise in subject areas. Informal leaders showed additional individual initiative and helped colleagues to learn through practical help and advice. They also helped their colleagues to be aware of others, modelled interdependence, facilitated the spread of ideas and the taking-up of responsibilities.

There is one other point to make. Throughout the book we emphasize the polyphonic nature of whole school curriculum development. Although in each chapter we focus upon specific characteristics, structures, and processes, all of them interact. Moreover, each serves more than one purpose. In short, whole school curriculum development is complex and dynamic, a point we make in the conclusions and to which we now turn.

Conclusions

There are a number of conclusions which we feel may be drawn from our study. They are presented here in three groups: the nature of primary schools as organizations; the complexity of whole school curriculum development; the importance of leadership and membership. They are major, and sometimes recurring themes in the book. We will consider each in turn.

The Nature of Primary Schools as Organizations

As organizations primary schools are complex. We have made this claim in other places. For example, we have said that primary schools are made up of a number of parts:

> A school is not, in fact, a monolithic organization. Rather, it is a composite of many different parts (people, buildings, teams and groups, beliefs and values) which all need to be accommodated or reconciled to one another before they fit together. The 'whole school' needs to be understood in terms of the complexity and number of its constituent parts. (*ibid*, p. 178)

This view is supported by this research whose evidence further suggests that primary schools have three structural characteristics which make them complex: interconnectedness; simultaneity; and redundancy.

Interconnectedness, a term which describes the close way each part of a school interrelated with one or more other parts, was a feature common to all the schools. For example, teacher development related to curriculum development; each of the seven characteristics of a 'whole school' interacted with one or more of the others; and attention to a single aspect of the curriculum had an impact upon other curriculum areas and organizational matters (for example, staff responsibilities; resources). In other words, whilst it was possible to focus, for a short time, upon a single aspect of the school or curriculum, one could not ignore its relationship with its context. Because of the way each aspect impinged upon others and intertwined with them, attention always needed to be given, often at the same time, to more than one aspect of the school.

These schools were also characterized by simultaneity, for not only did all aspects of the school impinge upon others but they did so at the same time. As the schools attempted to develop aspects of their respective curricula they were simultaneously engaged, or needed to embark upon: individual teacher developments; the modification and spreading of particular educational beliefs and practices; the absorption of externally generated and imposed changes (for example, the introduction of the National Curriculum, LEA curriculum initiatives); planning and preparing projects, concerts, holidays and visits; remaining alert to the concerns of parents; all the day-to-day tasks which need to be undertaken and discharged to keep a school functioning efficiently (for example, pastoral care for the children and staff; lesson preparation; pupil discipline; maintenance of equipment and resources). At any one time the staff of each school were dealing with a multiplicity of issues, concerns and tasks.

The combination of interconnectedness and simultaneity resulted in overlapping organizational and managerial arrangements. Many staff members worked on the same tasks either together or separately. Overall, there was much duplication of effort, with more than one person doing the same thing at the same or a different time. This reminded us of what Landau (1969) has described as redundancy. Like a commercial aircraft, every vital function in a primary school can be carried out by more than one component, creating in its members confidence in its strength (Nias, 1987). Hence, the duplication which occurred in these schools was not a weakness in their organization, but a strength. The redundant nature of the school structure provided opportunities for many, sometimes all members of staff to take part in developments and 'projects'. It created opportunities for all members of staff to become accustomed to taking on responsibilities beyond the confines of their classrooms and, sometimes, to lead colleagues and accept responsibility for them. Participation in common tasks also involved contact with colleagues and opportunities for mutual support. Another consequence of overlapping responsibilities was that some members of staff could usually act as substitutes for temporarily absent colleagues without causing undue stress or shock to the school's organization.

Together these three characteristics mean that the formal organizational and curricular structure of the project schools were neither neat nor tidy. Although in each school there was a measure of structural clarity, created by the use of job descriptions, defined roles, working parties, meetings and agreed plans for curriculum developments and projects, the formalized duties of members of staff became blurred because it was not always possible, nor desirable, to restrict individuals to a single-minded approach to developments. As organizational structures these schools can best be described as 'webs' rather than 'trees', since they consisted of dense networks of responsibilities and relationships which interwove and interpenetrated.

The Complexity of Whole School Curriculum Development

Given the intricate, interdependent nature of primary schools it is not surprising that the process of developing 'whole school' curricula within them should also be complex. There are five reasons for this. The first lies in the nature of complexity itself. LaPorte (1975) has suggested that the complexity of a system is a function of the number of components, how differentiated they are and the extent of their interdependence. Even in a small primary school such as Upper Norton the number of adults directly or indirectly involved with the curriculum is considerable and they are markedly interdependent for the fulfilment of their individual and shared tasks and responsibilities. To be sure, their roles are not always very strongly differentiated, but even with this qualification primary schools can, in LaPorte's terms, be described as very complex social systems. The second reason overlaps with this one; the very complexity of the school as a total organization is mirrored in its parts. The development of an agreed curriculum within a 'whole school' takes place by means of two processes: learning 'what' (i.e. gradually persuading staff members and others that the underlying curricular principles of an innovation can be reconciled with their developing or established beliefs) and learning 'how' (i.e. slowly enabling all the staff to acquire the technical competencies to translate these principles into action in ways that are compatible with their beliefs and consistent from one classroom to another). Yet because of the interdependent nature of the primary school as an organization these processes normally take place at the same time and by means of the same activities, events and structures.

There are three other reasons for the complexity of whole school curriculum development, each of them deriving from the central part that teachers' professional learning plays in such development. The phrase itself has two components which represent separate but inter-locking aspects of primary teachers' perspectives and aspirations. Be-cause teachers generally perceive the curriculum as their individual responsibility, under their control and mediated through their own interests, priorities and capabilities, they tend to see curriculum de-velopment as a matter of their own professional learning. But since many of them also want to work in 'whole schools', they are under a self-imposed pressure to develop with their colleagues shared educa-tional purposes and common classroom practices. They have to keep these two opposing tendencies in balance and daily find a compromise between them. Yet, second, this balance is a dynamic one, not just because the professional lives and circumstances of primary teachers are always changing, but because the learning which takes place when the curriculum is developed within a 'whole school' makes profession-al growth a corporate as well as an individual responsibility. During and as a result of this collective learning, the educational basis of the 'whole school' itself subtly changes, ensuring that staff members' need to go on learning is perpetuated. Moreover, third, the fact that the professional learning of adults is at the heart of whole school curric-ulum development is also significant, for such learning is not com-partmentalized, linear and easy to acquire but interrelated, erratic, wide-ranging and full of emotional risk.

Small wonder, then, that whole school curriculum development is also full of tension. In the project schools, this took many forms. For example, there were structural tensions arising from intercon-nectedness and simultaneity (for example, members of staff perform-ing the dual roles of classteacher and coordinator). There were tensions over the allocation of resources (for example, materials and equipment, use of time, use of ancillary staff). Other differences arose from personal likes and dislikes. All these were part of the underlying tensions between individual and collective goals which affected every-one in the school. When the teachers were actively concerned to move closer together in terms of educational beliefs and classroom practices, they could make progress towards this end only by overcoming or reconciling differences between them. Sometimes these differences touched upon strongly held beliefs about the nature of teaching and learning and those who held them did not always feel they could change them to fit in with others. At others they arose from the tension between change and continuity which existed when, for example, staff were determining which area or areas of the curriculum to focus upon. Individual teachers' preferences differed and not all were necessarily as committed to the collective choice as were their colleagues. The simultaneous existence of internal and external curricular demands further complicated the picture. The scheduling of National Curriculum requirements was quite arbitrary insofar as each school was concerned. All of them had already embarked upon their own programmes of curriculum review and development before the National Curriculum Council's programme cut across and ran counter to these plans. In some schools the arrival of the National Curriculum was sometimes a source of frustration, especially when it required staff to return to an aspect of the curriculum they felt they had already dealt with in sufficient detail, or when it prevented them from focussing upon an area which was currently of greater concern to them.

These tensions made whole school curriculum development a fragile business. Each form of tension could adversely affect the commitment of individual members of staff to agreed developments. Some forms of tension (for example, those associated with change and external demands; interpersonal tensions) could disturb the emotional climate within the school, unsettling some members of staff and hindering them, or making them reluctant to participate fully with others and with developments in the school. Where tensions adversely affected teachers' enthusiasm for working with others or their commitment to an agreed policy, progress towards whole school curriculum development was held back or halted.

However, the fragility of whole school curriculum development cannot simply be attributed to the attitudes of individuals or the emotional climate within the school. Changes in personnel, such as the departure of the head at Fenton, and the impending absence of the deputy at Orchard made it plain that such development could be impeded or set back by factors beyond the control of the school. Indeed, it could even, on occasion, be put into reverse. Although the staff in each school believed they had embarked upon a journey towards a whole school curriculum, their journeys were along pathways which sometimes ascended, sometimes fell away, sometimes moved steadily forwards and sometimes turned back. When the Head of Ingham said that she felt the school was edging towards the goal of becoming a 'whole school' she not only accurately captured the pace but also the precarious nature of the enterprise.

There is one further point to make. Whole school curriculum development is not a natural process. There are two reasons for this view. First, the individualistic traditions of primary teaching work against, rather than in favour of, developing a sense of a 'whole school'. Second, the teachers in the project schools had a felt need to control the curriculum which they saw as being an individual responsibility rather than a collective one. The teachers who initiated developments did not necessarily have a view of the curriculum offered to other pupils than their own. Generating a sense of community and collective responsibility was necessary, therefore, not just to establishing a sense of 'whole school' but also to the development of a whole school curriculum. It follows then that a 'whole school' is not an indulgence for the staff; it is not a comfortable and cosy 'club'. It has to be forged, long and painfully, if a whole school curriculum is to be a reality.

The Importance of Leadership and Membership

The headteachers and other leaders in the project schools played a crucial part in enabling their colleagues to develop the curriculum and to work together.

The heads played a prominent part in articulating a set of educational beliefs around which they expected the school as a whole to cohere. They were assiduous and persistent in promoting and sustaining these beliefs, both directly and indirectly. Using a mix of authority and influence, they sought to educate their colleagues so that they too would share those beliefs. In this task they were assisted by other leaders in the school (for example, deputies, coordinators), especially when these people too already shared the same educational values as their heads.

The heads also played an important role in trying to ensure that school policies and developments were adhered to and put into practice. They attempted to do this in two main ways. First, they monitored the extent to which practices in classrooms reflected agreed policies. They toured the school, visited classrooms with some regularity and attended 'showing' assemblies. Moreover, staff in the schools knew that their heads were observing them and saw this as a legitimate part of their leadership. Second, when the heads were aware that some individuals were finding acceptance of a school policy difficult, either because they were philosophically opposed to the policy or because they found it difficult to implement in practice, then the heads negotiated with them. When faced with differences between themselves and an individual the heads sought a compromise acceptable to themselves and their colleague. They did this because they were anxious to preserve an appearance, at the very least, of shared beliefs and common practice. Similarly, they also wished to avoid any differences which existed between themselves and members of staff from becoming so wide that they could not be bridged in the future. In both cases, they appeared to be trying to keep a sense of 'whole school' alive so that when circumstances once again became favourable they could resume the move towards it. As they fostered a feeling among the staff that theirs was a 'whole school' and developed a whole school curriculum, the heads acted as negotiators, much practised in the arts and skills of micropolitics and diplomacy.

However, the heads were assisted in this political activity by the fact that the teachers believed their heads should take the lead when differences emerged amongst them which they could not solve by mutual negotiation. Under these circumstances the teachers looked to their heads to help them reach workable agreements. In all the schools, staff tacitly accepted that the head should arbitrate on behalf on them all when no other consensus could be reached. The teachers also accepted the heads' right to have the final say on school policy decisions even when this involved a veto of staff decisions. These heads were usually consultative and all of them valued teacher participation in curriculum development and review, but their behaviour was consistent with the established picture of primary headship. They were central and powerful figures in 'their' schools and remained in control of developments which took place within them.

Although the heads were central figures in the schools, their leadership was supported by that of other colleagues. These other leaders also played a part in promoting the flow of ideas and initiatives, in helping to establish both commonly agreed policies and similar classroom practices, and in ensuring that developments occurred both within individual classrooms and across the school. Specific curriculum developments were often the responsibility of deputy heads or coordinators. However, in addition, other members of staff took on leadership roles in relation to particular areas of school life such as school journeys, parents' workshops, concerts and fund-raising events. By means of these activities they helped their colleagues to work together and modelled a pattern of widely dispersed leadership. Moreover, they demonstrated that teachers should be concerned with matters beyond the confines of their individual class-rooms. In ways such as these they contributed to creating a sense of 'whole school' and an awareness that the curriculum was a collective concern.

Although leadership was crucial to all these aspects of whole school curriculum development the leaders were reliant upon the active membership of colleagues. Groups are only as strong as their members. The willingness of individual members to join and actively participate in groups and teams was a notable feature of these schools. This was possibly due, in part, to the skill of the heads and other leaders, when, for example, they managed productive meetings and helped to establish a context where all felt valued and involved. Nevertheless, teachers themselves were also responsible for their own level of participation. However, not all members of staff in all of the schools were always willing to work with one another. On the occasions when they were ready to take part in school policy decisions, to accept responsibility for others, to be aware of events beyond the confines of their classrooms and to plan activities and projects which involved their colleagues, they helped to create a context to which everyone contributed and in which a sense of school identity was forged. Such involvement was particularly impressive given that participation in groups was a costly exercise. Involvement required each teacher to invest substantial amounts of time. Yet time was something of which all teachers felt very short, since they had many other demands upon their attention (for example, individual needs of children, preparation, marking, lesson planning, classroom organiza-tion, INSET). In other words, the extent of their involvement with others should neither be overlooked nor taken for granted.

Implications

We wish now to stress four implications of these findings for those who work in primary schools and are concerned with their develop-ment. They are concerned with: the way school development is con-ceptualized; collegiality; organizational culture; resource provision.

First, in recent years educationalists have advocated a systematic approach to school and curriculum development (for example, Joyce *et al.*, 1983; McMahon *et al.*, 1984; DES, 1990a). Such a systematic approach emphasizes the need for serialized, step-by-step planning and implementation. However, we have shown that development in these schools was seldom like that. Often it was neither sequential nor 'rational' in a linear sense. Particular curriculum developments were sometimes spontaneous, at others they seemed opportunistic, as heads or members of staff capitalized upon the curricular interest or class-room experiments of an individual. Curriculum review too was fluid and, sometimes, improvized. Neither development nor review were pre-arranged and pre-programmed except on a minority of occasions.

Yet there was no shortage of development. In part, the way the staff in these schools approached curriculum development can be explained by the complexity of the organization, particularly by the way developments interconnected and occurred simultaneously. Typi-cally, for example, these teachers were dealing with several concerns at once and, since one aspect of the school interrelated with many others, it was not always possible, nor practicable, to try to focus upon a single aspect of the curriculum. Moreover, the complexity of the organization was compounded by the complexity of the processes of whole school curriculum development.

Another complicating factor was the fact that whole school curri-culum development itself relied upon the willingness and the capacity of individuals and groups to learn. Yet, since the process of learning can cause learners to experience uncertainty, doubt, a loss of confi-dence and threats to their self-image, curriculum development is a rather more uncertain, painful and imprecise process than those who advocate a systematic approach assume. Nias (1991) has argued that the experience of widespread curricular change in primary schools is akin to bereavement. While this overstates the suffering and confusion caused by the learning which made whole school curriculum develop-ment possible in the project schools, it draws attention to the emo-tional costs of such learning and the fact that school leaders and improvers neglect them only at their peril.

There are two further objections to perceiving curriculum de-velopment as systematic. First, it takes little account of the way circumstances can alter in schools. Initiatives can be overtaken by events elsewhere (for example, legislation) or inhibited by changes in the school (for example, personnel). Either or both of these can have the effect of altering the pace and tempo of development. They can also make school initiatives redundant or adversely affect the staff to such an extent that developments temporarily halt or even regress. Insufficient attention has been paid to these aspects of curriculum development. Previously published work takes too optimistic, or even naive, a view of the complexities and inherent difficulties of whole school curriculum development.

Second, whole school curriculum development depends upon the acceptance, by at least a majority of the teaching staff, that the educational community to which they belong is built upon shared beliefs about its purposes and the best means of accomplishing these, and upon a willingness to act accordingly. Individual learning takes place within this context and cannot be seen as separate from it; indeed the two interrelate. Whole school curriculum development is therefore likely to involve the slow, halting and difficult process of persuading some teachers to change their educational beliefs and values. Moreover, not all teachers are likely to be willing to alter their professional values. Yet those who prescribe a systematic and holistic approach to school development tend to overlook how hard it can be to change individuals' beliefs and values. They have also failed to suggest that the process is likely to be a protracted one. Furthermore, the fact that the process of development requires teachers to change, modify or extend their beliefs raises questions about the wisdom of trying to apply to all schools a single approach to school development. Some schools will certainly not be able, because of the differences in educational beliefs which exist between members of staff, to undertake a holistic approach to the curriculum.

School development planners are not wrong to prescribe clarity and certainty, but they also need to recognize that ambiguity and uncertainty will have a major impact upon the process of curriculum development. Equally, we believe that whilst formal structures and a planned approach play an important role in such development, there is a need to appreciate the part also played by informal patterns of staff interaction. The two co-exist and complement each other. Only when there is appreciation of both will the nature and scope of the activity of whole school curriculum development be fully understood.

Moreover, it is much easier to call for 'whole school' policies and plans than to create the conditions in school for them to be realized. 'Whole school' approaches have an increasing currency. Indeed, the phrase is in danger of becoming a slogan (for example, DES, 1989a; Ainscow and Muncey, 1989), the use of which can distract attention from the inherent complexities, difficulties and fragility of the process of whole school curriculum development.

By the same token, our findings also have implications for the concept of collegiality. During the 1980s collegiality was advanced as the way forward for primary schools (Campbell, J., 1985 and 1989; Lieberman, 1986; DES, 1980, 1982 and 1984b; Welsh Office, 1985; ILEA, 1985; House of Commons, 1986). As Wallace (1988) argues, these writers consistently advocated a model of good management practice: all professional staff participate actively in negotiating an agreed curriculum and contribute jointly to planning, implementing and evaluating its delivery. Used in this sense, collegiality implies a high degree of consultation amongst staff, their collaboration in co-ordinating the curriculum and their participation in policy decision-making (Campbell, J., 1985). It is also sometimes taken to mean that curriculum decision-making in school will be democratic (Wallace, 1988). Furthermore, collegiality is often used as a synonym of 'whole school'.

However, we have noted in this project that the heads of the project schools were central, powerful figures who exercised a controlling influence upon the school and its development. Several writers have doubted the compatibility of such a role for the head with a collegial approach to management (Alexander, 1984; Campbell, J., 1985; Southworth, 1987; Campbell and Southworth, 1990). Certainly, we would not make the claim that the project schools were collegial ones. Rather, we believe it is necessary to draw a distinction between 'whole schools' and collegial ones. In 'whole schools' it appears to be acceptable to both the heads and the teachers that the head plays a powerful and pivotal role. By contrast, in collegial schools, because such a role conception for the head is regarded as a barrier to collegiality (Campbell, J., 1985), the head would act differently. Moreover, in 'whole schools' there is a high degree of consultation but, given the heads' role, this should not be mistaken for teacher democracy. Consultative schools are not necessarily democratic ones.

The third implication of our findings relates to school culture. When we completed the Primary School Staff Relationships Project (Nias *et al.*, 1989) we were left with a puzzle. The project identified and described a particular organizational culture which we called the 'culture of collaboration'. Whilst this culture appeared to be effective in enabling staff to work together, both socially and professionally, it did not always follow that the staff of these schools were developing their curricula. In other words, there was no unambiguous connection between a collaborative culture and curriculum development.

In this project we have shown that the key ingredient for school development is teacher learning. We now believe that the existence of a collaborative culture is a necessary condition for whole school curriculum development, because it creates trust, security and openness. Yet, these are not sufficient conditions for growth. For growth to take place, at the level of either the individual or the school, teachers must also be constantly learning. The challenge for staff in primary schools then, and for those who support them, is to establish a culture which facilitates teacher collaboration whilst, at the same time, enabling teachers to learn from each other and from courses outside the school. The presence of both these factors will enable professional debate and challenge to occur in a climate of trust and openness, thereby ensuring that the risks and discomforts of learning are counterbalanced by mutual support and a concern for individuals.

However, teacher learning, like the whole school curriculum development which it underpins, is not necessarily easy to achieve. Nor, like 'whole school' approaches, can it be achieved by simply making it into a slogan. Rather, anyone with a serious interest in the continuing professional development of teachers must consider the latter's reasons for wanting to start or to continue learning; the opportunities they have to do so; the means by which they learn; the conditions which facilitate their learning; and the content of that learning, in particular whether it most affects practitioners' educational beliefs or their technical competence. Further, whether teachers' development goes on outside the school or within it, school leaders and particularly their heads, must be aware of the central part played by learning in the twin processes of whole school curriculum development, and must be able to contribute to and guide it.

The fourth implication concerns resources. Whole school curriculum development needs two key resources: time and skilled, committed people. Interaction between teachers is crucial to the development of both the curriculum and a sense of educational community. Yet interaction takes time and the staff in the project schools were very short of it. Although the teachers and heads were creative in manufacturing opportunities to meet with others, observe one another at work, plan together and so on, they nevertheless felt hard pressed to fulfil in the time available all the expectations placed upon them. Consequently heads and teachers often used their own time (for example, evenings and weekends) to fulfil these expectations. Moreover, when the heads were frequently called out of school, as they all were during our period of fieldwork, their absence reduced the number of occasions when they or their staff could professionally interact during the school day. It follows then that whole school curriculum development will be impeded unless there is ample time for staff to interact and learn from one another. As others have previously noted (for example, House of Commons, 1986; Campbell and Neill, 1990) there is a crucial need for primary teachers to be given some relief from class-teaching duties during the school day in order that they are able to learn from one another and so develop the school's curriculum.

A second key resource for whole school curriculum development is teachers who possess specific skills and personal qualities. For example, these teachers worked in schools which were organizationally complex, where tensions were present, and where many tasks needed to be undertaken or kept in mind simultaneously. They had to be able to cope constructively with these conditions. They had to be tolerant of ambiguity, able to thrive in situations where not everything was tightly structured and clearly defined, and willing to accept that they would not be able to concentrate upon one thing at a time.

They also needed to be able to face the professional differences which existed amongst them. These differences were sometimes openly confronted. At others they were dealt with by negotiation. The latter occurred either on a one-to-one basis between teachers and teachers and the head, or in groups as, for example, part of staff meetings. Teachers therefore needed to have the interpersonal skills of negotiation and the willingness to reach compromises. Furthermore, they had to be able to negotiate in two different arenas: on an individual basis with their year partner, head, or neighbour; and in small groups or the full assembly of staff. In other words, it was important that heads and teachers had developed or were developing the micropolitical skills of communal life.

Finally, there is one other point to make. A great deal of what we have described will be well known to those who work in or are closely associated with primary schools. We make no apology for this, since it was one of our intentions to describe what was taking place in the schools in which we worked. If the data provide a familiar picture, this reassures us that we have captured some of the qualities and features of life inside primary schools. Indeed, we believe that the power of our research rests in its very familiarity. In a sense, what we have attempted to do is draw attention to those features of schools which are often taken for granted by researchers, academics, LEA officers, heads and, even, teachers. Our analysis has identified, clarified and emphasized some of the intuitive ways in which the staff in these schools worked. We have done this deliberately in order to stress the strengths of the staffs' existing approaches to collaboration and curriculum development, as well as to the challenges and problems they face. Moreover, we have tried to highlight those traditions and processes which, in our opinion, should be preserved. Schools presently face an unprecedented scale and pace of change. As their staff respond to these changes there is a danger that they may discard practices which have served them well in the past.

Bibliography

AINSCOW, M. and MUNCEY, J. (1989) *Meeting Individual Needs*, London, Fulton.

ALEXANDER, R. (1984) *Primary Teaching*, London, Cassell.

ALEXANDER, R. (1988) 'Garden or jungle? Teacher development and informal primary education' in BLYTH, W.A.L. (Ed.) *Informal Primary Education Today*, Lewes, Falmer Press.

BALL, S. (1987) *The Micro-Politics of the School*, London, Methuen.

BARNARD, C. (1938) *The Functions of the Executive*, Cambridge, MA, Harvard University Press.

BENNIS, W. and NANUS, B. (1985) *Leaders*, New York, Harper & Row.

BLUMBERG, A. and GREENFIELD, W. (1986) *The Effective Principal*, 2nd edn, Boston, MA, Allyn & Bacon.

BRADLEY, H.W. (1991) *Staff Development*, Lewes, Falmer Press.

CAMPBELL, J. (1985) *Developing the Primary School Curriculum*, London, Cassell.

CAMPBELL, J. (1989) 'The Education Reform Act: Some implications for curriculum decision-making in primary schools' in PREEDY, M. (Ed.) *Approaches to Curriculum Management*, Milton Keynes, Open University Press.

CAMPBELL, J. and NEILL, S. (1990) *1330 Days: Teacher time in Key Stage 1*, London, AMMA.

CAMPBELL, P. (1989a) 'A cord of three strands: A case study of leadership, individual initiative and teamwork at Fenton County Primary school, 1988–9', Cambridge Institute of Education mimeo.

CAMPBELL, P. (1989b) 'Keeping a step ahead of the game: A case study of Carey Infant school 1988–9', Cambridge Institute of Education mimeo.

CAMPBELL, P. (1989c) 'Edging forwards: A case study of Ingham County Infant school 1988–9', Cambridge Institute of Education mimeo.

CAMPBELL, P. and SOUTHWORTH, G. (1990) 'Rethinking collegiality: Teachers' views', paper presented at the annual meeting of the American Educational Research Association, Boston Cambridge Institute of Education mimeo.

CLEGG, A. (1980) *About Our Schools*, Oxford, Blackwell.

COULSON, A.A. (1980) 'The role of the primary head' in BUSH, T., GLATTER, R., GOODEY, J. and RICHES, C. (Eds) *Approaches to School Management*, London, Harper & Row.

DAY, C., JOHNSTON, D. and WHITAKER, P. (1985) *Managing Primary Schools*, London, Harper & Row.

DAY, C., WHITAKER, P. and WREN, D. (1987) *Appraisal and Professional Development in Primary Schools*, Milton Keynes, Open University Press.

DES (1978) *Primary Education in England*, London, HMSO.

DES (1980) *A View of the Curriculum: Matters For Discussion, an HMI series*, London, HMSO.

DES (1982) *Education 5 to 9: An Illustrative Survey of 80 First Schools*, London, HMSO.

DES (1984a) *The Organization and Content of the 5–16 Curriculum*, London, HMSO.

DES (1984b) *Education Observed*, London, HMSO.

DES (1985a) *Education 8–12 in Combined and Middle Schools: A Report by HMI*, London, HMSO.

DES (1985b) *The Curriculum from 5–16: Curriculum Matters 2, an HMI series*, London, HMSO.

DES (1985c) *History in the Primary and Secondary Years: An HMI View*, London, HMSO.

DES (1987) *Primary Schools: Some Aspects of Good Practice*, London, HMSO.

DES (1989a) *The Curriculum from 5–16*, London, HMSO.

DES (1989b) *School Teacher Appraisal: A National Framework, Report of the National Steering Group on School Teacher Appraisal Pilot Study*, London, HMSO.

DES (1990a) *Planning For School Development*, London, HMSO.

DES (1990b) *The Teaching and Learning of Language and Literacy, HMI An Inspection Review*, London, HMSO.

ELLIOTT, J. (1976) 'Developing hypotheses about classrooms from teachers' practical constructs: An account of the work of the Ford Teaching Project', *Interchange*, 7, 2, pp. 2–21.

ELLIOTT, J., BRIDGES, D., EBBUTT, D., GIBSON, R. and NIAS, J. (1981) *School Accountability*, Oxford, Blackwell.

FULLAN, M. (1982) *The Meaning of Educational Change*, New York, Teachers' College Press.

FULLAN, M. (1991) *The New Meaning of Educational Change*, 2nd edn, New York, Teachers' College Press.

GRIFFIN-BEALE, C. (Ed.) (1979) *Christian Schiller; In His Own Words*, London, A. & C. Black.

HOLLY, P.J. and SOUTHWORTH, G.W. (1989) *The Developing School*, Lewes, Falmer Press.

HOLMES, G. (1952) *The Idiot Teacher*, London, Faber.

HOUSE OF COMMONS (1986) *Achievement In Primary Schools, Report of the Committee of Enquiry*, Vol. 1 London.

HOYLE, E. (1986) *The Politics of School Management*, London, Hodder & Stoughton.

ILEA (1985) *Improving Primary Schools*, London, ILEA.

JACKSON, B. (1964) *Streaming: A System in Miniature*, London, Routledge & Kegan Paul.

JACKSON, P.W. (1968) *Life in Classrooms*, New York, Holt, Rinehart & Winston.

JOYCE, B., HERSH, R. and McKIBBIN, M. (1983) *The Structure of School Improvement*, New York, Longman.

LANDAU, M. (1969) 'Redundancy, rationality and the problems of duplication and overlap', *Public Administration Review*, 29, pp. 346–58.

LAPORTE, T. (Ed.) (1975) *Organised Social Complexity: Challenge to politics and policy*, Princeton, NJ, Princeton University Press.

LIEBERMAN, A. (1986) 'Collaborative work', *Educational Leadership*, 43, 3, pp. 4–8.

LORTIE, D. (1969) 'The balance of control and autonomy in elementary school teaching' in ETZIONI, A. (Ed.) *The Semi-Professions and Their Organization*, New York, Free Press.

LORTIE, D. (1975) *Schoolteacher*, Chicago, IL, University of Chicago Press.

McMAHON, A., BOLAM, R., ABBOTT, R. and HOLLY, P.J. (1984) *Guidelines for Review and Internal Development in Schools: Primary School Handbook*, York, Longman.

NATIONAL CURRICULUM COUNCIL (1989) *Curriculum Guidance One: A Framework for the Primary Curriculum*, York, NCC.

NATIONAL CURRICULUM COUNCIL (1990) *Curriculum Guidance Three: The Whole Curriculum*, York, NCC.

NIAS, J. (1987) 'One finger, one thumb: A case study of the deputy head's part in the leadership of a nursery and infant school' in SOUTHWORTH, G.W. (Ed.) *Readings in Primary School Management*, Lewes, Falmer Press.

NIAS, J. (1989a) *Primary Teachers Talking: A Study of Teaching as Work*, London, Routledge.

NIAS, J. (1989b) 'On the move; A case study of Upper Norton C of E Primary School, a school in transition, 1988–9', Cambridge Institute of Education mimeo.

NIAS, J. (1991) 'Changing times, changing identities: Grieving for a lost self' in BURGESS, R. (Ed.) *Educational Research and Evaluation: For Policy and Practice*, Lewes, Falmer Press.

NIAS, J., SOUTHWORTH, G.W. and YEOMANS, R. (1989) *Staff Relationships in the Primary School: A Study of Organizational Cultures*, London, Cassell.

PETERS, T. and AUSTIN, N. (1985) *A Passion For Excellence*, Glasgow, Collins.

POLLARD, A. (1985) *The Social World of the Primary School*, London, Cassell.

SARASON, S. (1971) *The Culture of the School and the Problem of Change*, Boston, MA, Allyn & Bacon.

SCHAEFER, R. (1967) *The School as a Centre of Inquiry*, London, Harper & Row.

SCHÖN, D. (1987) *Educating the Reflective Practitioner*, New York, Jossey-Bass.

SCHOOLS COUNCIL (1981) *The Practical Curriculum*, London, Methuen.

SCHOOLS COUNCIL (1983) *Primary Practice*, London, Methuen.

SCHOOLS EXAMINATIONS AND ASSESSMENT COUNCIL (1990) *Records of Achievement in Primary Schools*, London, SEAC.

SOUTHWORTH, G.W. (1987) 'Primary school headteachers and collegiality' in SOUTHWORTH, G.W. (Ed.) *Readings in Primary School Management*, Lewes, Falmer Press.

SOUTHWORTH, G.W. (1989) 'Pied pipers and distant drummers: A case study of the Orchard Community Junior School, 1988–9', Cambridge Institute of Education mimeo.

STENHOUSE, L. (1975) *Introduction to Curriculum Development*, London, Heinemann.

VIALL, P.B. (1984) 'The purposing of high-performing systems' in SERGIOVANNI, T.J. and CORBALLY, J.E. (Eds) *Leadership and Organizational Culture*, Chicago, IL University of Illinois Press.

WALLACE, M. (1988) 'Towards a collegiate approach to curriculum management in primary and middle schools, *School Organization*, 8, pp. 25–34.

WELSH OFFICE (1985) *Leadership in Primary Schools*, Cardiff, HMSO.

WHITAKER, P. (1983) *The Primary Head*, London, Heinemann.

WOLCOTT, H. (1973) *The Man in the Principal's Office*, Prospect Heights, Waveland Press.

WOODS, P. (1987) 'Managing the primary teacher's role' in DELAMONT, S. (Ed.) *The Primary School Teacher*, Lewes, Falmer Press.

Index